Edited by
Antonella Invernizzi
and **Jane Williams**

Children and
Citizenship

Edited by
Antonella Invernizzi
and **Jane Williams**

Children and Citizenship

Los Angeles | London | New Delhi
Singapore | Washington DC

First published 2008
Reprinted 2009

 SAGE Publications Ltd
1 Oliver's Yard
55 City Road
London EC1Y 1SP

SAGE Publications Inc.
2455 Teller Road
Thousand Oaks, California 91320

SAGE Publications India Pvt Ltd
B 1/I 1 Mohan Cooperative Industrial Area
Mathura Road
New Delhi 110 044

SAGE Publications Asia-Pacific Pte Ltd
33 Pekin Street #02–01
Far East Square
Singapore 048763

Library of Congress Control Number: 2007924344

British Library Cataloguing in Publication data

A catalogue record for this book is available from the British Library

ISBN 978–1–4129–3537–1
ISBN 978–1–4129–3538–8 (pbk)

Typeset by Newgen Imaging Systems (P) Ltd., Chennai, India
Printed in Great Britain by the MPG Books Group
Printed on paper from sustainable resources

Contents

Notes on Contributors

Priscilla Alderson is Professor of Childhood Studies, Social Science Research Unit, Institute of Education, University of London. Her research interests include children's competence and wisdom, and their share in making decisions that affect them, on which she has published numerous reports. She teaches on the Institute's MA Course in Childhood Studies and Children's Rights. See www.ioe.ac.uk/ssru

Joanna Birch is currently Research Associate working on an ESRC project based in the University of Sheffield's Centre for the Study of Childhood and Youth. The project, Space to Care, seeks to understand how different spatial environments impact upon children's experiences of hospitalization. Jo's previous research and her teaching background have been focused around children and young people, their conceptualizations and perceptions of the spaces and places that they experience.

Dr Samantha Clutton worked at University of Wales, Swansea for 10 years before joining Barnardo's Cymru Policy and Research Unit. She has completed two secondments to the Welsh Assembly Government where she was involved in the production of Welsh strategies on youth offending and child poverty. She is currently involved in developing a research and practice model around child sexual exploitation and development work around support for prisoners and their families.

Rhian Croke has been the UNCRC Monitoring Officer for Save the Children (UK) since April 2004. She coordinates the work of the Wales UNCRC Monitoring Group, a national alliance of agencies tasked with monitoring and promoting the implementation of the UNCRC in Wales. She is co-editor of *'Righting the Wrongs: The Reality of Children's Rights in Wales'*, an analysis of how far law, policy and practice have progressed in achieving compliance with the UNCRC in Wales. She previously worked for the University of Cape Town Children's Institute as a Senior Researcher in the HIV/AIDs Programme.

Penny Curtis works in the School of Nursing and Midwifery at the University of Sheffield and is a member of the University's Centre for the Study of Childhood and Youth. Ongoing empirical research includes an ESRC funded study 'Space to Care: Children's perceptions of spatial aspects of hospitals' (with Allison James and Jo Birch).

Judith Ennew Honorary Research Fellow in the Department of Applied Social Sciences, University of Wales Swansea, has been an activist and researcher in children's rights since 1979, specializing in child workers, 'street children' and child sexual exploitation. She has worked in Latin America, Africa, South and Southeast Asia and Eastern Europe on children's rights and child labour issues and is currently based in Bangkok as Head of Programme Development for the Thai NGO Knowing Children.

Jane Fortin is Professor of Law at King's College London. She writes widely on issues relating to child and family law and is co-editor of the *Child and Family Law Quarterly*. Her special interest in Child Law and children's rights led to her book *Children's Rights and the Developing Law* and to a variety of other publications considering the impact of legal principles on children and their families. For the last 12 years she has run a post-graduate programme in Child Studies for a wide range of senior practitioners.

Antonella Invernizzi is Senior Lecturer at the Department of Applied Social Sciences, Swansea University. Her work has focused on 'street children' in southern countries, children's work (Peru, Portugal), children's participation and children's citizenship.

Allison James is Professor of Sociology at the University of Sheffield. She has worked in the field of sociology/anthropology of childhood since the late 1970s and has helped pioneer the theoretical and methodological approaches to research with children. Her research has included work on children's language and culture, children's attitudes towards sickness and bodily difference, children's experiences of everyday life at home and at school and concepts of childhood. She has written numerous articles and books on childhood.

Gill Jones is Emeritus Professor of Sociology, Keele University, and is now semi-retired and living in Edinburgh. After an early career in social work, she became a sociologist in the early 1980s, and has been engaged in research on young people, their families and youth policies ever since. Books include *Youth, Family and Citizenship* (with Claire Wallace, 1992), *Leaving Home* (1995), *Balancing Acts: Youth, Parenting and Public Policy* (with Robert Bell, 2000), and *The Youth Divide: Diverging paths to adulthood* (2002).

Prof Dr Manfred Liebel is Sociologist, International Academy (INA) at Free University of Berlin; Scientific Coordinator of the European Network of Masters in Children's Rights (ENMCR); a collaborator of the movements of working children and adolescents in Latin America, Africa and Asia.

Ruth Lister is Professor of Social Policy at Loughborough University. She is a former director of the Child Poverty Action Group. She has published widely in the areas of poverty, gender, citizenship and welfare reform. Her most recent publications are *Citizenship: Feminist Perspectives* (2nd edn 2003) and *Poverty* (2004).

Andrew Lockyer is Professor of Citizenship and Social Theory in the Politics Department of Glasgow University where he has taught since 1970. He is the holder of the St Kentigern Chair and has written widely on political and social theory, children's issues, juvenile justice and citizenship education.

Brian Milne is a social anthropologist who has worked in the field of children's rights as a researcher, teacher and trainer since the mid-1980s. His work ranges from academic teacher and researcher to international consultancy as an evaluator, trainer and researcher in areas that include street children, child labour, children abuse and neglect and their participation in civil society. For at least the last decade and half he has been particularly concerned with theoretical and practical issues around child participation that have progressed on to deeper examination of children's citizenship and their relationship with the state.

Virginia Morrow is Reader in Childhood Studies at the Institute of Education, University of London. Children and young people have been the focus of her research activities since 1988. Her work has focused on methods and ethics of social research with children; social capital; children's work; children's understandings of family and other social environments. She is an editor of *Childhood: a global journal of child research*.

Christine Piper is a Professor in the School of Law at Brunel University. Her research and teaching interests are in child and family law and policy as well as youth justice and sentencing. She is on the Editorial Board of the *Child and Family Law Quarterly* and her recent publications include *Sentencing and Punishment: The Quest for Justice* (with S. Easton, OUP, 2005).

Helen Stalford is Senior Lecturer at the Liverpool Law School, University of Liverpool. She has been researching and publishing in the area of family law and children's rights under EU law for the past 10 years and is co-author of the book *A Community for Children?: Children, Citizenship and Migration in the European Union* (2004, Ashgate).

Jane Williams is a former UK and Welsh Assembly government lawyer now based in the School of Law, Swansea University where she teaches Public Law, aspects of Child Law and children's rights. She is a member of the Wales UNCRC monitoring group, the work of which is discussed in Chapter 15 in this volume.

Preface

The notion of children's citizenship has seen increased popularity in the last decade as a way of rethinking the position of children, mainly as members of the community or the nation and as rights holders. Discourses on children's citizenship often include claims for the recognition of selected rights for all children, or certain categories of children, and sometimes claims by children themselves. They thus relate to what Isin and Tuner portray as a 'major trend in western nation-states towards the formation of new claims for inclusion and belonging' where social issues (such as immigration, disability, gender, indigenous people) have been reframed in terms of rights and obligations, that is, within the language of citizenship (2002: 1). Within discourses on the citizen child, the UN Convention on the Rights of the Child (UNCRC) is often seen as a foundation for a new position of children in contemporary societies, in which rights to participation are often seen as pivotal, guaranteeing that the child is approached as a rights holder and subject (for instance Invernizzi and Milne, 2005). The child is thus to be considered as a 'citizen now', as opposed to a 'citizen becoming'.

Close examination of notions of children's citizenship, however, reveals further complex theoretical and practical issues. How does children's citizenship fit with established understandings of citizenship in general? How do notions of children's citizenship relate to children's own experiences, to theories of childhood and to the very different and contrasting images and discourses about children? And to what extent is the rhetoric of children's citizenship reflected in policy and legislation?

It was in order to explore some of these questions that an interdisciplinary research seminar was organized at Swansea University between 2005 and 2006, by the Department of Applied Social Sciences and the School of Law. It brought together leading experts from law, social sciences and politics in pursuit of better understanding of the different perspectives on the issue. Rather than producing a discourse or promoting a theoretical stance on children's citizenship, the seminar was intended to explore complementary as well as contrasting perspectives and to gain an overview of some of the many issues to be addressed. This book is the result of that collaboration. Some contributions contradict as well as complement others, raising further questions as well as proposing particular theoretical or practical approaches.

In view of the impetus brought to the debate on children's citizenship by the UNCRC, we were delighted that Jaap Doek, Chair of the UN Committee on the Rights of the Child, agreed to provide a Foreword to this volume. In it key elements of the emergent concept of 'child as citizen now' inherent in the UNCRC are outlined. The following chapters are organized in three parts dealing with notions of citizenship, constructions of childhood and experiences of children and finally, with policy and legislation. It is a rather arbitrary classification as authors often include reflections on more than one area. Nonetheless, such organization allows for some key questions to be mapped out and some contrasts in views to be highlighted. We hope that this rich collection will inform and stimulate further interdisciplinary consideration of what citizenship does and can mean for children and of their position in contemporary societies.

References

Invernizzi, A. and Milne, B. (2005) 'Conclusion: Some elements of an emergent discourse on children's right to citizenship', in A. Invernizzi and B. Milne (eds) *Children's citizenship: an emergent discourse on the rights of the child?*, *Journal of Social Sciences, Special Issue N. 9*, pp. 83–99.

Isin, E.F. and Turner, B.S. (2002) 'Citizenship studies: An introduction', in Isin, E.F. and Turner, B.S. (eds) *Handbook of Citizenship Studies*, London: Sage, pp. 1–10.

Foreword

Jaap E. Doek

Chairperson UN Committee
on the Rights of the Child

Citizen Child: A Struggle for Recognition

'The fundamental right to citizenship is still denied to some nine million persons' (Sokoloff, 2005: 5). These figures refer to the nine million stateless persons (UNHCR, 2006: 9). Contrary to what this statement suggests there is no provision in any international human rights treaty conferring on an individual the right to citizenship. Indeed, many may associate citizenship with being a national of a State, that is: you are the citizen of a State of which you are a national. But again: there is no right to the nationality of the State in which you are born. Human rights treaties do not contain a 'right to a nationality' (let alone to a nationality of choice). However, in the context of this volume it is important to note that 'every child has the right *to acquire* a nationality' (Article 24 (3) ICCPR; Article 7 (1) UNCRC (emphasis added)). To quote from the proposal of this book and as various contributions in this volume reflect, 'citizenship eludes definition (except in the [. . .] sense used in the field of nationality and immigration) and is variable, contextual and often contested. It is closely linked to but not synonymous with rights and implicitly confers on children the status of subjects. This links the issue of children's citizenship to that of "children's participation." '

It is tempting to engage in a discussion on the concept of citizenship and its constituting elements: Nationality? Right to reside permanently on the territory of a State? The right to be protected by the State? The right to vote, to hold office and to participate in decision making? The right to social action and to economic rights?

But I will limit myself to some observations about the citizenship of children in the context of the UN Convention on the Rights of the Child (UNCRC). Just as a starter: the citizenship of the child should not be dealt with only as a nationality issue. Nationality is undoubtedly an important element of citizenship. But I like to take a broader approach from the perspective of the child as a rights holder. Citizen Child may not vote or run for a public office, but is entitled to the enjoyment of all the rights enshrined in the UNCRC without discrimination of any kind. I don't pretend that the following observations cover all aspects of the child's citizenship but they are fundamental.

Key Elements for the Recognition of Citizen Child

Birth Registration (Article 7 UNCRC)

Article 7 UNCRC contains an important rule in very strong language: 'The child *shall* be registered at birth'. It affirms that registration of a child is a key condition for the recognition of her or his existence. Without a registration (at birth or as soon as possible thereafter) the child is most likely not acknowledged as a person before the law and in many countries it means no or very limited access to health care, education or social services. The Committee on the Rights of the Child (the UN Committee) has noted that lack of registration 'can impact negatively on a child's sense of personal identity and children may be denied entitlements to basic health, education and social welfare' (2005: para. 25). The UN Committee systematically recommends State Parties to the UNCRC to promote and facilitate proper registration of all children born on their territories, including children born to illegal immigrants, refugees and asylum-seeking people. In addition, it is important that all children arriving in a country as refugees or migrants are registered.

There are often different barriers to full implementation of the right to be registered at birth: political barriers (e.g. non-registration of some ethnic minority children), financial (charging of fees) or geographical barriers. It goes beyond the scope of this introduction to elaborate more in detail on the various aspects of birth registration: these are documented elsewhere (see UNICEF, 2002). But it is clear that Citizen Child will face serious problems in being recognized as such if he/she is not properly registered. That is even more so because in many countries there is a link between registration and nationality, as any person without a registration has no nationality.

The Right to Acquire a Nationality (Article 7 UNCRC)

The matter of nationality is a complex one and often politically sensitive. In principle the rules on nationality fall within the scope of domestic jurisdiction and therefore within the domain of national law. The different rules for granting or losing nationality have given rise to problems such as statelessness.

But Article 7 UNCRC is very clear: the child shall have the right to acquire a nationality and States Parties shall ensure the implementation of this right [. . .] in particular where the child would otherwise be stateless.

With regard to this article the UN Committee has expressed its concerns, in particular regarding children who are considered as non-citizens or who are stateless according to the national law of the country in which they live. From information submitted to the UN Committee it is clear that these children often suffer from serious discrimination and that they, by virtue of their lack of legal status, are unable to fully participate in their community/society and face many problems in integrating themselves in the society. To take just one example, Syrian-born Kurdish children are considered as foreigners or as *'maktoumeen'* (unregistered) by the Syrian authorities. They have no nationality at birth and face serious problems in acquiring Syrian nationality. Many remain stateless (UN Committee on the Rights of the Child, 2003: para. 32, 33).

The UN Committee has issued various country-specific recommendations. The core message was and is:

Prevent children from becoming stateless – for example as a result of their lack of a legal status at birth which is regularly a problem for children belonging to ethnic minorities, refugee and (im)migrant children. Measures recommended in this regard should aim at providing the child with a nationality either of the country of origin or of the country they are born in. This is not without legal complications if State A wants to provide a child with the nationality of State B because State B is considered to be the country of origin. It requires bilateral negotiations and agreements but the CRC Committee expects States Parties to undertake efforts in this regard and to include the possibility of providing the child, if no other options are available, with the nationality of the State in which the child is living.

It is also important that States, where necessary, take measures to ensure that children born out of wedlock do ex lege acquire the nationality of the mother. The Committee has also recommended States to introduce legal provisions allowing the child to acquire the nationality of both her/his father and mother. In the event of the parents' divorce or de facto separation, this may prevent the child from becoming stateless in the country where she/he continues to live with the mother. This also addresses a matter of non-discrimination between the mother and the father: accordingly the Committee on the Elimination of All Forms of Discrimination against Women regularly makes similar recommendations.

Equally important are measures to reduce statelessness of children, which may require amending existing nationality laws/regulations allowing children to acquire the nationality of the country they are living in. The UN Committee has recommended States to ratify the Convention on the Status of Stateless Persons (1954) and the Convention on the Reduction of Statelessness (1961).

Finally the child has not only the right to acquire a nationality but also the right to preserve her/his nationality. Article 8 UNCRC contains the unique provision in the field of human rights that the child has the right to preserve his or her identity which includes nationality, name and family relationship. Paragraph 2 of this Article requires that States Parties, in case the child is illegally deprived of, for example, her/his nationality, shall provide appropriate assistance and protection with a view to speedily re-establishing her/his nationality. This may be particularly important for children in conflict areas who are victims of cross-border displacements or of (forced) disappearances (see Doek, 2006; for more details on the recommendations made by the UN Committee in respect of the implementation of Article 7 see UN Committee on the Rights of the Child, 2006).

Citizen Child as a Rights Holder

Registration at birth (or later) and a nationality are indeed key elements for the recognition of the child as a citizen. But this recognition must not only depend on these formalities, but also and perhaps even more important, on the opportunities the child is given to become a full and active member of her/his community and society.

It should be noted that these opportunities should be provided to every child on the territory of the State Party to the UNCRC regardless of whether he/she is registered at birth or has a nationality. This is in line with what I would call one of the characteristic features (or: goals if you want) of the UNCRC: the full and harmonious development of the child's personality, not only with a view to becoming an individual with her/his own personality, but also with a view to becoming a full member of her/his community and/or society (see the Preamble to the UNCRC and also Article 29).

The Preamble to the UNCRC states the conviction that a child should be afforded the necessary protection and assistance so that he/she can fully assume his/her responsibilities within the community.

This role as an active member of the community is not only something exclusively meant for mainstream children with a birth certificate and a nationality. It is meant for all children and, to underscore this, Article 23 UNCRC states that a child with disabilities should enjoy a full and decent life in conditions which [. . .] facilitate the child's active participation in the community. A similar provision in Article 40 UNCRC dealing with the not so popular group of children in conflict with the penal law, also known as juvenile delinquents. These children have the right 'to be treated in a manner consistent with the child's sense of dignity and worth which [. . .] takes into account [. . .] the desirability of promoting the child's re-integration and the child's assuming a constructive role in society' (Article 40 (1) UNCRC).

This characteristic feature or goal of the UNCRC requires that the child is fully recognized as a rights holder who shall be allowed to exercise her/his rights. But in doing so, the parents have the responsibilities, rights and duties to provide the child in a manner consistent with her/his evolving capacities with appropriate direction and guidance (Articles 5 and 14 UNCRC).

In the recognition of Citizen Child as a rights holder the concept of evolving capacities is crucial. It is impossible to discuss the many aspects of this concept in this introduction (see Lansdown, 2005 for an excellent elaboration of the various aspects of this concept). This concept represents a recognition of the growing autonomy of the child and the need to respect the gradual acquisition of independent exercise of the rights enshrined in the UNCRC such as the right to freedom of expression, the right to freedom of thought, conscience and religion and freedom of association (see Articles 12–17 UNCRC).

But as Lansdown (2005) observes, the concept of evolving capacities has implications for all rights in the UNCRC and demands significant changes at all levels of society. It represents a fundamental challenge to conventional attitudes towards children, questioning some of our deeply held assumptions about children's needs, children's development, protection of children and children's agency. As discussed in a number of the contributions to this volume, many lessons can be found in the real experience and practice of children. In societies throughout the world more could and should be done to create environments in which children achieve their optimum capacities and greater respect is given to children's potential for participation in and responsibility for decision making in their own lives – within the family, in school, in respect to their own health care, education, in courts, in local communities and in local and national political forums.

Some Concluding Observations

The recognition of the child as a citizen requires some concrete measures such as an immediate registration at birth and the provision of a nationality. But from the UNCRC perspective a broader approach is needed. Every child, and not only those with a birth certificate and a nationality, should be treated as a citizen. This means inter alia the full respect for and implementation of the rights of every child in order to allow her/him to live an individual and decent life in society and to facilitate her/his active and constructive participation in the community.

It requires that we acknowledge the child's growing autonomy and that we respect the gradual acquisition of independent exercise of rights.

Quite often children are presented as the citizens of tomorrow. It is undoubtedly important that we invest to the maximum extent of our available resources in the implementation of the rights of the child in order – to quote Article 29 UNCRC – to prepare the child for a responsible life in a free society in the spirit of understanding, peace, tolerance, equality of sexes and friendship among all peoples ethnic, national and religious groups and persons of indigenous people.

But that citizenship starts today and from birth. The Citizen Child is a citizen of today and the full recognition of this fact is one of the fundamental requirements of the UNCRC.

References

Doek, J.E. (2006) 'The CRC and the right to acquire and to preserve a nationality', *Refugee Survey Quarterly*, 25(3): 26–32.

Lansdown, G. (2005) *The Evolving Capacities of the Child*. Innocenti Insight, Florence: UNICEF/Innocenti Research Centre.

Sokoloff, C. (2005) 'Denial of Citizenship: A Challenge to Human Security', Report prepared for the Advisory Board on Human Security, February 2005.

UN Committee on the Rights of the Child (2003) *Concluding Observations on the Syrian Arab Republic*, CRC/C/15/Add. 212, 10 July 2003.

UN Committee on the Rights of the Child (2005) *General comment No. 7 on Implementing Children's Rights in Early Childhood*, CRC/CGC/7, 1 November 2005.

UN Committee on the Rights of the Child (2006) *Compilation of the practice of the Committee on the Rights of the Child as related to the Prevention and Reduction of Statelessness and the Treatment of Stateless Children, January 2003–January 2006*, prepared by Protection Policy and Legal Advice Section, Department of International Protection of the UNHCR (February 2006, Geneva).

UNHCR (2006) *Refugees by Numbers*. Geneva: UNHCR.

UNICEF Innocenti Research Centre (2002) *Innocenti Digest N. 9: Birth Registration: Right from the Start*, March 2002, Florence: UNICEF.

PART I

NOTIONS OF CHILDREN'S CITIZENSHIP

Introduction

The contributions in Part I address the broad question of how children's citizenship may be understood or defined. A number of notions are embedded in discourses and theories of citizenship: these include rights and obligations, equality and difference, status and practice, membership, dignity, competence, autonomy, dependence, independence and participation. Defining these notions is as important as understanding different ways in which scholars in the different disciplines use and make connections between them. The authors of the chapters included here address, from their different perspectives, approaches to citizenship, children's rights and the underlying philosophies.

In Chapter 1, Lister outlines different components ('building blocks') of citizenship: 'membership', 'rights', 'responsibilities' and 'equality of status, respect and recognition'. Both citizenship and rights can be read in relation to status and practice. Among the many lessons to be taken from her contribution is acknowledgement of the risk identified by Cohen (2005) of confusing one component with the whole of citizenship. No 'building block', in Lister's terms, 'can be discarded'. However, some building blocks can be remoulded and some appear more compatible with childhood. In order to do this, suggests Lister, there is a need to move away from a debate on children being or not being citizens. One can, thus, suggest that age should not be the sole or central criterion in the debate, a proposition also developed later in this volume (Jones) and with reference to the many experiences of children (Part II). In Lister's terms, citizenship is not a 'unitary phenomenon'.

The idea that 'no building block should be discarded', and thus the need for a more holistic approach, is underscored by other authors. Fortin identifies, for instance, the risk of exclusively addressing individual rights without consideration of the rights of others, which one could easily reframe in terms of obligations. Similarly, the absence of debate on children's obligations or responsibilities within the children's rights discourse does not equate with absence of obligations (for instance, Liebel). Rather, it points to a need to link consideration of children's rights to recognition of their responsibilities and the expectations made of them (Lockyer).

Most of the contributions acknowledge the significance of the UN Convention on the Rights of the Child (UNCRC) in the process of rethinking the position of children in contemporary societies. Jaap Doek's Foreword to this volume identifies features of the UNCRC-based approach, putting forward a notion of the child as a *citizen now*:

> The recognition of the child as a citizen requires some concrete measures such as an immediate registration at birth and the provision of a nationality. But from the UNCRC perspective a broader approach is needed. Every child, and not only those with a birth certificate and a nationality, should be treated as a citizen. This means inter alia the full respect for and implementation of the rights of every child in order to allow her/him to live an individual and decent life in society and to facilitate her/his active and constructive participation in the community. It requires that we acknowledge the child's growing autonomy and that we respect the gradual acquisition of independent exercise of rights. [. . .] But that citizenship starts today and from birth.

In the Foreword, among the key features one can identify in the UNCRC approach to the citizen child are:

- Non-discrimination in the exercise of rights, as a means of redressing the exclusion of some children not recognized as members of a nation (right to acquire a nationality and registration at birth (or later)) as well as children who require particular assistance and protection (for instance, children with disabilities or in conflict with the law);
- The child as rights holder in her/his present life, since 'the recognition [of the child as a citizen] depends [. . .] on the opportunities the child is given to become a full active member of her/his community';
- The goal of ensuring 'the full and harmonious development of the child personality, with the view to become and individual [. . .] [and] a full member of her/his community and/or society'. Provision of necessary protection and assistance without discrimination is the means to achieve this goal;
- The recognition of the child's evolving capacity as 'the growing autonomy of the child and the need to respect the gradual acquisition of independent exercise of the rights enshrined in the UNCRC such as the right to freedom of expression, the right to freedom of thought, conscience and religion and freedom of association'. Participatory rights are thus pivotal but rather than being understood in a narrow manner, they appear to have implications for all other rights and require significant changes in society.

The significance of the UNCRC-based notion of children's citizenship is more evident in Part III where the UNCRC is implicitly or explicitly referred to as a standard against which other legislation and policies are measured. By contrast, a number of authors in this part critically examine the UNCRC by resituating the children's rights approach in a broader theoretical framework of citizenship.

Fortin lays emphasis on the vague formulation of some UNCRC Articles (related to health) that are not readily enforceable, a point also made by Milne in respect of participatory articles in the UNCRC. From the perspective of law, Fortin further warns about the risks of proliferation of claims which might somehow devalue the entire category of rights. One could argue that while lack of precision within the UNCRC may affect the possibility of defining the formal status of children, the same rights, particularly participatory ones, might be and indeed are the source of inspiration or validation for claims for inclusion and for a practice of active citizenship. The changes promoted by the UNCRC at social and legal level would have to be simultaneously explored here. However, in this respect, Lister identifies 'something of a conundrum: children can make their claim to be members of the citizen-community through active participation in it; but in order to be able to participate they first need to be accepted as members of the citizen-community.'

Milne's contribution further addresses the UNCRC-based approach to children's citizenship by detailing its history. On the one hand, his analysis suggests that the Convention only partly reflects the philosophy and pioneer experiences of those who inspired it, such as Janus Korczak. Its distance from children's lives in southern countries has also regularly been underlined (see also Invernizzi and Liebel, in this volume). On the other hand, examination of history underlines the original concerns for children's welfare which fall short of contemplating the rights usually included within notions of adult citizenship (see also Ennew) and particularly, as Lister and Lockyer also point out, political rights. The participatory rights included in the UNCRC should therefore be understood as reflecting a particular social and legal construction of the child as subject rather than as holder of formal political rights. In relation to human rights, Ennew has identified the underlying philosophy of the UNCRC participatory rights as follows: 'just as dignity is the undefined basis and touchstone of human rights, participation is the basis and touchstone of ensuring that children are subjects of those same human rights' (1998: xix).

Despite growing interest and publications over recent years, children's participation remains, however, difficult to conceptualise. Different definitions coexist and no clear and holistic theoretical framework or agreed tools for evaluation of children's participation seem to be available at this point in time (Beers et al., 2006a). Often defined as 'involvement of children in decision making', experiences classified as participation might have very different aims. Among them for instance, empowerment or education (as discussed below), increased children's self-confidence and self-esteem or increased efficiency of projects and policies. An illustration of this lack of clarity can be found in a recent evaluation of children's participation in Vietnam (Beers et al., 2006b) which concludes that definitions used by professionals are mainly teleological, that is describing what is done in the field in the name of participation rather than what participation is intended to be and to achieve.

Ennew's contribution addresses the issue of children's citizenship within the United Nations (UN) by examining their experiences of participation as well as identifying some mechanisms of exclusion. Examining concepts of citizenship at international level is highly relevant for at least two reasons. First, because of the human rights instruments' potential for counteracting mechanisms of exclusion generated by concepts of citizenship based on nationality. Indeed, human rights instruments allow services and provision to be claimed for children who are often excluded, such as refugee or asylum seekers. In the Foreword to this volume, Doek stresses the importance of registration in the struggle for the recognition of children's rights. When examining experiences of children's participation within the UN, Ennew observes however that the UN structure relies substantially on nationally based definitions and thus brings nationally defined forms of exclusion into the UN function. Children who have no passport, nationality, are not registered or who are simply assimilated into a majority, as are many minority groups, will not be likely to be able to represent their interests within UN structures of participation. UN structures for children's participation are not representative. As Ennew provocatively suggests, should they be representative they would then surpass adult ones. The second reason is that it is in human rights instruments that reference is found to participatory rights. Albeit children's rights to participation are limited compared to adult political rights, they do reflect many provisions commonly made in human rights instruments. Here also, Ennew's contribution points out the limitations of any straightforward suggestion about children being citizens within the UN structure. She outlines a number of issues to be scrutinized within debates on children's participation. Difficulties with accommodating children in adult-specific arenas of decision-making and sometimes with respecting their rights go hand in hand with a very limited real impact in many of the events she analyses. Ennew's conclusion stresses indeed the limitations of current structures and processes in providing opportunities for citizenship in practice for children within the UN.

Another key issue discussed in this part is that of the different political traditions, presented in particular by Liebel and Lockyer. They focus particularly on liberal and republican (or social) traditions which put very different emphasis on rights and obligations of the individuals, their active involvement in the public sphere and the role of the state. Liebel further refers to the neoliberal approach to citizenship which advances policies reducing state provision of welfare and services, with especially negative implications for children in so-called developing countries.

Although they both refer to the republican tradition when conceptualizing citizenship and also refer to children's participation as part of active citizenship, Liebel and Lockyer each delineate very different practical interpretations of the same notion. Liebel locates what he calls 'citizenship from below' within children's everyday lives and refers to both welfare rights and active citizenship as the practice of citizenship. 'Citizenship from below' relates to the active role of children who generate incomes and contribute to the well-being of others in very difficult socio-economic circumstances. Citizenship also relates to their active learning through valuing their role, defining their rights and common interests as they emerge from everyday lives, promoting their rights and negotiating solutions and policies with the authorities.

Lockyer examines the underlying philosophy of citizenship education in England, in which he identifies references to both republican and liberal traditions in a 'blend' stressing the reciprocity of rights and duties. He conversely associates the children's rights discourse with a liberal approach to citizenship and sees age as a central criterion for determination of political and welfare rights. Within the English context, the main areas of citizenship education are 'social and moral responsibility, community involvement and political literacy'. It is within this framework that active citizenship is considered and pupils' involvement in communities is meant to be a process of learning civic responsibilities as well as values such as 'tolerance' 'fairness', 'respect for truth' and 'respect for difference'. Participation in school is also promoted as 'engagement of pupils in discussion and consultation' and giving 'responsibility and experience in running parts of the school'.

Albeit apparently starting from similar conceptualizations, the rights and practices of children in relation to their citizenship are extremely different in these two contributions. Among the key contrasting facets is that Liebel's approach is 'bottom-up' whereas Lockyer's discussion of policies and their application in schools centres on a 'top-down' approach. Lockyer's examination addresses the issue of the balance between rights and duties and the learning potential within the citizenship education curriculum that promotes democracy within the communities in general. Liebel instead refers to a model of the citizen emerging from everyday experiences of excluded communities. As he states, rights so constructed do not necessarily conform to rights included in international instruments. Liebel's focus is on citizenship and rights of children in their present lives whereas Lockyer's presentation of citizenship education refers principally to education for 'adult citizenship' and children's activities within participatory settings as 'learning by doing'. Qvortrup's (1990) distinction between children as 'human beings' and 'human becomings' helps to contrast these two approaches. Thus one could oppose 'citizenship education', as a matter of children as 'human becomings', to 'citizenship from below' as a matter of children as 'human beings'. The first would be about learning for future citizenship and, for this reason, pupils' experiences of participation and engagement in school would be promoted as educational; that is promoting or inculcating specific values, rules, skills and knowledge of rights and duties. The second would refer to empowerment of children in their present lives, recognition of their positive but already existing contribution to the community, definition of their needs and interests based on everyday lives. Indeed, as reflected in Part II, debates on participation often make reference to education and protection as discourses that undermine access to participatory rights. However, things are not so simple. On the one hand, Lockyer puts forward key arguments suggesting that citizenship education might provide a space for promoting young people's inclusion as well as for debating their experiences within communities. He suggests this requires reconceptualizing the political and puts forward ways of doing so. Particularly, he considers that there is potential for 'children to be politically active citizens [. . .] without insisting either on their being prematurely autonomous, or requiring the institutions they inhabit to be prematurely democratic'. On the other hand, Liebel does not reject the educational dimensions involved in experiences of 'citizenship from below', which he sees as 'the result of a learning process among children (and among adults in relation to the children)'. In his approach, the learning process does not consist of 'an induced growth of competence' but instead relates to learning 'concrete experiences of "being needed" and of their own contributions to the life of society, and become aware of their own "importance"'.

The argument originally put forward by Qvortrup's distinction between 'human becomings' and 'human beings' relates to a critique of policies and legislation making children solely 'human becomings', that is objects of socialization, education and care and thus denying their rights and status of subjects in their present lives. The impact of these and other conceptualizations of children and childhood on policies and legislation is developed by contributors in Part III (Piper, Stalford, Clutton) and in Part II (James et al. and Alderson). Children's rights reduce the impact of a 'human becoming' approach by giving children status as legal subjects and rights holders in their present lives. However, when considering experiences of children's participation, much may be gained by accepting that practice may involve *both* learning *and* empowerment rather than separating and opposing these two very much interconnected dimensions. Both children and adults are simultaneously 'human beings' and 'human becomings'.

One can return to Lister's suggestion that citizenship is not a 'unitary phenomenon' with a number of illustrations, relating to the different components she outlines in her contribution, to different levels and membership (for instance, UN, national, community levels) as well as to different political traditions. But when considering the different contributions included in Part I, one has also to stress what Lister calls the 'contextualized' and systematically 'contested' character of the concept of citizenship (2003 and in this volume). This can be easily assessed within what can be seen as the arena of different and contrasting claims made for, in the name of or by children and young people. One could further argue that children's participation appears to be an equally 'contested' and 'contextualized' concept.

Perhaps the central lesson to be drawn from Part I is that we need a more holistic approach to the notion of children's citizenship. Pursuing Lister's theoretical developments, one can argue not only that discussion of children's citizenship exclusively in terms of full citizenship versus non-citizenship provides limited depth but also that sectoralized approaches considering exclusively one or another component (i.e. rights, obligations, membership, etc.) or approach (for instance as 'human becoming' or 'human being', as above) gain by being situated in a more holistic picture. A further expansion, as contributors show in Part II, is to ensure that account is taken of knowledge about children's positions, practices and experiences in society. Discussion of what might constitute children's citizenship in general brings about several contradictions that might make more sense when related to such knowledge. Perhaps we still know very little when we consider different stages of childhood – from early childhood to youth – different contexts, cultures, societies and economic conditions. Greater appreciation of such diversity might enable us to understand more exactly the different and occasionally contradictory positions reflected here.

References

Beers, H. van, Invernizzi, A. and Milne, B. (eds) (2006a) *Beyond Article 12. Essential Readings on Children's Participation*. Bangkok: Knowing Children.

van Beers, H., Chau, V.P., Ennew, J., Khan, P.Q., Long, T.T., Milne, B., Nguyet, T.T.A., and Son, V.T. (2006b) *Creating an Enabling Environment: Capacity Building in Children's Participation, Save the Children Sweden, Viet Nam, 2000–2004*. Bangkok: Save the Children Sweden.

Cohen, E.F. (2005) 'Neither seen nor heard: children's citizenship in contemporary democracies', *Citizenship Studies*, 9(2): 221–40.

Ennew, J. (1998) 'Preface' in V. Johnson, E. Ivan-Smith et al. (eds), *Stepping Forward: Children and Young People's Participation in the Development Process*. London: IT Publications.

Lister, R. (2003) *Citizenship: Feminist Perspectives*. Basingstoke: Palgrave.

Qvortrup, J. (1990) 'Childhood as a social phenomenon: an introduction to a series of national reports', *Eurosocial Report 36*, Vienna: European Centre.

1

Unpacking Children's Citizenship[1]

Ruth Lister

Introduction

This chapter attempts to answer a question posed by Hill and Tisdall: 'whether the concepts of "childhood" and "citizenship" are compatible. 'This question', they point out, 'depends just as much on how "citizenship" is defined as it does on childhood's definition. Certainly, a definition of "citizenship" could be made that would definitely include children.... But would such a definition of "citizenship" retain the basic building blocks of the concept?' (1997: 38).

Having first briefly outlined the main 'building blocks of the concept', the chapter unpacks them in order to see how far they are able to accommodate children. It then suggests a number of lessons that can be learned from the feminist critique of citizenship. The conclusion returns to Hill and Tisdall's question and argues for a child-sensitive theorization and practice of citizenship.

The Building Blocks of Citizenship

At the formal level, citizenship simply denotes the legal status of membership of a nation-state, as symbolized by the right to a passport. However, at a substantive level it means much more than this legally, politically and socially. It is at this level that citizenship is frequently described as 'an essentially contested concept', reflecting different political traditions and, today, the challenges of various social movements. It has also been described as 'a contextualised concept' (Siim, 2000: 1). In other words, 'vocabularies of citizenship' and their meanings vary according to social, political and cultural context and reflect different historical legacies (Lister et al., 2007). The discussion of children's citizenship here needs therefore to be read in the UK context within which it is written.

As a contested concept, there is no one single definition of citizenship. One, which contains the basic building blocks used in many conceptualizations, is that provided by T.H. Marshall: 'a status bestowed on those who are full members of a community. All who possess the status are equal with respect to the rights and duties with which the status is endowed' (1950: 28–9). The key elements here are membership of a community, the rights and duties that flow from that, and equality of status.

Although Marshall placed considerable emphasis on full membership, he did so largely from the perspective of the status that derives from membership. Today the literature is interrogating the meaning of membership in a way that earlier writings did not, for instance placing more emphasis on identity and a sense of belonging and on the relationship between individual citizens.

For Marshall, rights (especially social rights) were pivotal to membership as an integrative force. Marshall's triad of the three elements of citizenship – civil, political and social rights – is well known. It is worth noting, from the perspective of children, Keith Faulks' (2000) distinction between 'civil rights' as 'market rights' (for instance the right to own property) and 'civil rights' as civil liberties (such as freedom of speech). Rights are central to the liberal citizenship tradition but the validity of social rights is contested by neoliberals. Other forms of rights have been identified since Marshall including – of particular relevance to children – participation rights: 'the right of participation in decision-making in social, economic, cultural and political life' (Gould, 1988: 212).

Here citizenship as a status becomes forged with citizenship as a practice (Oldfield, 1990). Indeed, rights more generally are today being theorized in terms of practice as well as status that is, as constituting citizens as active claim-makers rather than passive recipients and as not fixed but open to reinterpretation and renegotiation and needing to be defended and extended through political action.

Citizenship duties also bridge the status/practice divide. In Marshall's definition, they stand as part of the status of citizenship. Yet, fulfilling the duties and responsibilities of citizenship constitutes a practice. In civic republicanism, the other main citizenship tradition, the obligations of citizenship are primarily political. Political activity is not a means to an end, but an end in itself associated with the pursuit of the 'public' or 'common good', although it is also regarded as contributing to the self-development of the individual citizen. In recent years, however, it is paid work which has emerged as the primary citizenship obligation in many welfare states.

The final building block identified by Marshall is that of equality, which understood as equality of status is linked to notions of dignity and equal worth that in turn underpin the notion of human rights.

From this discussion it can be seen that in its substantive form, citizenship is not a unitary phenomenon. Elizabeth F. Cohen (2005) has, rightly, criticized accounts of children's citizenship, which treat one element as if it were the whole. A more differentiated analysis suggests that some of the building blocks of citizenship are more compatible with childhood than others.

Children's Citizenship

Membership

At one level, children's claim to citizenship lies in their membership of the citizenship community. A study of young people's perceptions of citizenship found that the most common model to which they subscribed was that of citizenship as a 'universal status', enjoyed by virtue of membership of the community or nation (Lister et al., 2003).

Children's relationship to that community may be different from adults' but that does not necessarily affect the claim to citizenship status. Jeremy Roche proposes that 'the demand that children be included in citizenship is simply a request that children be seen as members of society too, with a legitimate and valuable voice and perspective' (1999: 479). He later equates 'being counted as a member of the community' with participation (1999: 484). He cites Martha Minow's observation that 'including children as participants alters their stance in the community, from things or out-siders to members' (1999: 485). This points to something of a conundrum: children can make their claim to be members of the citizen-community through active participation in it; but in order to be able to participate they first need to be accepted as members of the citizen-community. Yet that acceptance is, in practice, partly contingent on children demonstrating their capacity to be participatory citizens.

Evaluations of initiatives that have enabled children and young people to participate, as well as research into children's participation in social action groups, testify to how they 'strengthen young people's sense of belonging to the community' as well as equipping them with the skills and capacities required for effective citizenship (Cutler and Frost, 2001: 6).

This all suggests that, while at one level all children are members of the community and therefore have the status of citizens in a thin sense, recog-nition of children as citizens in a thicker sense of active membership requires facilitating their participation as political and social actors. This is about more than just participation in individual decisions about one's own life made by parents and professionals, for it also implies participation in wider collective decision-making.

Rights

Children's right to express an opinion and to have that opinion taken into account in any matter or procedure affecting the child is enshrined in Article 12 of the UN Convention on the Rights of the Child (UNCRC). In the UK, such a right is contained in various pieces of children's legislation. There is no general legal right to participation for either children or adults. However, arguably participatory rights are of particular significance for children and young people aged under 18 who do not have the vote (Cutler and Frost, 2001). This is even more the case in the context of social exclusion, where children's voices (as well as adults') are even less likely to be heard.

It is the lack of the vote that perhaps raises the biggest question mark over the status of children's citizenship. The right to vote in national elec-tions is what divides denizens (people with a legal and permanent resi-dence status) from citizens, since denizens in theory normally enjoy full social and civil rights. It could be argued that without the vote a person is not a full citizen. As against that, the vote does not seem to figure very prominently in public understandings of citizenship, including those of the young people in the study mentioned earlier. Moreover, given the low turnout in recent elections, particularly among young people, participation in informal politics, social action or public decision-making that affects their lives may constitute a more important signifier of effective citizenship for many people. That is not, however, a reason for rejecting current demands for extension of the right to the vote down to age 16, endorsed by the Power Inquiry (2006). With the advent of citizenship education and the spread of participatory initiatives among children and young people, the case for this has arguably been strengthened.

Education was identified by Marshall as a 'genuine right of citizenship', although he regarded it 'not as the right of the child to go to school, but as the right of the adult citizen to have been educated' (1950: 25). It is only recently that a clear legal right to education has been enshrined in law, and in England and Wales the right is framed with reference to parental preferences. Social security, including child benefit, is a social-citizenship right that children receive only 'by proxy' through their parent(s) and it is a right which became increasingly age-structured in the late twentieth century (Jones and Wallace, 1992: 49; Jones and Bell, 2000; Jones in this volume). With regard to civil rights, Cohen suggests that many of them are typically 'regarded as irrelevant or inappropriate to the circumstances of childhood' (2005: 224).

Children's disqualification from adult-citizenship rights is justified on grounds of their need for protection and their dependence on adults. Few would question that some distinction is valid on those grounds. However, the widespread use of age as 'the key determinant in the acquisition of formal rights' creates an inflexible model which 'does not reflect children's actual and differing capacities' (Lansdown, 2005: 49–50). Nor is it consistent with the increased emphasis today on children's responsibilities.

Responsibilities

In the study mentioned earlier, the young people found it much harder to articulate their rights as citizens than they did their responsibilities (Lister et al., 2003). Although they tended not to think of citizenship in terms of formal rights and responsibilities, for a number of them the essence of citizenship was constructive social participation. Good citizenship, in particular, meant 'taking a socially constructive approach to the community. At its more proactive, it entailed contributing to society, helping the community, being a good neighbour and supporting the vulnerable. At its less proactive, "good citizenship" meant being polite, courteous and considerate, and abiding by the law and being non-destructive' (Smith et al., 2005: 437).

This suggests two overlapping aspects to citizenship responsibilities: those that are imposed and/or encouraged by the State and those that are exercised by choice. As the young people acknowledged, a key imposed minimal responsibility of citizenship is to obey the law. The effective age of criminal responsibility is only 10 in England and Wales and eight in Scotland, in defiance of the recommendations of the UN Committee on the Rights of the Child. Children are a prime target of anti-social behaviour orders and they can now be subject to special 'child curfews' (Tisdall, 2006).

However, policy is not consistent. Such and Walker contrast the responsibilities attributed to children in crime and anti-social-behaviour policies with the lack of responsibility accorded them in family policy. They observe that 'it is notable that children appear only to be granted agency and autonomy in the context of wrong-doing: children are able to be wilfully irresponsible but not wilfully responsible' (2005: 46). Their article reports on an exploratory study of children's own understandings of responsibility in the context of family life. They conclude that 'responsibility is a meaningful and everyday aspect of many children's lives. To shy away from recognising this . . . serves to deny children social citizenship' (2005: 54–6) (for a discussion of children's contributions see also Liebel, Alderson and Invernizzi in this volume).

It's possible to point to examples of how children assume responsibility in both the private and public spheres. In the private sphere, an important example highlighted in the literature is the heavy responsibility adopted by children who take on the role of young carers. In the public sphere, a number of research studies as well as media reports reveal a fair amount of formal and informal volunteering and social action among children and young people, although this can be obscured by narrow interpretations of what counts as 'constructive social participation' (Smith et al., 2005).

Equality of Status, Respect and Recognition

To treat others with respect is seen by the general public as a key responsibility of citizenship (Home Office, 2004; Almond, 2005); one that children are as capable of exercising as anyone else. Conversely, Bren Neale defines citizenship for children 'as an entitlement to recognition, respect and participation' (2004: 1). Yet, as hinted at already, a common theme in the literature is the *lack* of recognition and respect for the responsibilities that children and young people exercise. This reflects a wider sense that children are not respected and therefore do not enjoy genuine equality of status as citizens in the here and now. This is particularly true of children being brought up in poverty.

It has been argued elsewhere in the context of gender and citizenship that 'lack of recognition implies exclusion and marginalization from "full participation" in the community' (Hobson and Lister, 2002: 41). The children's movement, which, according to Stasiulis, 'enacts an alternative imaginary of children's active citizenship' (2002: 532), can thus be understood as a struggle for recognition as well as for participatory and other rights.

Lessons from the Feminist Critique

This brings us to the possible parallels between feminist critiques and those made of the construction of children's citizenship. First, just as feminists have exposed the male template underpinning traditional meanings of citizenship (see Lister, 2003a), so can we argue that it is an adult template, which measures children against an adult norm and which ignores the particularities of children's relationship to citizenship. The difference is that, in modern times, citizenship's universalism is supposed to cover women, in theory at least, whereas mainstream accounts of citizenship do not typically make any claims to include children.

Capacity

The reasons used to justify women's earlier exclusion from citizenship are very similar to those used to justify children's exclusion: notably their lack of competence, in particular to be rational, and their dependency. Hill and Tisdall (1997) question the use of rationality as a criterion, pointing out that adults do not necessarily always act rationally in decision-making whatever their capacities. Priscilla Alderson states that 'competence seems to be as much in the eye of the beholder as the ability of the child' (1992: 175). This, she suggests, points to a need to develop new ways of defining and assessing children's competence.

A UNICEF report provides a compass to help navigate the difficult question of age and capacity. It explores the meaning of Article 5 of the UNCRC, focusing on evolving capacity rather than age in relation to the balance between participatory and protection rights. While capacities evolve with age, in practice the actual ages at which a child acquires competencies vary according to her life experiences and social and cultural environment on the one hand and the nature of the competencies and the situations in which they are required to be exercised on the other. At every stage, the report argues, regard must be had to 'children's right to respect for their capacities' and to children's agency. In practice, 'adults consistently underestimate children's capacities', raising questions about their *ability* to assess them (Lansdown, 2005: 15, 30–1). The report suggests that most of the thinking on capacity hitherto has been in relation to medical consent. What is needed is the same kind of assessment of the capacities necessary for citizenship.

While there is a legitimate question concerning the competence for citizenship of babies and very young children, the literature is abound with examples of where even young children have shown themselves to be competent in the skills and capacities required for participation as citizens (Cutler and Frost, 2001; Marchant and Kirby, 2004). Moreover, as Alderson has pointed out, 'treating children with respect can markedly increase their competence' (1992: 175 and in this volume).

(In)dependence

The treatment in the literature of dependence as an obstacle to children's citizenship echoes some of the arguments in the feminist literature. Jones and Wallace (1992) explicitly draw parallels to argue that the extended dependence of young people as a result of policy developments has damaged their status as citizens. More recently, Jones and Bell claim that 'citizenship is meaningless without economic independence' (2000: 60). Children in industrialized societies lack such independence, except for whatever part-time wages they may earn.

As noted earlier, any social security rights for children are by proxy. A key feminist policy argument has been that women's right to social security should be individualized and not mediated through their partner. This is a more difficult argument to apply to children who, so long as they are required to attend school and do not have the potential to earn a wage to support themselves, are necessarily dependent economically upon parents or other adults who are responsible for their protection (see also Jones in this volume).

While children's economic dependence on adults may be incompatible with full rights as *social* citizens, it does not follow that they lose their claim to be *active, participating* citizens. Dependency arising from the need for protection is not incompatible with the right to participation. 'A framework of rights that implies that only fully autonomous people may enjoy participation rights normalizes individual independence. . . . Indeed, the mutual reinforcement of protection and participation rights is integral to the model of children's citizenship advanced in the children's movement' (Stasiulis, 2002: 513–14).

The critique of the normalization of independence chimes with a strand of feminist argument. Iris Young's (1995: 548) distinction between independence as autonomy (the ability to make and act upon one's choices) and as self-sufficiency ('not needing help or support from anyone in meeting one's needs and carrying out one's life plans') is helpful here, for the autonomy associated with citizenship does not require an illusory self-sufficiency. Moss and Petrie (2005) point out that feminist arguments about human interdependence can be applied to children as well as adults. This claim is supported by Such and Walker's exploratory study, which indicated that 'crucial components of responsibility were found to be its interdependence and relational nature' (2005: 48).

Although children's dependence is a product of the care they *receive*, whereas women's stems from the care they *provide*, as observed earlier, some children are also care-providers (Dearden and Becker, 2005). As such, the work involved would be recognized as the exercise of citizenship responsibility in some feminist frameworks. Children may also help adult care providers in the home in various ways, particularly in two-earner and in lone-parent families (Miller, 2005; Such and Walker, 2005; Ridge, 2006). In their discussion of children's dependence, Moss and Petrie endorse the feminist critique of 'the normative image of the independent wage-earning citizen which is at heart of contemporary notions of social participation and citizenship' (2005: 85). The displacement of that normative image in feminist critiques is thus also relevant for children in education, whose claim to citizenship cannot, in Western societies, lie through wage-earning, even if some children do earn a part-time wage.

The Public–Private Divide and Power

For both women and children, the link between (in)dependence, care and citizenship is mediated by the public–private divide. Cohen draws the analogy between coverture, under which married women forfeited independent legal status, and the way in which children are 'folded into the legal identity of their parents upon birth' (2005: 229). So, she argues, 'where women once ceded a public identity to their husbands and retreated (often reluctantly) to the private realm, children remain privatized by analogous forces' (2005: 229). Wyness et al. argue that children are 'located within the hidden private sphere and at best viewed as political animals in potentia' (2004: 86). Whereas women are now generally part of the public as well as the private sphere, commentators have pointed to how children are increasingly excluded from public space (or are concentrated in adult-controlled spaces) (Prout, 2000). According to Save the Children 'children's use of public space has decreased significantly since the 1970s' (2005: 3). Within the private sphere, in the same way that it was once considered permissible for men to inflict violence upon their female partners, so, in the UK, it is still as lawful for parents to hit their children but within legal limits.

This right reflects the power that adults have over children. Roche notes that 'one constant theme in much writing about children's rights is the deep sense of powerlessness and exclusion felt by children and young people' (1999: 478). The economic dependence of both women and children is closely linked to unequal power relations. Women's and children's groups are fighting for more power as citizens and both have, inevitably, encountered resistance.

Equal or Different?

A final parallel between the gendered citizenship and children's citizenship literatures lies in the question as to whether claims to citizenship are made on the basis of sameness/equality or difference. The argument for children's citizenship is predicated in part on a fundamental sameness and equal worth as human beings. Moreover, to state the obvious, children become adults, whereas women do not typically become men. Any arguments based on difference are therefore arguments that pertain only to a particular stage of the life-course. Nevertheless these arguments are salient.

Mehmoona Moosa-Mitha asserts children's 'rights to belong as "differently equal" members of society, outside the private–public dichotomy that results in marginalizing children's interests and needs' (2005: 386). She does so within the framework of a 'difference-centred', feminist model of citizenship, which acknowledges the multiple- subject positions occupied by citizens. Nevertheless, the appeal to equality also represents a claim on citizenship's universalist promise. I have suggested elsewhere that we can characterize such tensions between universalist and difference-centred models of citizenship as a 'differentiated universalism' (Lister, 2003a: ch. 3).

The notion of a 'differentiated universalism' helps to capture children's particular relationship to both citizenship and human rights. Roche comments that 'save for the "child liberationists", no one is arguing that children are identical to adults or that they should enjoy exactly the same bundle of civil and political rights as adults' (1999: 487). Some rights are shared with adults in the form of human rights, some are particular to children in the form of children's rights and some are denied to children.

The idea of a differentiated universalism also provides a lens through which to acknowledge the responsibilities children exercise and the ways these may simultaneously reflect adult responsibilities and their own position as children (Bessell, 2006). Following Roche, no one is arguing that children should exercise exactly the same bundle of responsibilities as adults – rather, again redolent of feminist arguments, that the responsibilities they do exercise should be recognized. In particular, some advocates of 'the imaginary of the active child citizen' (Stasiulis, 2002) acknowledge the dangers of casting participation as a responsibility for children. The right of the child not to participate must also be respected. Stasiulis, for instance, asks 'does children's citizenship then tend to devalue the right of children to remain children with all its implications – such as playfulness, lightness and "childishness"?' (2002: 509). Proponents of children's active citizenship need to be wary of subordinating children's right to be children (as understood in its particular cultural context) to the higher calling of the demands of citizenship. Otherwise there is a danger of mirroring the dominant instrumental construction of children as social investments who represent the citizens/citizen-workers of the future (Lister, 2003b).

Conclusion

Returning to Hill and Tisdall's question posed at the beginning of this chapter, the conclusion reached from the above analysis is that we cannot discard 'the building blocks of citizenship' in order to accommodate children. However, feminist critiques have shown how some of those building blocks can be reshaped in order better to do so. A key move is to get away from the construction of substantive citizenship as an absolute – the idea that a person is either a citizen or she/he is not. That has been the purpose of this chapter in unpacking the building blocks and analysing children's citizenship in relation to each one of them. Cohen uses the term 'semi-citizenship' to denote a 'middle ground' in which children 'are citizens by certain standards and not by others' (2005: 234).

I have elsewhere drawn a distinction between being a citizen and acting as a citizen: 'to be a citizen, in the legal and sociological sense, means to enjoy the rights of citizenship necessary for agency and social and political participation. To act as a citizen involves fulfilling the full potential of the status. Those who do not fulfil that potential do not cease to be citizens; moreover, in practice participation tends to be more of a continuum than an all-or-nothing affair and people might participate more or less at different points in the life-course' (Lister, 2003a: 42). This formulation does not work for children. Rather, some children are deploying their agency as citizens without first enjoying the full rights of citizenship.

In fact, much of the literature that is making the case for recognition of children as citizens is not so much arguing for an extension of adult rights (and obligations) of citizenship to children but recognition that their citizenship practice (where it occurs) constitutes them as *de facto*, even if not complete *de jure*, citizens. It is also calling for adults to transform their relationship to children particularly in terms of respectful behaviour and changes in the way participatory citizenship is practised in order to accommodate children.

Note

1 A longer version of this chapter will be published in Theoretical Inquiries in *Law*, 8(2), July 2007. The author is grateful to Kay Tisdall for helpful comments on an earlier version.

References

Alderson, P. (1992) 'Rights of children and young people', in Anna Coote (ed.) *The Welfare of Citizens*, London: IPPR/Rivers Oram Press, pp. 153–80.

Almond, M. (2005) 'An Investigation into the Meanings of Good Citizenship', PhD thesis, Loughborough University, Loughborough.

Bessell, S. (2006) 'Children, Human Rights and Social Policy: Is Citizenship the Way Forward?', paper presented at Crawford School of Economics and Government Seminar series, The Australian National University, 9 May.

Cohen, E.F. (2005) 'Neither seen nor heard: children's citizenship in contemporary democracies', *Citizenship Studies*, 9(2): 221–40.

Cutler, D. and Frost, R. (2001) *Taking the Initiative: Promoting Young People's Involvement in Public Decision-making in the UK*. London: Carnegie Trust.

Dearden, C. and Becker, S. (2005) 'Growing up caring: young carers and vulnerability to social exclusion', in M. Barry (ed.) *Youth Policy and Social Inclusion*, London and New York: Routledge, pp. 251–69.

Faulks, K. (2000) *Citizenship*. London and New York: Routledge.

Gould, C. (1988) *Rethinking Democracy*. Cambridge: Cambridge University Press.

Hill, M. and Tisdall, K. (1997) *Children and Society*. Harlow: Prentice Hall.

Hobson, B. and Lister, R. (2002) 'Citizenship', in B. Hobson, J. Lewis and B. Siim (eds) *Contested Concepts in Gender and Social Politics*, Cheltenham: Edward Elgar, pp. 23–54.

Home Office Research, Development and Statistics Directorate (2004) *2003 Home Office Citizenship Survey*. London: Home Office.

Jones, G. and Bell, R. (2000) *Balancing Acts. Youth, Parenting and Public Policy*. York: Joseph Rowntree Foundation.

Jones, G. and Wallace, C. (1992) *Youth, Family and Citizenship*. Buckingham: Open University Press.

Lansdown, G. (2005) *The Evolving Capacities of the Child*. Florence: UNICEF Innocenti Research Centre.

Lister, R. (2003a) *Citizenship: Feminist Perspectives*. Basingstoke: Palgrave.

Lister, R. (2003b) 'Investing in the citizen-workers of the future: transformations in citizenship and the state under New Labour', *Social Policy & Administration*, 37(5): 427–43.

Lister, R., Smith, N., Middleton, S. and Cox, L. (2003) 'Young people talk about citizenship: empirical perspectives on theoretical and political debates', *Citizenship Studies*, 7(2): 235–53.

Lister, R., Williams, F., Anttonen, A., Bussemaker, J., Gerhard, U., Heinen, J., Johansson, S., Leira, A., Siim, B., Tobio, C., and Gavanas, A. (2007) *Gendering Citizenship in Western Europe*. Bristol: The Policy Press.

Marchant, R. and Kirby, P. (2004) 'The participation of young children: communication, consultation and involvement' in B. Neale (ed.) *Young Children's Citizenship*, York: Joseph Rowntree Foundation, pp. 92–163.

Marshall, T.H. (1950) *Citizenship and Social Class*. Cambridge: Cambridge University Press.

Miller, P. (2005) 'Useful and priceless children in contemporary welfare states', *Social Politics*, 12(1): 3–41.

Moosa-Mitha, M. (2005) 'A difference-centred alternative to theorization of children's citizenship rights', *Citizenship Studies*, 9(4): 369–88.

Moss, P. and Petrie, P. (2005) 'Children – who do we think they are?' in H. Hendrick (ed.) *Child Welfare and Social Policy*, Bristol: The Policy Press, pp. 85–105.

Neale, B. (2004) 'Introduction: young children's citizenship', in B. Neale (ed.) *Young Children's Citizenship*, York: Joseph Rowntree Foundation, pp. 6–18.

Oldfield, A. (1990) *Citizenship and Community, Civic Republicanism and the Modern World*. London and New York: Routledge.

Power Inquiry (2006) *Power to the People*. York: York Publishing.

Prout, A. (2000) 'Children's participation: control and self-realisation in British late modernity', *Children & Society*, 14(4): 304–15.

Ridge, T. (2006) 'Helping out at home: children's contributions to sustaining work and care in lone-mother families', in C. Glendinning and P.E. Kemp (eds) *Cash and Care*, Bristol: The Policy Press, pp. 203–16.

Roche, J. (1999) 'Children: rights, participation and citizenship', *Childhood*, 6(4): 475–93.

Save the Children (2005) *The Well-being of Children in the UK: Summary*. London: Save the Children.

Siim, B. (2000) *Gender and Citizenship*. Cambridge: Cambridge University Press.

Smith, N., Lister, R., Middleton, S. and Cox, L. (2005) 'Young people as real citizens: towards an inclusionary understanding of citizenship', *Journal of Youth Studies*, 8(4): 425–43.

Stasiulis, D. (2002) 'The active child citizen: lessons from Canadian policy and the children's movement', *Citizenship Studies*, 6(4): 507–38.

Such, E. and Walker, R. (2005) 'Young citizens or policy objects?' *Journal of Social Policy*, 34(1): 39–57.

Tisdall, K. (2006) 'Antisocial behaviour legislation meets children's services: challenging perspectives on children, parents and the state', *Critical Social Policy*, 26(1): 101–20.

Wyness, M., Harrison, L. and Buchanan, I. (2004) 'Childhood, politics and ambiguity: towards an agenda for children's political inclusion', *Sociology*, 38(1): 81–99.

Young, I.M. (1995) 'Mothers, citizenship and independence: a critique of pure family values', *Ethics*, 105: 535–56.

2

Education for Citizenship: Children as Citizens and Political Literacy

Andrew Lockyer

Introduction

The adoption of the UN Convention on the Rights of the Child (UNCRC, 1989) and the implementation of the Crick Report on *Education for Citizenship and Teaching of Democracy in Schools* (1998) have both given impetus to the debate about the status of children as citizens in the UK. It has become a contested issue whether children, defined as young people below the age of majority, are to be viewed as current citizens, or merely future citizens, partial citizens, or citizens-in-the-making. Conceptualizing active citizenship is at the heart of the matter. On the face of it, the UNCRC and the Crick Report point in different directions; the former focuses on the distinctive rights of children, and the latter gives equal emphasis to their duties or responsibilities. Central to the issue of children's actual or potential citizenship is their political standing – their lack of voting rights, against their putative obligation to be politically educated.

My argument is that despite the UNCRC's definition of children by their lack of the political and civil rights, the attribution to them of participatory rights (especially those embedded in Article 12) both entitles and obliges them to become politically engaged. The UNCRC should be interpreted in the light of the Crick Report rather than viewed as at odds with it. The republican model of citizenship that is embedded in the Crick Report is potentially transformative. It allows children to be politically active citizens (in the sense prescribed) without insisting either on their being prematurely autonomous, or requiring the institutions they inhabit to be prematurely democratic. I suggest that the compulsory education in political literacy that derives from the Crick Report, consistent with Article 12, has the potential to impact upon and transform relationships beyond the public sphere.

Crick Report

The Crick Report, whose recommendations led to citizenship education becoming an examinable subject in the National Curriculum in England and adopted as an element in the curriculum in other parts of the UK, was in aspiration a radical document.

We aim at no less than a change in the political culture of this country both nationally and locally: for people to think of themselves as active citizens, willing, able and equipped to have an influence in public life and with the critical capacities to weigh evidence before speaking and acting; to build on and to extend radically to young people the best in existing traditions of community involvement and public service, and to make them individually confident in finding new forms of involvement and action among themselves.

The Crick Report (paragraph 1.5)

The impetus behind the Crick Report is its concern about the health of contemporary British democracy. It speaks of 'the worrying levels of apathy, ignorance and cynicism about public life' (paragraph 3.5). It links political disengagement, evidenced by poor election turn out amongst first-time voters and distrust of politicians, with the wider social ills associated with youth alienation and decline in 'traditional forms of civic cohesion' (paragraph 3.6). The proposed citizenship education is therefore to produce a 'nation of engaged citizens'. In this sense the Crick Report aims at what Parry calls a 'transformative' agenda of citizenship education rather than a merely 'reproductive' one (Parry, 2003).

Liberalism and Republicanism

The Crick Report is widely recognized to embody competing elements of liberalism and republicanism in the conception of citizenship that it endorses (Lockyer, 2003). One of the key differences between the two traditions is the extent to which the State should prescribe the way of life for its citizens. This of course has implications for the character and content of citizenship education.

For the liberal the primary function of education is to facilitate autonomy and maximize the opportunity of persons to live their chosen ways of life (Gutmann, 1987; Callan, 1997). Democratic politics has largely instrumental value in preventing governments from abusing power. Political and civil liberties include the *right* to take part in public affairs but no *obligation* to do so.

Republicanism by contrast is grounded on the ethic of civic engagement, which entails a duty of public service, and an obligation to contribute to the common good of the community, or communities, with which the citizen identifies (Dagger, 1997).

The republican ethic derives from an Aristotelian conception of mankind as *zoon politikon*, in essence a political being (Aristotle, *The Politics*, 1948 Bk I). Thus what is public and civic is privileged as a way of life over what is personal and private (Arendt, 1958). Although classical republicanism embodied a gendered conception of citizenship by endorsing a peculiarly masculine conception of virtue and reason (Elshtain, 1982; Okin, 1989), the extension of the contemporary State to deliver welfare and distributive justice within civil society provides a more gender-neutral foundation for the ethic of service.

One way in which the Crick Report seeks to accommodate the two traditions, or value systems, is by stressing the need for 'reciprocity' between the rights and duties. It criticizes T.H. Marshall (Marshall, 1950) whose liberalism led him to place too much emphasis on 'individual rights' to the neglect of 'obligations'. The Report praises *Encouraging Citizenship*, the House of Commons Commission on Citizenship, 1990, for seeing that rights and responsibilities must be viewed together (paragraphs 2.3).

The curriculum is expected to teach a good deal about rights, both human rights in an international setting (paragraph 6.12), and rights which more particularly affect students directly in their daily lives – including those embedded in the UNCRC.

Schools should not only facilitate talk about rights and responsibilities, but also enable students to put them into practice 'within the school and within the local community' (paragraph 5.3.1).

The Crick Report puts the substance of citizenship education under three heads – 'social and moral responsibility, community involvement and political literacy' (paragraph 1.8). Members of the Crick Committee, who had a diversity of political and professional backgrounds, may well have attached different weights to the three elements – they may be variously construed from more or less liberal and republican perspectives. Bernard Crick has subsequently 'wondered . . . how many of my group realised that they were signing up to the radical agenda of civic republicanism rather than the less demanding "good citizen" and "rule of law" imperatives of liberal democracy' (Crick, 2002: 114).

Active Citizenship

Among the three aspects of active citizenship, the requirement to become 'politically literate' is the most problematic. Nobody could object to the teaching of 'social and moral responsibility' since this can incorporate an infinite variety of values, attitudes and beliefs. Standing alone it would seem to allow the moral perspective to be entirely open – compatible with an extreme liberal, tolerant or permissive perspective, or even a highly illiberal one. However, the report suggests that 'in a parliamentary democracy' moral responsibility must include political responsibility (paragraph 2.12), which is already to say something about the moral citizen. On these terms it would be socially and morally irresponsible not to become politically engaged.

Community involvement might be understood in a variety of ways; there are notably different ideas about serving 'the community' and about which is (or which are) the most morally relevant community (or communities) to serve. Influenced by *Encouraging Citizenship*, the report makes explicit the desirable connection between local voluntary community service and political activity. It suggests an 'interactive role between schools, local communities and youth organisations' which 'could help make local government more democratic, open and responsive' (paragraph 1.11). This echoes the prescription of writers within the American civic republican school (Barber, 1984; Putnam, 2000) who identify the need to replenish the stock of 'social capital' to combat the loss of community consequent upon the pursuit of market individualism. Crick acknowledges the influence here of Alexis de Tocqueville and John Stuart Mill who teach that the nursery of democratic practice is to be found in local participation in neighbourhoods and the small associations of civil society (Crick, 2000).

Where the Report's recommendations directly challenge received values is in their insistence that the school itself is the place to engage with politics both in the classroom and in the school community as a whole. This is at the centre of Parry's claim that the citizenship education in the Crick Report is transformative. The aim is to prepare all for civic and political participation – 'The purpose of citizenship education in schools and colleges is to make secure and to increase the knowledge, skills and values relevant to the nature and practices of participative democracy' (paragraph 6.6).

The reservations about teaching politics are confronted head on. These were in part the product of legislation expressly forbidding the pursuit of politically partisan activities in schools (in the Education Acts of 1986 and 1996), the origin of which was the always-exaggerated fear of indoctrination by 'leftist' teachers (Scruton, 1985). The 'safe' option is to teach political history or institutions – something akin to the American teaching of civics. Bernard Crick elsewhere calls this 'safe and dead, dead-safe, old rote learning' (Crick, 2000: 119).

The Crick Report argues that in the first place the potential for ideological bias in teaching is not confined to teaching about politics, it can occur elsewhere in the curriculum – in History, Geography and English Literature, for instance (paragraph 10.3). More importantly, in a liberal democracy learning about controversial issues 'constitutes the essence of worthwhile education' as distinct from training (paragraph 10.4).

Equipping students to understand and debate controversial issues requiring them to effectively participate in classroom discussion is closely tied to political literacy. This involves learning to engage in political argument, demanding an ability to understand and deploy relevant concepts and to operate within the conventions that accommodate 'reasonable disagreement.' This in turn requires the inculcation of what Bernard Crick calls 'procedural values' – those of 'tolerance, fairness, respect for truth and reasoned argument' (Crick, 2000: 68). These both facilitate reasonable debate and promote respect for difference, which together underpin the values of a liberal–pluralist education.

Considerable weight is attached to participating in the community of the school beyond the classroom. This is described as the 'whole school approach'. The 'ethos of the school' must be one which encourages pupil participation. This may be facilitated by the schools having 'informal channels' which make the school responsive to the student's voice and through setting up class and schools councils. The significance attached to these might be thought to exaggerate their role – they are said to give 'practical experience of decision-making and democratic processes' (paragraph 3.19).

Certainly, if the transformative aspiration of citizenship education depended upon the opportunity for democratic participation in schools, the aspiration identified by Parry must appear to be a distant ideal. But perhaps the requirement to democratize schools is not a prerequisite. It may be sufficient to liberalize and/or politicize them. This will be considered later.

A Liberal Objection

Before leaving the Crickian model of active citizenship we should note that it is considered to be too prescriptive for some liberal commentators. Its specification of moral, social and political education is arguably at odds both with individual autonomy and with value pluralism. The latter objection carries the greater weight in the context of seeking an appropriate form of education for a multicultural and multinational State (Kymlicka, 1995; Macedo, 2000). Where there are community identities claiming greater affective allegiance than State membership a thick conception of citizenship is thought to be especially problematic.

Graham Haydon (2003), for instance, argues that grounding citizenship on a shared civic ethic rather than on external compliance with norms and principles embodied in the law, risks excluding those whose values and beliefs are inimical to it. This can be understood as an objection to viewing citizenship as a species of 'virtue ethics'. It requires citizens to be people motivated to act on certain beliefs, and exhibit certain attributes of character, that may confront or be at odds with the persons they are, or required to be by other identities or ethical commitments.

Haydon's complaint is that in privileging political literacy the republican model constrains and tends to exclude. Minimal citizenship will better accommodate a multicultural, multi-faith society. External compliance with legal norms is sufficient, and there is no requirement to favour civic engagement or national or State identity above others. On this view, there need be no general obligation to act politically, so compulsory education in political literacy is a questionable imperative.

It is sufficient for now to notice that this minimal citizenship comports with the conception of representative democracy that views politics in the main as a specialized activity of elites. Democratic liberty is preserved so long as 'there is competition amongst elites for the people's vote' (Schumpeter, 1943). There need be no general obligation on citizens to be engaged with or participate in politics, so long as these are available careers to pursue. This is exactly what the Crick Report rejects in endorsing the participatory model embodied in civic republicanism.

The UNCRC: Participation, Rights and Responsibilities

The adoption of the UNCRC (1989) is seminal to any contemporary discussion of children's citizenship. There is no space here to give a full assessment of the implications of its provisions (other contributors to this collection provide some of this); it is appropriate to comment on those aspects of the convention which bear on the issue of political rights, and to briefly suggest how the significance of participatory rights comes to be underrated.

The UNCRC includes some universal rights which children share with adults and some rights which are peculiar to children. Implicit in the definition of a child is a category of rights, linked to 'majority', which children lack. It is useful to employ Feinberg's classification, adopted by Archard (2004), and call the first 'ac' rights, the second 'c' rights and the third 'a' rights. Foremost among 'a' rights are political rights associated with the democratic franchise and those 'liberty' or 'autonomy' rights grounded on the right-holder being deemed the best judge of their own interests. On the face of it, withholding political rights and denying autonomy are on all fours.

Among the rights peculiar to children ('c' rights) there are some which treat them as objects, or recipients, of protection and welfare (beyond what is afforded to adults), in virtue of their 'immaturity' and need for 'special safeguards and care' (UNCRC, 1989: Preamble). There are others which treat children as agents with developing capacities to exercise some legitimate freedoms and to participate in decisions which affect them. It is the latter, the participatory rights of the UNCRC, that represent an advancement in empowering children, albeit they are often thought to be insubstantial, subject to limitation, or unrealizable (see Milne; and Liebel in this volume).

Article 12 contains the most important formulation of participatory entitlement.

12 (1) 'States Parties shall assure to the child who is capable of forming his or her own views the right to express those views freely in all matters affecting the child, the views of the child being given due weight in accordance with the age and maturity of the child'.

Commentators commonly gloss Article 12 by pointing to its conditions and qualifications (Archard, 2004). The provision is typically interpreted (especially by lawyers) to predicate due-process rights, as specified in Article 12(2).

More profoundly Article 12 is typically considered as a substitute for the exercise of adult autonomy. Thus a child's right to be heard is understood to allow her/him a share in decisions which might otherwise be made for them. Article 12 is thus juxtaposed with Article 3, whereby consideration of a child's interest trumps acting on their views, especially when the child's interest is the only or 'a primary' object of the decision.

But Article 12 is much wider than this. It includes the child's right to express a view and have it considered on 'all matters that affect the child'. This must include any area of private life or public business. There is no confinement of this right to where the interest of a child, or children, are being exclusively considered. At least in theory Article 12 extends a right to children to influence all decisions which affect them as well as others (not a right that is generally granted to adults). If the reality is that in practice the implementation of this right is limited, it does not negate its importance.

The liberal disposition to implicitly treat autonomy rights (or elective rights) as the paradigm case in rights discourse (see Fortin in this volume), not only presents an obstacle to a proper grasp of participatory rights, but also impedes a sophisticated understanding of the complex relation between rights and responsibilities (Lockyer, 2003). The idea that 'the right holder has exclusive control more or less extensive over the other person's duty so that in areas covered by the law, the individual who has the right is a small scale sovereign' (Hart, 1982: 170) makes little sense when applied to the interwoven rights and responsibilities that express the relation between children and parents, let alone the obligations which citizens have to each other and the community as a whole.

What is clear in the formulation of most of the UNCRC participatory rights is that they impart to children neither adult autonomy nor adult responsibilities. Yet, 'consistent with their evolving capacities' children are granted sufficient competence to exercise some rights, and this same competence presupposes that they are capable of taking some responsibilities. Children who exercise participatory rights must also acknowledge their duties to others. Some rights and duties are peculiar to the relations of parents and children and some obligations require considering the interests of others beyond the family (see Article 5). Neither the rights of children nor parents typically make them 'sovereign' over the other's duties. This suggests that their pursuit of collective 'goods', especially where there is disagreement, will typically require to be negotiated.

Reconceptualizing the Political

Returning to political literacy in the Crick Report we noted: first, it was identified with knowledge of political concepts; second, it required the adoption of procedural values that demand respect for truth and reasoned argument; and third, it involves learning by doing, and thus required political engagement.

We noticed that Crick himself identified political citizenship with republicanism rather than liberalism. This entails not only developing appropriate skills but also acquiring attributes and particular virtues of character, to which State education is committed. The State should not merely provide the opportunity for young people to become politically educated, it is a compulsory obligation of citizenship – needing to be learned like other forms of literacy.

If we look closely at Bernard Crick's understanding of politics as an activity, drawn from over 40 years of reflection, it has undergone some extension and has come to implicitly merge the boundaries between the public and private spheres. His argument *In Defence of Politics* (1962) is concerned to delineate political rule from the varieties of non-political rule. There is politics where there is the peaceful resolution of conflict; where there is no monopoly of truth, or claim to legitimate power, but where there is plurality of values; and, where there is accommodation and compromise without resort to coercion.

In more recent times his idea of the political has developed, not least as a result of the influence of feminist writers, to recognize the practice of politics beyond the institutions of the State embedded in the associations of civil society. In his essay on 'Political Literacy' first published in 1978 (with Ian Lister) and republished in his collection of *Essays on Citizenship* in 2000, he argues that there is a form of politics in 'everyday life – in the family, the locality, educational institutions, clubs and societies and in informal groups of all kinds' (Crick, 2000: 65). It occurs wherever there are 'actions and interactions between groups' who recognize a mutual entitlement to influence decisions. Politics encompasses activity where 'ordinary people' share in decision-making that aims at peacefully resolving disagreement and the pursuit of collective ends (Crick, 2000: 59–74).

The skills of politics are classically identified with the attributes of rhetoric and dialectic – the use of language to advocate, explain, justify and persuade. The skills of argument are to be deployed in those locales, or relationships, where obedience cannot be instructed or demanded. In this sense political literacy is a necessary life-skill even if there is thought to be no obligation to participate in public life beyond the parochial.

It is in the context of politics thus understood, that the participatory rights and responsibilities of children specified by the UNCRC should be seen. Attributing to the young the right to have their views listened to and given due weight vests them with some power. Right holders need not be mini sovereigns to be acknowledged as political actors, rather they must be viewed as simultaneously bearing rights and duties. In a sense the lack of autonomy of young people, whose views can be overruled by others even on matters that primarily affect them only, makes the 'political' skills of persuasion even more important to them than to adults. Moreover, even if for enfranchised adults the locus of political citizenship remains primarily focused on the formal institutions of the State, this may not be so for young people both because the decisions which affects them are made closer to home and because the public institutions they inhabit are not principally those characteristically regarded as sites of political action (There is clearly a parallel between children and women here. See Lister in this volume.).

There are a number of obvious objections to my suggested reconceptu-alizing of the political, not least its disturbance of the distinction to be drawn between activity appropriate to the separation of public and private spheres. In its classical republican formulation (following Aristotle) the public sphere, where politics is located, is an association of equals free to decide upon collective goods by the application of reasoned argument, and thereby superior to the private sphere where relations are hierarchical and ends are fixed by necessity (Arendt, 1958). The idea that there can only be politics where there are relations of equality, and scope for rational disagreement about ends, is a potent one.

But the pertinent question is, what kind of equality is a prerequisite for politics? Even for Aristotle political equality is proportionate rather than arithmetic. That is, it should take into account relevant differences amongst citizens – only in extreme democracy where political 'offices' are distributed by lot is there absolute political equality (Aristotle Politics: Bk IV). The ideal of equal citizenship holds so long as citizens are considered to be equal in those matters where there is no legitimate ground for discrimination – equality of respect, equality before the law and equal opportunity to achieve advantaged positions. This does not require that relevant differences be set aside.

The minimalist liberal conception of democracy (already mentioned) where the principal political activity of citizens is voting in State elections, embodies an arithmetic conception of equality – 'each is to count as one and nobody more than one'. Where voting is understood instrumentally as the representation of individual interests (such that the collective interest can be aggregated), it is both hard to find a rationale for political education and difficult to see how the interests of non-voters can be accommodated (Plamenatz, 1973). The expected competence of voters is so low that the case for extending the vote to children seems the obvious solution.

Dissatisfaction with the minimalist model of liberal democracy has been central to the revival of civic republicanism, and the pursuit of more sophisticated models of democracy and participation (Pateman, 1970). The ambition has been to theorize the ethical practices of a democratic society not only where collective decision-making is principled, but also where social interactions are informed by principles of equality or mutuality. There are two notions (sometimes run together) that democracies should be 'deliberative' and 'discursive' (Elster, 1989; Dryzek, 1990). The focus is on the character of the process of decision-making, so that outcomes are informed by reasoned and fair argumentation, where competing points of view are taken seriously and respected. The core of discursive democracy is 'communicative rationality' which provides the grounding of open and equal political discourse. An important point to take from these ideas is that democratic discourse has to be learned by being practiced, so our institutions must provide the opportunities or 'space' for such learning.

My claim is that where there are interactive relationships and where there is no monopoly power, such that there is room for deliberative discussion about ends, there is the possibility of politics. The powerless cannot participate in politics. But where persons have participatory rights they have some power. There can be politics where there are legitimate inequalities, including those relating to the right to decide. We may express this by saying that relations need not be founded on democratic equality to count as political, or that democratic discourse can be practised outside wholly democratic institutions. The prerequisite for acquiring political literacy through practice is to be found in non-autocratic settings. Whether or not the home or the school are such settings depends on whether they permit the exercise of participatory rights and facilitate communicative rationality.

Conclusion

The school is an arena in which children act and interact with others, and as such is public space in which politics may be experienced. If a classroom teacher brooks no discussion or elicits no account of views in class, there is no opportunity for the exercise or development of political literacy. The teacher–student relationship may be deemed autocratic. Similarly, where parent(s) or guardian(s) take every decision regarding a child's welfare with neither consultation nor explanation of their reasoning, the possibility of politics is excluded from their interactions. However, if Article 12 is taken seriously and children are acknowledged as having a legitimate perspective on matters affecting them and others, however naïve or imperfect, then they are recognized as having rights and capable of responsibilities to influence decisions through engaging in political discourse.

The school as a whole is a form of community and a class within it capable of acting as one. As in any community, certain norms of conduct must be established and followed in order for interactive discourse with the potential for political engagement. Therefore, the aim of citizenship education ought to be the inculcation of the procedural values associated with public reasonableness (toleration, receptiveness towards interlocutors, respect for argument and the possibility of persuasion). While on the one hand citizenship education uses the classroom to instil such values in young people ahead of their future deployment in the formal institutions of the public sphere, on the other the classroom itself is a political forum on the definition here outlined. These norms of public reasonableness become valuable in themselves to the wider learning environment in and beyond the school.

The procedural values are not only relevant to discourse in the classroom where young people are in fact exercising their rights and acknowledging their responsibilities, they enable young people to conduct themselves appropriately in other contexts where opportunities arise in any form of community to participate in discourse about collective ends or purposes. Citizenship education also comes to represent a means of influencing the private sphere through the public, since the tenets of public reasonableness absorbed at school may come to animate discourse in the domestic arena.

Since matters emanating from the domestic sphere frequently affect the public domain engagement with issues which traverse the business of home and school is inevitable. Just as encounters between different primary values or conceptions of the good are bound to occur where young people who are members of diverse cultural communities are brought together, school in effect becomes the site of such intersubjective encounters which provide learning experiences that promote understanding and accommodation within pluralist civil society.

It is sometimes objected that fundamental values and inherited identities are threatened by the promoting of autonomy in liberal education. But equipping young people to think for, and be, themselves, in a context of respect for reasoning, where there is also respect for difference, can validate as well as undermine. Students are equipped to express and defend their inherited views and values in the language appropriate to public discourse. Grounding members of communities in discursive ethics and practice, allows them to more effectively represent their own particular conceptions of the good in the formal political sphere. Moreover, the exposure to democratic discourse does not require rejection of the 'self identity' acquired through familial socialization; it enables the developing self to negotiate new identities through the interaction with peers and in confronting public issues. Civic virtues promoting justice and service to others make calls upon the familial values of loyalty and care, which are part of normal parental upbringing. Rather than my extension of the 'political' constituting an alien imposition on a hermetically sealed private sphere, it acknowledges the interconnectedness of the personal and the public.

It should be said that my argument is not that we merely redraw the boundaries of political citizenship, ascribing value to previously neglected forms of activity, and then redefine our existing institutions, including schools, as conducive to political participation. There is much that needs to change within the existing regimes of schools, domestic life and the other institutions of civil society for political literacy to flourish, not least the need to challenge unjustifiable autocracy. My claim is we do not need to require schools (or families) to be wholly democratic institutions to admit political engagement. They may acknowledge children to be equally citizens without denying them differential status in relation both to rights and responsibilities.

Redefining the ambit of the political to non-autocratic social interactions where there is legitimate disagreement, respect for rights and responsibilities, where communicative rationality prevails, helps bridge the divide between the private and public spheres. The status of young people is thereby changed. They are recognized as legitimate political actors with a stake in the decisions that affect them inside and outside the institutions which have the greatest influence on their lives – arguably, families and schools. It is therefore necessary to take seriously the civic–republican political component of citizenship education since it empowers young people to be active and responsible citizens in advance of them enjoying full autonomy rights and the entire range of civic duties expected of enfranchised democratic agents.

References

Archard, D. (2004) *Children: Rights and Childhood* (2nd edn). London: Routledge (1st edn, 1993).

Arendt, H. (1958) *The Human Condition*. London: Cambridge University Press.

Barber, B. (1984) *Strong Democracy*. Berkeley, CA: University of California Press.

Barker, E. (Ed. and Trans) *The Politics of Aristotle*. Oxford: Clarendon Press.

Callan, E. (1997) *Creating Citizens*. Oxford: Oxford University Press.

Commission on Citizenship (1990) *Encouraging Citizenship*. London: Her Majesty's Stationery Office.

Crick, B. (1962) *In Defence of Politics* (1st edn). London: Weidenfeld and Nicolson. (5th Edn. 2000 London: Contiuum).

Crick, B. (2000) *Essays on Citizenship*. London: Continuum.

Crick, B. (2002) *Democracy: A Very Short Introduction*. Oxford University Press.

Crick Report: Education for Citizenship and Teaching of Democracy in Schools (1998) Final Report of the Advisory Group on Citizenship, Qualifications and Curriculum Authority.

Dagger, R.J. (1997) *Civic Virtues: Rights, Citizenship, and Republican Liberalism*. Oxford: Oxford University Press.

Dryzek, J.H. (1990) *Discursive Democracy: Politics, Policy and Political Science*. Cambridge: Cambridge University Press.

Elshtain, J.B. (1982) *The Family in Political Thought*. Amherst, MA: University of Massachusetts Press.

Elster, J. (ed.) (1989) *Deliberative Democracy*. Cambridge: Cambridge University Press.

Gutmann, A. (1987) *Democratic Education*. Princeton, NJ: Princeton University Press.

Hart, H.L.A. (1982) *Essays on Bentham: Jurisprudence and Political Theory*. Oxford: Clarendon Press.

Haydon, G. (2003) 'Aims in citizenship education: responsibility, identity, inclusion', in A. Lockyer, B. Crick and J. Annette (eds) *Education for Democratic Citizenship: Issues of Theory and Practice*, Aldershot: Ashgate, pp. 78–88.

Kymlicka, W. (1995) *Multicultural Citizenship: A Liberal Theory of Minority Rights*. Oxford: Oxford University Press.

Lockyer, A. (2003) 'The political status of children and young people', in A. Lockyer, B. Crick and J. Annette (eds) *Education for Democratic Citizenship: Issues of Theory and Practice*, Aldershot: Ashgate, pp. 120–38.

Macedo, S. (2000) *Diversity and Distrust: Civic Education in a Multicultural Society*. Cambridge, MA: Harvard University Press.

Marshall, T.H. (1950) *Citizenship and Social Class and Other Essays*. Cambridge: Cambridge University Press.

Okin, S.M. (1989) *Justice, Gender and the Family*. New York: Basic Books.

Parry, G. (2003) 'Citizenship education: reproductive and remedial', in A. Lockyer, B. Crick and J. Annette (eds) *Education for Democratic Citizenship: Issues of Theory and Practice*, Aldershot: Ashgate, pp. 30–46.

Pateman, C. (1970) *Participation and Democratic Theory*. Cambridge: Cambridge University Press.

Plamenatz, J. (1973) *Democracy and Illusion*. London: Longman.

Putnam, R. (2000) *Bowling Alone: The Collapse and Revival of American Community*. New York: Simon and Schuster.

Schumpeter, J. (1943) *Capitalism, Socialism and Democracy*. London: Allen and Unwin.

Scruton, R. (1985) *World Studies: Education or Indoctrination?* London: Institute for European Defence and Strategic Studies.

3

Citizenship from Below: Children's Rights and Social Movements

Manfred Liebel

Introduction

In the social sciences, the question of children's rights is being discussed increasingly with regard to the citizenship of children. This addresses in a general way the question whether children do not only possess rights, but also make extensive use of these, and are able to confer rights upon themselves. Such a perspective goes beyond the mere assumption of the 'usefulness' of the UNCRC and other legal norms for children codified by the State, and raises the question to what extent children themselves can play an active and effective part in the formulation and implementation of their rights.

In this chapter, the question will be discussed as to what the citizenship of children in contemporary societies can consist of and what its preconditions are. To this end, I will introduce various concepts of citizenship, and discuss their relevance and their chances of realization for children. In doing so, I will pay particular attention to two questions: On one hand, what 'equal' citizenship of children can imply and how it can be implemented, on the other hand, what kind of citizenship arises in the context of social movements of children, which in the following is termed 'citizenship from below'.

What Does 'Citizenship' Mean?

The use of the concept 'citizenship' is closely connected with notions of democracy and participation. It is a product of the emergence of predominantly urban societies and the demands of the residents to no longer leave public affairs to a high-handed ruling class, but to take them into their own hands. In eighteenth-century Europe, with the rise of bourgeois societies and the connected desire of the new bourgeoisie for a State with clear territorial delimitations serving their interests, citizenship gradually became a 'national' concern. With the introduction of universal franchise, citizenship was expanded, at least formally, to all (enfranchised) members of the nation-state, and is today increasingly also extended to interstate and suprastate political systems. Meanwhile, continental citizenships (' "citizens" Europe'), not to mention a global citizenship (that could be connected with the UN system or transnational civic society networks) remain abstractions without clear contours.

In modern Europe, two fundamentally different concepts of citizenship can be distinguished: on the one hand the liberal concept, and on the other the republican (or social) one (see Fernández Steinko, 2004; and Lockyer in this volume).

The *liberal* conception stresses the individual liberty of the citizen, and assigns to the State the function of guaranteeing private property and the scope for action of the individual citizen based on this by means of corresponding constitutions and laws.The function assigned to the State here is not a formative one but a regulating one. The role of the citizens in public affairs is confined to periodic elections of representative bodies. The emphasis is on 'participation' in the private sphere, whether in economic or family matters. In neo-liberal variants of citizenship, this can reach the point where the public sphere, when relating to matters of 'public welfare', is completely privatized, that is, absorbed into the private sphere.

The *republican* (or *social*) conception of citizenship, in contrast, stresses the dominance of the public sphere and of the community, based on solidarity of all citizens identified with it, without regard to their private possessions or their individual social position. The individual's scope for action is seen as dependent on economically conditioned positions of power, and the State is expected to intervene in the interests of social levelling. The liberty of the citizens is then expressed, conversely, by the fact that they are able to exert a continual and as far as possible extensive influence on public affairs. The corresponding State form is mostly termed 'participatory' or 'direct', in contrast to 'representative', democracy. In contrast to socialist (or social democratic) views, libertarian (or anarchistic) variants of the republican conception of citizenship ascribe greater significance to the self-organization of the citizens outside of the State than to the State itself. But in contrast to the (neo)liberal conception, society is not regarded as a conglomeration of private individuals; instead, the social interrelations and mutual obligations of the members of society are stressed.

Today, the fundamental differences between (neo)liberal and republican concepts of citizenship have sometimes been extended by the notion of 'active citizenship'. This term implies that citizens – as in traditional socialist or social democratic conceptions – not only function as (passive) recipients of governmental provision services but as individuals that actively participate in society. The understanding of 'own activity' can however vary largely. Here again the neoliberal understanding of replacing state responsibility by complete individual self-responsibility (which leaves those perceived as too 'passive' to their own fate) is opposed by a social or republican understanding, which desires extension of the realm of action and responsibility of the citizens, yet in a sense of extended influence on political decisions and state action. The ideas and strivings for a citizenship of children presented below will be discussed in the light of the republican conception of citizenship.

Partial Citizenship or Equal Rights with Adults?

In the social sciences that deal with children, there is agreement that so far there is no 'citizenship as a whole of rights' (Jans, 2004: 38), not even in States with democratic constitutions. This takes into account that, together with civil rights, political, social, economic and cultural rights are fundamental to citizenship. Jens Qvortrup (2005: 11) expresses this succinctly in the statement that 'children do not enjoy economic and political rights as autonomous citizens'. Those who take children's rights seriously are bound to imagine citizenship also of children and to take action for it.

However, there are differing ideas of children's citizenship and possible ways for its implementation. On one hand there is support for the idea that children have the possibility to have an influence on society not only in 'children's affairs', but also in all matters affecting the present and future of societies. This position is at times described as *'equality* between children and adults' yet does not – as the history of the child rights movements demonstrates (see Liebel et al., 2001: 321–48; Liebel, 2007: 18–26) – automatically imply an *equation* of children and adults. On the other hand 'child-friendly' or 'child-size' forms of citizenship are supported that are understood as preparation for future citizenship and are therefore seen more than anything as learning process (see Jans, 2004; Roche, 1999). An equal citizenship is seen as being problematic since it would burden the children with the full responsibility, and would ignore or endanger specific peculiarities and needs of children that are founded in human development. This understanding of child-friendly or child-size citizenship is therefore also critically termed 'partial citizenship' by Invernizzi and Milne (2005: 3), and connected to the question whether the citizenship of children requires special 'children's structures', or whether we are to understand them 'as inclusion and collaboration with adults'.

Based on the above described republican concept of citizenship I will argue in the following, to what extent an 'equal citizenship' of children can not only consider differences between children and adults but is virtually dependent on taking into account the inferior social status of children. To this end it seems useful to imagine citizenship not only in a legal sense as a 'bundle of rights', but in a sociological sense as a social relationship, in which norms, institutional practices, meanings, cultural assumptions, and the sense of belonging are combined (see Isin and Turner, 2002). This understanding of 'lived citizenship' (Lister) is based on a dynamic, process-oriented understanding of rights. Following Ruth Lister (2007), this is particularly important for 'societies where rights are under-developed or are under threat or for groups who are denied full citizenship rights'.

Tom Cockburn (1998) notes, with reference to the citizenship concept of Thomas H. Marshall (1950), that the full citizenship of children is prevented by their marginal social status. They are placed under the direct responsibility of their parents or – in exceptional cases – the State. Children do meanwhile have certain rights, such as the right not to be killed or physically abused, but they remain nevertheless dependent on the goodwill of adults. In conceptions of political citizenship, children are by definition non-political subjects with the right neither to vote nor to strike, and have only limited and, as a rule, strictly controlled access to the media. In this connection, Cockburn calls to mind that over the past 150 years, children have successively been excluded from almost all spheres of public life.

According to the notions of childhood that predominate in the world today, children are primarily regarded as potential for the future or as future citizens. Like women in earlier times, and as 'ethnic' minorities still are today, they are considered as 'outsiders', who (still) fail to possess all the qualities that go to make a 'proper citizen': 'Children are almost everything that the non-citizen is: they are irrational, incapable, undeveloped or dependent and are defined in terms of what they are not, that is adult, responsible, rational and autonomous' (Cockburn, 1998: 107). Their lack of qualification for citizenship is, as a rule, 'justified on grounds of children's need for protection and their dependence on adults' (Lister, 2006: 24).

One particular feature of the citizenship of children consists in the fact that children require a special degree of protection, and their dependence on adults can also mean vital security and support. Arguments in support of the citizenship of children do not need to claim (or insist) that they have to be like adults, or possess the same qualities that are ascribed to adults or which adults claim for themselves. Indeed, children may possess other qualities that can be particularly fundamental to citizenship, such as the 'intuitive' feeling for what is phoney, or for discrepancies between words and deeds. Their supposed lack of competence is also not an argument against the citizenship of children, as this cannot simply be deduced from their time of life, but is connected with specific circumstances of their lives and with their experience. 'Incompetence is not something natural or innate but is socially produced' (Cockburn, 1998: 109).

According to Marshall, social and economic rights and safeguards are the necessary preconditions for the ability actually to exercise civil and political rights. This connection, which is formulated in particular with a view to socially disadvantaged and excluded sections of the population, does not, however, include children. Although Marshall sees in the right of children to education a sign of their social citizenship, he also notes: 'Fundamentally it should be regarded not as a right of the child to go to school but of the adult citizen to have been educated' (1950: 25). Also, with the expansion of compulsory schooling and the length of school attendance, children are refused the opportunity to engage in generally recognized and paid 'productive work'.

Proceeding from Marshall's position, the view could also be supported that 'social citizenship' has been extended to children, in the sense that they are able to claim a degree of protection, that society is responsible for them. But this has not so far been combined with the right for children to exercise political power themselves. Children have merely a 'welfare role' that grants them a certain amount of care and protection, but which conversely plays down their social and economic contributions. Moreover, during the past 25 years, the social citizenship of children, even in the relatively affluent societies of the North, has been undermined by a dramatic growth of poverty. The attitude to rights and laws that has spread under neo-liberal influence since the 1980s devalues social citizenship, while stressing a form of citizenship that is to a high degree individualistic.

Here, the question is not least whether the concept of citizenship is related to the community or rather to the market, whether as consumer or as (potential) member of the labour force. According to the latter concept – which may be termed neo-liberal – the public and private spheres are no longer distinguished; the relation to the community is replaced by individual behaviour of choice in the sense of personal advantage (e.g. the ability to choose from a large number of TV channels). This concept is currently being energetically furthered in the sphere of the European Union, for example, by an increase in the 'economic orientation' of the (still State-run) school system and its opening up for 'marketing' of large enterprises.

Some authors refer – with Great Britain in mind – to the children who, because their parents live in poverty, have to take on responsibility in the family themselves, especially in taking part in looking after other family members (younger siblings, sick or handicapped parents, or other relatives). Roche (1999: 478) calls it 'ironic that those children who act in that highly responsible way (the way in which it is often regretted they do not act) in relation to their family are "made to disappear" by adult practice. [. . .] What the young carers are doing does not really have to be taken seriously, they are just "helping out".' Aldridge and Becker (2002: 218) point out that in the media they are represented either as 'little angels' or 'little victims' of practices of exploitation.

In the case of the children in the countries of the South living in great poverty, this paradoxical situation is even more acute. The 'privilege' of being largely unburdened by duties and responsibilities promised by the status of childhood in the relatively affluent countries of the North, is totally denied to them. Although the UNCRC asserts their rights to care and protection as well as participation, in practice they are hardly able to avail themselves of these, and have little but duties. Indeed, even when, for instance, out of a feeling of solidarity with their families, they fulfil these duties, they receive no recognition for this in society or from political quarters. Their situation becomes completely paradoxical when, as working children who are forbidden to work, and whose working it is aimed to abolish, they are placed in a situation of lack of rights which can even extend to their criminalization.

From this, Giangi Schibotto (2005: 182) draws the conclusion that it is not possible to strive for children's citizenship without 'in some form addressing the problem of the exclusion of children and adolescents'. With regard to working children, Alejandro Cussiánovich (2007: 202) adds that it makes sense to talk of citizenship only if this is understood 'as a social relation on the basis of equality and liberty, but not of subjection and dependence, and not within a hierarchy which discriminates and excludes'. A real citizenship of children is, he states, possible only when they are not seen and recognized as the 'object of investments' in the future, or even only as a 'cost factor', but as 'productive economic subjects' who carry out vital tasks for society and their families (2007: 204).

Citizenship Despite Powerlessness?

One constant topic in writings on children's rights is the fact that children and young people have a profound feeling of impotence and exclusion, and the question arises what this means for the view of children as subjects or actors which is a central element of the childhood studies of today. Are children degraded to the status of objects by exclusion, marginalization and the withholding of political rights, or is the feeling of impotence and exclusion precisely an indication of the fact that children do regard themselves as subjects, which prevents them from resigning themselves to being reduced to the status of objects? In other words, can one imagine that children could effectively influence political life, or at least attempt to do so, despite their feeling of impotence and inadequate political rights?

I see the key to the answer to this question in the fact that children are becoming aware of or being involved in many ways in social and economic life today. This participation frequently takes on forms which, as shown above, bring disadvantages rather than advantages for the children, and as a rule does not meet with appropriate recognition. But it can form a basis for children to be assured of their importance to society, and to claim a not merely recognized but also influential role in society (see Invernizzi in this volume).

Citizenship in this sense is the result of a learning process among children (and among adults in relation to the children). I do not, however, see this learning process as is still common in education for citizenship – namely that the children require to be made capable of citizenship by means of an induced growth of competence – but instead that they relate to concrete experiences of 'being needed' and of their own contributions to the life of society, and become aware of their own 'importance'. The framework of such learning processes can be either educational projects directed towards the empowerment of children and the fostering of their self-confidence, or social movements organized and managed by the children themselves (frequently with support from adults acting out of solidarity with them).

In all societies – whether in the North or the South – 'children are social participants – participating in homeworking, child labour, political protest, caring, keeping the family "on the road," etc.' (Roche, 1999: 484). From this can ensue a conception of citizenship that does not only focus on the dependence of children on adults, but also brings out the (as a rule concealed) mutual interdependence of children and adults in the sense of 'giving and taking' (Alderson, 2000: 62). This also applies to quite young children who, although they are more dependent on adults than older children, are also at least emotionally important to the adults.

In the question of citizenship, children should not be seen and treated as if they were adults, but can meet with recognition on the basis of 'social difference'. 'Children should be regarded as equal citizens with the right to belong as "differently equal" members of society' (Lister, 2006: 25; see also Lister in this volume). It must also be remembered that not all children are equal, but differ as to age, situation in life, and social competences. Where these differences are not taken into account and expressly thematized, there is a danger that children from privileged social backgrounds will dominate over socially disadvantaged children, and thus additionally contribute to discrimination against them.

Citizenship from Below

I understand the cultivation of 'citizenship from below' as a form of everyday action that may appeal to rights, but can also take place totally independently of these, for example in protest movements with deliberate infringements of rules, whose actors do not wait for their rights to be granted. Precisely because as a rule by such action children incur the accusation of being 'bad citizens' (Milne, 2007), it is important to take note of the manner in which it is performed, and to recognize the way 'in which children do resist and challenge adult practices, though not necessarily in obvious or constructive ways' (Roche, 1999: 478). Faced with a world of adults in which children are hardly listened to and their political rights largely refused, they do not have many opportunities to take part in recognized political action. 'Children have to start from where they are socially positioned. This means that they have to make their own space in spaces not of their making' (1999: 479).

Citizenship from below is in this sense not an individual matter, subject to the whim of individual children. It only has a chance of being realized where an awareness of common interests comes about among the acting children. This is not possible for all children in the same way or to the same extent, for common interests are not only a question of a common age-group (a 3-year-old and a 13-year-old may not have much in common, but they certainly share the desire for distinction). As with adults, with children too a fusion of interests must first take place, in which similar experiences are put together in a push for common action.

In the children's movements of the South, what is doubtless the main motor of common action is the shared experience of fulfilling vital tasks in everyday life despite widespread disadvantage and discrimination. The necessity to do something in order to survive leads many children to take part in the spontaneous formation of groups whose self-help is frequently denigrated and criminalized as an early or concealed form of delinquency. While these spontaneous groups often see themselves in the paradoxical situation of offending against laws in order to realize their rights, in the more organized forms of children's movements a marked sense of justice arises. They act intrepidly, expressly demanding the realization of rights, and in some cases even formulating such themselves.

This is remarkable inasmuch as thinking in terms of codified 'rights' is alien to children in everyday life. In general, they have a sceptical attitude towards everything to do with the law and laws, or show little interest in them. The sphere of laws is a domain of adults. Children can (up to the present) neither pass laws nor be involved in jurisdiction. As a rule, laws are accompanied by unpleasant experiences for children, by primarily restricting their freedom of action, either by certain actions being prohibited for them as 'minors', or by laws, when they involve advantages, only applying to adults (from a particular age). For instance, African children are confronted by laws dating from the colonial era which forbid them to engage in 'hawking' or to 'loiter' in the street in order to sell things or beg (see Coly and Terenzio, 2007). Children who work in the street in Latin America are at present experiencing how laws and conventions which are supposed to be for their protection lead to harassment by the police or 'social cleaning-up' operations. Such laws place children, particularly those who live in poverty and try to assist their families, in a state of 'illegality' that means still greater problems for them than that of merely having 'no rights' (see Liebel, 2004).

If they nevertheless appeal to their rights and insist on rights, this is no doubt to do with the fact that with their movements they have fought for and acquired social areas of their own, in which they can experience mutual respect and the application of their own rules. The rights that they formulate are, it is true, influenced by the discourse on children's rights that has been welcomed by the children too since the passing of the UNCRC, but these rights are primarily founded on their own experience, and are immediately related to the reality of their lives. They are not formulae of compromise or general principles that leave broad, almost unlimited scope for interpretation, but concrete programmes of action in experienced or conceivable situations in life. I like to illustrate this with two examples from Africa.

At a meeting of children from South African townships that took place from 27 May to 1 June 1992, a *Children's Charter* was adopted (archive of *terre des hommes*, Germany), which states amongst other things:

- All children have the right to be protected against political violence and violence in townships, and to find a "safe place," and they have a right to institutions to which they may turn for assistance and protection from violence.
- Children have the right to say "no" to violence [. . .] and [. . .] to found youth groups to protect them from abuse.
- All children have the right to demand health and medical care, without obtaining permission from their parents or mentors.

- All teachers should be qualified and should treat the children with patience, respect and dignity. All teachers should be trained and prepared to guarantee that they protect the children's rights.
- All children that have no family should be given a proper and clear place within the community in which they live, where they are accommodated and receive food and clothing.
- All children have the right to protection from slavery and from obligations to work inherited as a duty from their parents or relatives.
- All children have the right to participate in governing the country, and particular attention should be paid to negotiations with children on their rights and their situation.

At the founding meeting of the Movement of Working Children and Youth of Africa, which took place from 18 to 23 July 1994 in Bouaké (Ivory Coast), the delegates formulated *12 Rights*, detailing them as follows (quoted in Liebel et al., 2001: 208–9)

- *The right to be taught a trade.*
  Organize ourselves so that we can take part in our own training schemes, and those set up by the government or others. Get sponsors for this training, work for the realization to training even for those that work during the day.
- *The right not to have to migrate (to stay in our villages).*
  We, the working children, work a lot in the cities and earn very little. We are not respected, we are exploited and we are afflicted by many sicknesses for which we get no treatment. We want to remain in our villages to develop the activities that allow us to be responsible for our own future. To do this, we must organize ourselves in our villages.
- *The right to security when working.*
  To work without being harassed by the authorities and people in general (not to be man-handled, to be trusted).
- *The right to access to equitable legal aid (in case of trouble).*
  Children never win against employers, authorities and those who have the money even though everyone is supposed to be equal in the eyes of the law. We demand this equality and the possibility to be given aid to establish the truth if we are not satisfied with the official version.
- *The right to play.*
  There should be both recreation time and space available to children, house workers should be allowed to watch the television. We should be allowed to play with our friends on Saturdays and Sundays.
- *The right to be listened to.*
  Respect us and pay attention to what we say. Adults and authorities should consult us when making decisions that affect us.
- *The right to light and appropriate work (adapted to our ages and abilities).*
  When we take up the work, we negotiate the type of work which is appropriate to our age, but this agreement is never respected. There are no fixed hours, we start early and finish late. We ask that we not be given hours of work and tasks that you would not ask your own children to do.
- *The right to respect.*
  Recognize our jobs, our contribution to the economy. Recognize that we are human beings, children and full actors in the development of our country.
- *The right to rest when sick.*

We should be given rest when we are sick to allow us to fight the illness and recover.
- *The right to health care.*
  We should be able to take care of ourselves if we do not have enough money to get professional help. We should have access to cheaper health services, just like school-children do.
- *The right to learn to read and write.*
  To learn how to read and write in French or Portuguese . . . and then in our own languages. Lend support to the training schools that we create in our neighbourhoods.
- *The right to self-expression and to form organizations.*
  To assemble, unite, speak as one and defend our group interests. Speak without gags, to say what we think, to be listened to and to give our opinion. We have to believe in what we are doing, believe that our strength lies in our unity, organize ourselves and set up legally recognized associations.

In other children's movements, too, and at other meetings conducted by children, comparable rights are repeatedly outlined. To some extent, they are oriented to the UNCRC, but they go beyond this in essential points, or touch on questions and problems that are not discussed in the UNCRC, or if so only in general formulations. It is typical of such rights not only that they are mostly concrete and related to particular situations, but that, wherever possible, they are also put into practice by the organized children themselves, or their application is demanded with the support of demonstrations. Thus the children organized in the African movement re-examine, at their meetings, which occur every two years, the extent to which their *12 Rights* have been implemented, and the reasons for particular obstacles or difficulties.

In other cases, negotiations are carried out with authorities, and occasionally agreements are also reached which translate the rights demanded into reality. Thus, for instance, the movement of the working children of Bolivia concluded an agreement with the mayor of La Paz that guarantees the children the free use of public places in the city for their work, instead of being, as hitherto, repeatedly dispersed by the police or private security guards. In the Peruvian capital Lima, the children's movement agreed with the city administration on a working and training project for children who had previously been obliged to survive by begging, stealing or prostitution in the streets. In other countries, it was achieved that the police recognize the membership passes of the children's movement, and protect the children from aggressive drivers or pedestrians. Or again – with the support of NGOs or neighbourhood groups – children's workshops and schools of their own were set up, in which working and learning are combined, and the dignity and experience of the children are respected.

Conclusion

The rights that have come into existence in the manner described, and the actions in favour of their application, are an expression of what I call 'citizenship from below'. In them are manifested not only claims for protection, State benefits and participation, but also a practice that rests on self-organization and stresses the possibility of a formative part that children can play in society.

Citizenship from below in the sense described here is significantly different to participation approaches in which children are offered participation in adult decision-making. Even if such offers go beyond mere non-binding consultations or symbolic forms of participation, children's possibilities for action stay limited within a space predefined by adults. Tacitly, this is expressed in the often used articulation that children are 'being involved'. In contrast, citizenship from below is expressed by children themselves setting goals they want to reach and choosing the way they want to act.

It is not guaranteed that this means children achieve what they want, but it shows clearly what has to be changed in children's environment and society in order to be able to speak of (equal) citizenship of children in a meaningful way. To trigger the citizenship of children, collective demonstration is indispensable since children can only reach the required respect and power through this in order to influence decisions or change reality in the way they desire. Such expressions do not necessarily and always have to take on the form of supra-regional social movements or organisations, but can be found in local, informal groups and cultures of peers that are commonplace in the everyday life of most children. The question remains how collective will grows out of these group configurations and cultures to not only preserve their own space or conquer it but also influence the environment or wider society.

References

Alderson, P. (2000) *Young Children's Rights. Exploring Beliefs, Principles and Practice.* London and Philadelphia, PA: Jessica Kingsley.

Aldridge, J. and Becker, S. (2002) 'Children who care: rights and wrongs in debate and policy on young carers', in B. Franklin (ed.) *The New Handbook of Children's Rights*, London: Routledge, pp. 208–22.

Cockburn, T. (1998) 'Children and citizenship in Britain: a case for a socially interdependent model of citizenship', *Childhood* 5(1): 99–117.

Coly, H. and Terenzio, F. (2007) 'The stakes of children's participation in Africa. The African movement of working children and youth', in B. Hungerland, M. Liebel, B. Milne and A. Wihstutz (eds) *Working to Be Someone. Child Focused Research and Practice with Working Children*, London: Jessica Kingsley, pp. 179–86.

Cussiánovich, A. (2007) *Ensayos sobre Infancia. Sujeto de Derechos y Protagonismo.* Lima: Ifejant.

Fernández Steinko, A. (2004) *Clase, trabajo y ciudadanía. Introducción a la existencia social.* Madrid: Ed. Biblioteca Nueva.

Invernizzi, A. and Milne, B. (eds) (2005) 'Children's citizenship: an emergent discourse on the rights of the child?' *Journal of Social Sciences*, Special Issue No. 9, Delhi: Kamla-Raj Enterprises.

Isin, E.F. and Turner, B. (eds) (2003) *Handbook of Citizenship Studies.* London: Sage Publications Ltd.

Jans, M. (2004) 'Children as citizens. Towards a contemporary notion of child participation', *Childhood*, 11(1): 27–44.

Liebel, M. (2004) *A Will of Their Own. Cross-cultural Perspectives on Working Children*. London and New York: Zed Books.

Liebel, M. (2007) *Wozu Kinderrechte. Grundlagen und Perspektiven*. Weinheim and Munich: Juventa.

Liebel, M., Overwien, B. and Recknagel, A. (eds) (2001) *Working Children's Protagonism. Social Movements and Empowerment in Latin America, Africa and India*. Frankfurt M. and London: IKO.

Lister, R. (2006) 'Children and citizenship', *Childright – A Journal of Law and Policy Affecting Children and Young People*, 223: 22–5.

Lister, R. (2007) 'Why citizenship: where, when and how children?', *Theoretical Inquiries in Law*, 8(2), Article 13. Avilable at: http://www.bepress.com/til/default/vol8/iss2/art13.

Marshall, T.H. (1950) *Citizenship and Social Class*. Cambridge: Cambridge University Press.

Milne, B. (2007) 'Do the participation articles in the Convention on the Rights of the Child (CRC) present us with a recipe for children's citizenship?' in B. Hungerland, M. Liebel, B. Milne and Wihstutz, A. (eds) *Working to Be Someone. Child Focused Research and Practice with Working Children*, London: Jessica Kingsley, pp. 205–09.

Qvortrup, J. (2005) 'Varieties of childhood', in J. Qvortrup (ed.) *Studies in Modern Childhood. Society, Agency, Culture*, Houndsmills, Basingstoke: Palgrave, pp. 1–20.

Roche, J. (1999) 'Children: rights, participation und citizenship', *Childhood*, 6(4): 475–93.

Schibotto, G. (2005) 'Reflexiones sobre el paradigma de la ciudadanía y sus aporías', *NATs – Revista Internacional desde los Niños y Adolescentes Trabajadores*, 9(13/14): 177–82.

4

From Chattels to Citizens? Eighty Years of Eglantyne Jebb's Legacy to Children and Beyond

Brian Milne

Introduction

This chapter sets out to explore the history of children's rights from what one might call 'prehistory' until the present. Despite specifying 80 years of Eglantyne Jebb's legacy in the title, the 'prehistory' certainly deserves a mention, if only to set the scene for the rest of the story. The object of recounting that story is to examine the possibility that the advent of children's rights as they stand has contributed to the emergent discourse on children's citizenship.

Whilst in principle examining a global phenomenon, the UK is often used as a point of reference. There is good reason for doing so. The UK was one of the first countries to have legislation specifically aimed at children and has borne a great deal of influence on processes that led to the 'era' of children's rights. If we also bear in mind that many significant changes began during the age of Empire and those laws were applied in many, if not most colonies, the influence on the rest of the world becomes clearer. Likewise, French and Portuguese empires were similarly ruled from the centres in Paris and Lisbon, with corresponding laws being applied in their colonies. Although declining during the early nineteenth century, Spanish colonies experienced some measure of the same. Much of the former British Empire still has secular legal systems with roots traceable back to the Anglo-Saxon legal system. Dutch, Belgian and German colonies experienced some comparable changes. Even as colonies gained independence, deeply implanted legal and social systems influenced much of their early development. Therefore we begin to gain a sense of the proportion of the influence of Western European reform worldwide. Therein notions of 'protection' and 'rights' have become so intertwined that rather than attempt to separate them it appears increasingly useful to look at one as the antecedent of the other. This is where we briefly look at the prehistory.

'Prehistory'

The history of child protection is older than often imagined. In 1794, magistrates at the Lancashire Quarter Sessions passed a resolution seeking to protect children in the care of a number of authorities by not allowing apprenticeship to masters who would work them for long hours. The Health and Morals of Apprentices Act 1802 and the Factory Act 1819 laid down principles but failed to provide adequate inspection and enforcement of the Acts since until the Registration Act 1836 introduced birth certification age was not a useful criterion for deciding who was or was not a child. In 1825 the 'Hobhouse Act' allowed employment of 'free' children beyond legal hours if parents consented. It was difficult to differentiate between a 'pauper' and 'free' child. By 1830, the government became aware of a number of problems in factories with which it intended to deal.

One of the problems was deciding who was really responsible for children who were effectively considered a residual category of persons who, in most European societies, were the property of parents. Some legal commentaries in England noted that child-stealing was not theft unless the child wore clothes which could be stolen. In fact, child theft was more like the theft of a corpse whereby the body was not inhabited by a legal person in either case (Ennew and Milne, 1989: 12). From the 1830s onward a series of industrial laws were passed in the UK and other nations, including parts of what are now Germany, Norway and Sweden, gradually removing children from the regular workforce. Depending on what one reads, historians tell us that this was either a move towards child protection or means of reducing the labour force as fewer but more skilled workers specialized in new technologies. In England and Wales, the Elementary Education Act 1870 introduced compulsory universal education for children aged 5 to 13 years and the Education Act 1880 tightened up school attendance laws. It is again debatable whether or nor this was for the wellbeing of children depending on whom one reads. Some authors (i.e. Goodman, 1971; Illich, 1971; Corrigan, 1979) occasionally cite or use examples of nineteenth- and early-twentieth-century political arguments for compulsory education as a means of removing idle, unemployed youths from streets and public places. Arguably, what appears a nascent move towards protection of children and improvement of their living standards was almost always inclusive of the element of increased control over them. What is certainly most clear from political history is that there was a real fear of the potential disruptive force of young people, leading to every consideration of one of the more important products of education that turned out people who would be part of a disciplined, punctual labour force. Providing a bourgeois moral and religious code to the working class within education would counter potential for revolutionary activity, a latent force under the material conditions of working-class existence at that time. Thus, their position in the social hierarchy would be an outcome of the refinement of educatedness that schooling with its routines and disciplines taught (i.e. Corrigan, 1979: 29–43).

However 'anti-child' much of that may sound, it was part of what drove reform in Europe and the Americas as the nineteenth century drew to a close. Anti-cruelty laws and age of sexual consent laws were amongst many that came either side of the change of century in Europe, parts of the USA, South America as too large parts of the colonial world. The early twentieth century was, however, to be by far the beginning of change for children. So-called child sciences such as developmental psychology, paediatrics and child psychiatry became formally accepted disciplines. It was a period in which, as Zelizer (1994) describes in relation to the USA, where between efforts to capitalize and even attach financial value to children, they were sentimentalized to the degree of making them almost 'revered'. This is when moves away from the child as simply a chattel of parents, especially the father, toward individual bearer of rights emerges and begins to develop. Undoubtedly some of the greatest steps towards what we recognize as child protection and welfare occurred at that time.

Eglantyne Jebb and the Foundation of Children's Rights

The period leading up to, during and in the immediate aftermath of the First World War mark the end of the 'prehistory'. In the wake of war in England, Dorothy Buxton initiated a group that began to campaign on behalf of European children, especially of the defeated Germans and their allies whose chances of enjoying good health and survival were beyond the comprehension of human compassion. Eglantyne Jebb, Buxton's sister, was a member of that group. It led to the launch of the Save the Children Fund, by Buxton, in 1919 as an initiative to raise money for children affected by war throughout Europe. Jebb was a physically sick but mentally very vigorous woman who went to live in Geneva where she began the Save the Children International Union, often called the Alliance for Children. As Buxton became less engaged with Save the Children, Jebb became a highly persuasive and committed figurehead of the charity. Through her influence Rädda Barnen, Swedish Save the Children, was set up and subsequently around 70 other national 'Saves' were launched worldwide. Her other main contribution to children was that in 1921 she formulated a 'Children's Charter', adopted by the International Union in 1923. In 1924 this was adopted almost verbatim by the League of Nations as the *Declaration of the Rights of the Child*, known as the Declaration of Geneva. It was a five point set of non-binding declarations to be used as 'guiding principles' in provision of *protection and care* of children by the League's members. Jebb died in Geneva in1928 having made what were the first of great strides forward for children.

The ILO, League of Nations and the 1959 UN Declaration

After the ILO was created in 1919, some of the international labour standards they adopted focused directly on children. They helped develop a notion that children who worked should possess particular rights. Their earliest conventions included the Night Work of Young Persons (Industry) Convention, No. 6, 1919; Minimum Age (Sea) Convention, No. 7, 1920; Minimum Age (Agriculture) Convention, No. 10, 1921; and Medical Examination of Young Persons (Sea) Convention,

No. 16, 1921. Subsequently, in matters in which children were significantly affected such as exploitative labour, slavery and trafficking, the League of Nations came to play a key role. This was assured by the League's Covenant, Article 23 including:

Subject to and in accordance with the provisions of international conventions existing or hereafter to be agreed upon, the Members of the League:

Will endeavour to secure and maintain fair and humane conditions of labour for men, women, and children, both in their own countries and in all countries to which their commercial and industrial relations extend, and for that purpose will establish and maintain the necessary international organisations;

[. . .]

Will entrust the League with the general supervision over the execution of agreements with regard to the traffic in women and children, [. . .].

To implement those provisions the League set up a Child Welfare Committee consisting of 12 government representatives and 13 'assessors' representing foremost NGOs with the ILO and League's Health Organization. This later amalgamated with the committee dealing with trafficking of young women and became the Advisory Committee on Social Questions. It was broadly speaking protectionist and not inclusive of children as subjects of rights.

Despite the goodwill of membership of the League of Nations, in reality few nations were members (63 was the greatest number ever). Following the promulgation of the Geneva Declaration, there were more obstacles than ways forward. In the wake of war came the massive influenza epidemic across Asia and most of Europe, killing hundreds of thousands of young adults. Immediately thereafter, the Great Depression caused global economic crisis, which brought about political developments that led to the Second World War. Thus little really changed. Hence, when the successor to the League of Nations, the United Nations, began to promulgate new human rights declarations it was almost natural to use the older declaration as basis for a new seven-point version in 1948. That was used as the source for the 1959 Declaration of the Rights of the Child which is still valid today and used as 'springboard' for the initiative to draft and adopt a legally binding set of principles within a convention.

The Road to the UNCRC

During the 1960s, the General Assembly approved a motion that 1979 be nominated as the International Year of the Child (IYC). In 1978, during the run up to the IYC, the Polish delegation to the 34th session of the UN Commission on Human Rights formally tabled a motion that the UN should adopt a convention on the rights of the child. Poland had, in fact, tabled a similar motion in 1959 in preference to adoption of a declaration. Poland stated concern for children regularly in international fora and often referred to its recent past as a pioneering nation. Indeed, the champion of children's rights representing Poland was Adam Lopatka, one of their most senior judges and legal academics who was a passionate believer in the ideas of Janusz Korczak. Returning briefly to the prehistory, Korczak was the pseudonym of Henryk Goldszmit, Polish–Jewish paediatrician, pedagogue and children's author. His biographers recall a variety of versions of where he began to seriously give children's rights any form of consideration but what is certain is that during 1911–12 he became the director of a Jewish orphanage, Dom Sierot, in Warsaw. Before becoming a military doctor in 1914, he formed a simple children's republic with a small parliament, court and newspaper within the orphanage. After 1918 he returned to the orphanage and helped found another until again called up for military service during the Polish–Soviet War. He contracted typhus, was demobilized and resumed work in Warsaw. In 1926 he allowed children to start their own newspaper which, in due course, was published as a regular supplement to the main national Jewish newspaper. His work continued into and during the Second World War. The children and he were moved to the Warsaw Ghetto in 1940. In August 1942 they were removed to Treblinka where all were presumed to have been gassed on arrival.

There is a niggling background debate about whether we should consider Jebb or Korczak as the real originator of the definitive notion of children's rights. It is almost arbitrary: another possible contender might be Maria Montessori, born before and outlived both (1870–1952), whose work included consideration of children's rights early on in the twentieth century (i.e. Montessori, 1964: 196–7). Stretching the point, among others one might consider Reverend Benjamin Waugh (1839–1908), philanthropist and founder of the NSPCC in England. Korczak (1879) was born two years after Jebb (1877), thus were absolute contemporaries, and whatever he may or may not have done or said including, as biographers claim, demanding a charter for children's rights, the fact remains that she drafted the declaration that was adopted. However, within reason, it is possible to extrapolate Korczak's view that children deserved a greater share in running the world than Jebb considered in attempts to primarily give children greater protection. Whoever it was, the fact remains that there is an identifiable starting point for where we are at present. What is incontrovertible is that each of them came from a particular background which influenced what they thought and we do not know an enormous amount about the input of children and how that was initiated anyway. Korczak might, if anything, have the edge on origination of an essentially generic vision of what those rights might be.

Although Korczak was not the only figure in recent Polish history he is certainly the most significant one in putting his nation at the forefront of attempts to see a convention some day, including and perhaps especially during years of Soviet domination. A group of people, including Professor Lopatka, set about drafting a convention they wished to see adopted during the IYC. In fact, what was presented was broadly speaking based on the existing Declaration, thus lacked many innovations inspired by

Korczak some people had wanted to see included, and actually better reflected the position of the Polish government. It was presented to the UN General Assembly for examination, then passed on to the 35th Session of the Human Rights Commission which took account of all comments and criticism of the draft. Rather than attempt to achieve the impossible by the end of the IYC, it was decided that a drafting process be initiated towards final convention within a maximum of ten years.

An open-ended Working Group was set up by the Commission, enabling any of 43 member nations to participate in the drafting process. Any other UN Member State was able to send observers who could take the floor and thus make ad hoc contribution to the drafting process. Intergovernmental organizations were given the same status and NGOs with consultative status to the Economic and Social Council of the UN were extended the right to attend meetings with no absolute right to speak or otherwise contribute. Lopatka became Chair and Rapporteur to the Working Group. A number of nations such as the UK, German Democratic Republic, USSR, Portugal, Norway, Finland and Netherlands were consistently at the heart of the drafting process although notably four poorer nations, Algeria, Argentina, Senegal and Venezuela, made regular and outstanding contributions. All in all it was a largely international effort although Western countries in due course dominated the drafting process. There was paucity of participation by the countries of the south. Nigel Cantwell, then with Defence for Children International, the NGO which was central to the process of drafting, observed that, ' . . . industrial countries were significantly over-represented at all stages. Fears that the outcome would be a heavily Northern-orientated text were widespread and justified' (1992: 23). Delegates from developing countries were not entirely satisfied with the composition of the drafting group. Cultural viewpoints and economic situations were seldom adequately taken into account although Islamic Sharia law was carefully considered. Paradoxically, participation of predominantly Western NGOs in drafting marginalized views of Eastern European and developing countries. The outcome is that it is often viewed as being in a Northern language by the nations of the South. While Poland proposed and submitted the first draft and Lopatka chaired the working group drafting the Convention they also delayed ratifying because of disagreements over the final version.

Non-governmental organisations initially showed enormous enthusiasm, waning after about 1981. A small core of NGOs formed an *ad hoc* group, including Defence for Children International, the first organization set up to solely work with children's rights in 1979 that became central to the work of the NGO group. During 1987, the NGO Group was not only able to revive diminishing interest in drafting but joined together with UNICEF to promote completion of drafting in time for adoption of the completed Convention by the General Assembly in 1989. In fact, extraordinarily UN agencies, including UNICEF, generally showed little interest in the Convention until after its completion and adoption at the end of 1989. Indeed, UNICEF was originally opposed to a convention on the rights of the child because the agency's leadership considered it a distraction from improvements in the field of child health and welfare through its development strategies.

Thus the drafting process began. There were often arguments on minutiae of small issues of little more importance than dotting an 'i' or crossing a 't'. Other issues such as the question of freedom of choice of religion that is virtually impossible within Islam required delicate diplomacy and negotiation to resolve, whereas an issue such as age at which children be permitted to take part in armed conflicts led to uncompromising debate that occasionally jeopardized the possibility of drafting ever being completed and Convention coming about at all. However, by the second half of 1989, after 11 meetings of the Working Group and hundreds of submissions by contributing nations, UN agencies, INGOs and NGOs this had been achieved and the final draft sent to the Commission on Human Rights, ECOSOC and General Assembly. It was adopted by the General Assembly on 20 November 1989. The Convention was opened for signature on 26 January 1990 by all UN Member States. On 2 September 1990, 30 days after deposit of the 20th instrument of ratification, the Convention entered into force. At present all member nations of the UN are signatories and one, the USA, remains to ratify. Somalia ratified twice but because of problems of recognition of their 'government' by the international community it is often said that they have not yet ratified. In the case of the USA there is some concern about its inability to join the international community in support of what is the most successful instrument of international law ever.

Of course, had the story ended with universal ratification and implementation and full acquisition of civil and human rights by all children then the proposition of a shift from being *chattel to citizen* would be assumed to have been largely concluded without further explanation. Indeed, this is not the case. In fact, it is largely based on a Western model of childhood that in turn is based on the idea that children should be protected from the adult world (i.e. Bar-On, 1997). It is a time of play and training for adulthood that has become the universal standard deemed obligatory under the Convention from birth to age 18 years.

The Content of the UNCRC: The 'Three Ps' and Categories of Rights

During drafting the most easily identifiable group of so-called participatory articles, 12 to 16, emerged out of what had only been Article 7 in the first draft. In essence, the original draft placed enormous emphasis on child protection with provision following, the notion of child participation was little more than a gesture. However, near the end of the drafting process, Defence for Children International was asked to identify the main categories of remit for all operative Articles (see Beers et al., 2006: 12). They established *protection, provision* and *participation*, commonly known as the 'Three Ps', and identified each article within the appropriate category. This particularly drew attention to participatory articles and in very little time a miniature 'industry' grew up that especially drew on Article 12 as its natural core. In due course this led to the misapprehension that the Convention potentially increased children's participation in civil society through its participatory articles and principles, thus drawing them closer to status of full citizenship than hitherto.

It is a convention drafted by consensus of a large number of disparate nations. Most contributions were submitted by diplomats to the UN, normally resident in New York or Geneva. Whilst many of them may have studied law, few were in fact experienced, practising lawyers. Few knew much about the real situation of children in any country including their own. It is, consequently, a human rights law and thus inevitably less likely to be taken as seriously as less 'idealized' sets of principles may be. It also includes a phrase at the end of the preamble: 'Recognizing the importance of international co-operation for improving the living conditions of children in every country, in particular in the developing countries . . . ' that renders it a 'charter for children in poor countries' in the view of some wealthier and more self-assured nations. This tends to undermine the fact that many, probably most, developing countries have basic laws offering protection and provision similar to Northern countries but economic problems and sometimes sheer population numbers inhibit or thwart delivery. It is also probably part of the attitude that led the former UK Minister for Children, Young People and Families, Margaret Hodge, to tell a House of Lords Standing Committee 'The UNCRC provides a set of principles or an ethical framework' (Hansard, 12 October 2004) during the drafting of the Children Act 2004. There is, accordingly, tension between less developed nations who have good intentions but few means of applying the Convention and wealthier nations who have ratified and appear not to have subsequently acted.

Debatably, some rights are regarded adequately described by civil and social rights; hence, for example, the right to life (civil right) is protected and provision (social right) should be made for its maintenance. Thus, Article 6 UNCRC reflects Article 3 Universal Declaration of Human Rights and Article 6 International Covenant on Civil and Political Rights, exemplifying how natural rights are adopted into legislation (see Milne, 2005: 34).

The Qualification of Rights in the UNCRC

Likewise, it sometimes appears to offer something with one hand then keep the other hand ready to take it away. Article 14 gives a good example:

1. States Parties shall respect the right of the child to freedom of thought, conscience and religion.

However, it goes on

2. [. . .] respect the rights and duties of the parents and, when applicable, legal guardians, to provide direction to the child in the exercise of his or her right in a manner consistent with the evolving capacities of the child.

The notion of 'evolving capacities' appears early in the Convention in Article 5:

> States Parties shall respect the responsibilities, rights and duties of parents or, where applicable, the members of the extended family or community as provided for by local custom, legal guardians or other persons legally responsible for the child, to provide, in a manner consistent with the evolving capacities of the child, appropriate direction and guidance in the exercise by the child of the rights recognized in the present Convention.

It offers proviso for subjective exclusion from any parts of the Convention that *directly* appear to extend rights to children. This exclusion may be for almost any reason adults consider justifiable and notionally extend for the entire duration of childhood, thus until age 18 years, if an adult's opinion is reasonable in their own mind rather than allowing for the child's view. Thus Article 12 may be more an ideal than a reality:

> 1. States Parties shall assure to the child who is capable of forming his or her own views the right to express those views freely in all matters affecting the child, the views of the child being given due weight *in accordance with the age and maturity of the child.* (my italics)

Likewise Article 13 may be equally idealized rather than realized:

> 1. The child shall have the right to freedom of expression; this right shall include freedom to seek, receive and impart information and ideas of all kinds, regardless of frontiers, either orally, in writing or in print, in the form of art, or through any other media of the child's choice.

Conclusion

Returning to the original proposition that children have somehow moved from being chattels to citizens, it is possible to imagine that the 80 or so years of the development of international human rights and liberal national reforms worldwide have begun to take children down that road. The UNCRC was most certainly never drafted with that in mind and interpretation of participation articles as such is essentially far more laden with enthusiasm and wishful thinking than accurate understanding of what is intended. There is probably much to be said of recent growth in the number of Ombudsmen and Commissioners around the world, some of whom have probably made more substantial steps forward than the Convention has made possible alone.

This chapter may appear highly critical of the UNCRC. However, we should not 'throw the baby out with the bathwater'. It is what we have and is still in its own infancy, needing many more decades before coming into its own. Despite the best efforts of the Committee on the Rights of the Child examining and reaching conclusions on what appears to be happening in States Parties as periodical reports are submitted, there is no means of measuring its effect on children. Oslo-based Childwatch International spent several years developing indicators that could be modified country by country to monitor delivery of children's rights and consequences of changes often required to achieve standards demanded it. Thus far, they seem not to have been used by anybody. Lack of indicators together with little analytical and theoretical work on what future steps might be is an enormous hurdle for us to overcome. Perhaps a push for a theoretical base for understanding exactly what children's rights are and how to work with that concept using tools for monitoring and measuring progress would be a good starting point. It may then begin to be feasible to draw together notions of children as bearers of rights and corresponding concepts of citizenship. Whether or not it will contribute towards children moving towards full citizenship imaginably depends on the extent to which all forms of analysis, including critique, are used in developing more solid theoretical bases out of which we are able to work towards delivery of the rights it describes. The fact that the UNCRC exists and has been ratified by so many nations changes little.

The UNCRC was born out of an interpretation of child protection that delivers welfare in a broad sense, which is to say includes such provisions as education and health. It also lacks any real political or economic rights that compare with those adults have (see Milne, 2005: 32–5; chapters by Jones, Lister and Lockyer in this volume) and the 'duties and responsibilities' experts such as Thomas Marshall attach great important to (Milne, 2005: 34). Since it is an instrument of international law, it has been 'claimed' by the legal establishment as its own. There is, thus, clear tension between how it is understood by social theoreticians, policymakers and where lawmakers place it in the greater scheme of things. However, even the most cursory glance at national reports to the Committee on the Rights of the Child reveal that politically it appears to be taken less seriously than it should, as most human rights instruments tend to be. Simultaneously, it generally appears that the human rights community has not really taken it on board (Flekkøy, 1991: 214–18; Himes, 1994: 2–4) because it does not explicitly address the *problems* and *injustices* other conventions embrace. Essentially it has potential for contributing to recognition of children as citizens but without yet having a precise identity, location and status in that discourse and lacks a 'high profile' advocate for the promotion of the process that might lead to that end.

References

Bar-On, A. (1997) 'Criminalising survival: images and reality of street children', *Journal of Social Policy*, 26: 63–78.

Beers, H. van, Vo, Phi Chau, Ennew, J., Pham Quoc, K., Tran Thap, L., Milne, B., Trieu Thi Anh, N. and Vu Thi, S. (2006) *Creating an Enabling Environment: Capacity Building in Children's Participation, Viet Nam, 2000–2004*, Bangkok: Save the Children Sweden.

Cantwell, N. (1992) 'The origins, development and significance of the United Nations Convention on the Rights of the Child', in S. Detrick (ed.) *The United Nations Convention on the Rights of the Child: A Guide to the 'Travaux Preparatoires'*, Dordrecht: Martinus Nijhoff.

Corrigan, P. (1979) *Schooling the Smash Street Kids*, London: Macmillan.

Ennew, J. and Milne, B. (1989) *The Next Generation: Lives of Third World Children.* London: Zed Books.

Flekkøy, M. (1991) *A Voice for Children: Speaking Out as Their Ombudsman.* London: Jessica Kingsley Publishers.

Goodman, P. (1971) *Compulsory Miseducation.* Harmondsworth: Penguin Education.

Hansard, Standing Committee B, 12 October 2004, Children Bill (Lords) 1st Sitting, Col. 21, London: HMSO.

Himes, J.R. (1994) *Implementing the Convention on the Rights of the Child: Resource Mobilization in Low-Income Countries.* Dordrecht: Martinus Nijhoff.

Illich, I. (1971) *Deschooling Society.* Harmondsworth: Penguin Education.

Milne B. (2005) 'Is "participation" as it is described by the United Nations Convention on the Rights of the Child (UNCRC) the key to children's citizenship?', in A. Invernizzi and B. Milne (eds) 'Children's citizenship: an emergent discourse on the rights of the child', *Journal of Social Sciences*, Special Edition 9, Delhi: Kamla-Raj Enterprises.

Montessori, M. (1964) *Spontaneous Activity in Education.* Cambridge, MA: Robert Bentley Inc.

Zelizer, V. (1994) *Pricing the Priceless Child: The Changing Social Value of Children.* Princeton, NJ and Chichester: Princeton University Press.

5

Children as Rights Holders: Awareness and Scepticism

Jane Fortin

Introduction

There is today a greatly heightened awareness that children in the UK are an important minority group with rights of their own. A lawyer might argue that this increasing appreciation of the concept of children's rights has been driven by two events: first, the ratification by the UK of the United Nations Convention on the Rights of the Child (UNCRC) in 1991; second, the implementation in October 2000, of the Human Rights Act 1998 (HRA). But others might urge that the introduction of citizenship education into primary and secondary schools in 2000 and 2002 respectively, will probably have a far greater long-term impact on children's own ideas than either of these developments. The Crick Report recommended that by the end of Key Stage 3, pupils should 'understand, at a basic level, the legal rights and responsibilities of young people with particular reference to the UN Convention on the Rights of the Child ... understand the rights and responsibilities underpinning a democratic society, with particular reference to the European Convention on Human Rights. ...' (Crick, 1998 para 6.13.2). It seems clear that there is enormous variation in the extent to which such aims are being realized in schools today (UNICEF, 2004 and Ofsted, 2006). Nevertheless, there is now a new generation of pupils emerging from full-time education very aware of their own important status as rights holders.

Children's Rights – Adult Scepticism

Those teaching citizenship in schools today will know that the factors driving an increased awareness of children as rights holders are of crucial importance. Nevertheless, teachers should also be aware that the concept of children's rights is not one that fills all adults with great enthusiasm. Whilst it is very easy to rubbish the idea, some concerns are valid. For example, how does the idea of children being rights holders affect their relationships with their parents? Indeed, it is the possibility of family conflicts that has led some writers to question the whole concept of children possessing rights at all. They argue that family relationships can be damaged by rights assertions. O'Brien Steinfels summarizes these concerns well:

> There is a deep contradiction between the political theory underlying our law with its impulse to protect individuals by an appeal to rights, and the biological

and psychological requirements for successfully rearing children to participate as adults in such a polity. In effect, one of the most perplexing questions raised by these changes is whether the efforts to extend rights of citizens to minors will not inhibit and undermine the kind of parental authority and family autonomy necessary to foster the qualities and virtues adult citizens must possess and be able to exercise in our society.

(1982: 232)

This argument however suggests that family relationships can *either* be based on mutual affection *or* the existence of rights and duties, but not both. This, as David Archard urges, is far from the truth. For a child to have rights against his or her parents is not evidence that parental love is not forthcoming. But as he says, even if that love has broken down, it

is a matter for regret, and recourse to rights may well be second-best. But this is not by itself a reason not to have rights . . .

(1993: 91)

There is also the argument that a system which allows children to enforce their rights against their parents, may *of itself* create division within families and break them apart. But Martha Minow answers that argument most effectively. As she points out, if rights need asserting, conflict has already occurred and the process of enforcing those rights merely gives such conflict expression and a method of resolution (1987: 1890–1).

There are other good reasons for the public's scepticism about the concept of children's rights. An American academic, Carl Wellman, warned against what he calls the 'proliferation of alleged moral rights'. He gives, as examples, the reformers who argue for wild animals' rights to be taken seriously, with the consequent closing of zoos; of those who claim that giant redwoods and virgin forests have legal rights not to be destroyed. He argues that the inflation of rights devalues their currency, so that the assertion of ungrounded rights discredits the ones that are genuine (1999: 1–3, 6–7). There is certainly a risk of this happening in the context of children's rights. Practitioners not uncommonly use rights talk to substantiate exaggerated claims on behalf of children. Another American writer, Martin Guggenheim, observed recently

The concept of 'Children's rights' is both deeper and more shallow than is often recognized. It has less substantive content and is less coherent than many would suppose. It has provided very little by way of a useful analytic tool for resolving knotty problems.

(2005: xii)

Children's Rights – Theoretical Underpinnings

Guggenheim has good grounds for being sceptical about the ability of children's rights, as a concept, to resolve 'knotty problems', but he is right only up to a point. In the hands of those who fail to reflect on the meaning of rights themselves, the concept certainly cannot resolve 'knotty problems'. But he perhaps overlooks the fact that its usefulness as an analytical tool can be improved upon, especially when underpinned by a sound theoretical understanding of the concept of moral rights itself (Fortin, 2003: 12–27). Indeed, those making overambitious claims on behalf of children should perhaps reflect on the work of the moral philosophers and their theoretical debates over the meaning of rights and the part they play in the moral order. Neil MacCormick produced an 'interest theory' of rights which is particularly apposite when applied to children. He argues that a moral right is 'a good of such importance that it would be wrong to deny it to or withhold it from any member of a particular group of people' (1982: 160). Nevertheless, even this theoretical guidance leaves room for uncertainty. Campbell, whose definition of moral rights is not dissimilar to that of MacCormick, admits that it may be a weakness of the interest theory of rights that 'it leaves us with a very open-ended basis for determining which interests are to serve as the ground of rights' (1992: 16).

Whilst MacCormick's interest theory of rights certainly qualifies children as being rights holders, it probably does not prove or disprove the validity of every rights assertion. Furthermore, society's views change – what might be of little importance in one century becomes a unanimously agreed moral right in the next – with legal support following closely afterwards. Thus whilst a century ago society condoned domestic violence, including marital rape, today such behaviour carries severe criminal sanctions. Society's views on the physical punishment of children appear to be undergoing a similar transformation.

Some might argue that we should dispense with the highly theoretical work of moral philosophers like MacCormick. Instead, we should consult the UNCRC which contains a long and clear list of 39 substantive children's rights. But matters are not quite so simple. Lawyers consider that to qualify as a right, an interest has to be capable not only of definition but also of enforcement. As many have pointed out, numerous so-called rights in the UNCRC are couched in such vague and idealistic language that they fall very far short of being rights at all. The doubts about the status of some of the so-called rights have been discussed by many authors (Fortin, 2003: 12–13). For example, Articles 24 and 27 respectively require States to recognize the child's right to 'the enjoyment of the highest attainable standard of health' and to 'a standard of living adequate for the child's physical, mental, spiritual and social development'. Everyone in society would relish such ideal conditions, old and young alike, but it is difficult to conclude that these are moral rights, as such. As another American writer, Joel Feinberg has observed, these are no more than 'manifesto rights' (1980: 153). Nevertheless, he, like many others, sympathizes with the use of rights language in such an international context. After all, it is a powerful way of expressing the conviction that these claims *ought* to be recognized by States, here and now, as 'potential rights'.

Children's Rights – Children's Autonomy?

There is a further reason for approaching the concept of children's rights with a degree of caution. Many people assume that the concept is all about giving children the right to make their own decisions. Indeed, today's proponents of children's rights often appear to place far greater emphasis on children's decision-making rights than on any of their other rights. A concentration on children's right to autonomy is not new. In the late 1970s and early 1980s, the writings of the American 'children's liberationists' provoked considerable controversy. They saw children as having an oppressed status and claimed that they should be liberated from adult domination. They argued that since adults value greatly the right to autonomy, they should not deny it to children. They attacked the laws which prohibit children from taking part in various adult activities until they attain formal and arbitrary age limits. Some even drew up charters of rights for children of *all* ages, including the right to vote, the right to determine their own education, to decide where they were to live, and whether to take paid employment.

Whilst predictably, these ideas attracted considerable criticism, (Fortin, 2003: 4–7) some were sensible. The arbitrary age limits imposed by the law in this country are indeed difficult to justify. For example, 10-year-olds are held responsible for criminal offences, 14-year-olds may ride a horse on a public road, and 16-year-olds may consent to medical treatment, marry (with parental consent), smoke and leave full-time education. Whilst at 17 teenagers may drive a car, they must wait until they are 18 to vote, sign leases, make wills and claim income support. Many adults lack the intelligence to exercise all the rights that, as adult citizens, they are automatically entitled to. Contrarily, countless children who, despite having that mental competence, are denied them, solely by virtue of their minor status. Indeed, given such illogicality, the American liberationists' claims for children to have a far more extensive list of rights, all based on notions of autonomy, might appear attractive. If the right to autonomy is an important aspect of civilized life for adults, should we not agree with them and acknowledge children's need for self-determination? After all, highly developed societies require children who can rapidly become adult citizens with sophisticated abilities. Citizens like this do not emerge from an overprotected childhood; they need their capacity for decision-making to be encouraged as early as possible.

Meanwhile, in this country, the House of Lords in *Gillick v West Norfolk and Wisbech Area Health Authority* [1986] AC 112 indicated very dramatically that they had considerable sympathy with the notion of adopting a more intelligent approach to assessing children's legal competence. Lord Scarman commented (at p. 186):

> If the law should impose on the process of 'growing up' fixed limits where nature knows only a continuous process, the price would be artificiality and a lack of realism in an area where the law must be sensitive to human development and change.

According to the House of Lords, a teenage girl who is of sufficient understanding to comprehend the matter in hand (in that case the need to receive contraceptive advice and help) has the legal capacity to approach her doctor without her parent's knowledge or consent. Indeed, the decision in *Gillick* reflected a more liberal view of the status of children in society and the ability of teenagers to take responsibility for important decisions regarding their health and their future generally.

At first sight, the *Gillick* decision appears to provide support for those who, like the American liberationists, still claim that teenagers under the legal age of majority should be entitled to adult freedoms (Franklin, 2002: 21–28). Nevertheless, whilst the importance of the *Gillick* decision cannot be discounted, it did not give teenagers complete autonomy. Nor does Article 12 of the UNCRC, despite the views of many that it is one of the most important of the Articles in the Convention. It guarantees participation rights, not autonomy (Lockyer, in this volume). Furthermore, the contemporary supporters of teenage autonomy should not overlook the criticisms of the work of the American children's liberationists, which retain their validity today. As the critics pointed out, children are different from adults in a variety of ways and therefore it is not unreasonable to deny them adult freedoms (Fox Harding, 1997: 123–37). Even as teenagers, the majority of children lack the intellectual developmental capacity for decision-making that the majority of adults have and so they should not be given all adult freedoms. Furthermore, children are physically vulnerable and cannot survive without special protection. They are therefore dependent on adult carers and, to a certain extent, do not need adult freedoms. Since children need protecting, the most obvious people to do so are their parents, and parents have rights too. They should be left alone to carry out their parental role, without undue State interference.

It seems unlikely that the children's rights enthusiasts who today concentrate so heavily on children's decision-making rights, always face up to the impact of their ideas. They imply that since children have rights, including the right to make choices, those choices have to be respected (Franklin, 2002, ibid.). But such a view is not supported by sound philosophical and jurisprudential argument. Children have a variety of rights and their decision-making rights may actually conflict with their other rights, especially the right to be protected. Teenagers may be intellectually mature enough to decide whether to undergo medical treatment, or to attend school, but their rejection of treatment or school may endanger their right to realize their long-term mental and physical potential. The difficulty is to achieve a balance between promoting a teenager's eventual capacity for independence, whilst also protecting his or her right to self-fulfilment (Fortin, 2003: 19–27, 2006).

Children's Rights – Legal Tensions

The discussion so far suggests that a healthy scepticism about the concept of children's rights is no bad thing. Nevertheless, so far as the law is concerned, children are undoubtedly legal rights holders. Indeed, since implementation of the HRA 1998 in October 2000, they have gained the legal protection of all the rights listed in the European Convention on Human Rights (ECHR). As discussed above, the Crick Report stressed the importance of the new citizenship education instilling in Key Stage 3 pupils a knowledge of their rights under both the UNCRC and the ECHR. The UNCRC is enormously influential and contains a long list of rights covering the broad spectrum of children's needs and expectations. In contrast, bar the right to education, the ECHR only protects the traditional civil and political rights that adults, but not necessarily children, normally value. Nevertheless, the ECHR is considered by lawyers to be of far more immediate relevance. Although the domestic courts are more routinely referring to its provisions (as, for example, in the first of the two cases discussed below), the UNCRC lacks teeth. Unlike the ECHR, the UNCRC has not been made part of domestic law; it remains 'unincorporated'. Consequently the British government is not obliged to comply with its provisions and, without any court attaching to it, individual children are unable to claim legal redress for infringements of the rights it contains.

By incorporating all the rights listed in the ECHR into domestic law, the HRA allows children, or adults on behalf of children, to appeal to any court in this country for a remedy if their rights under the ECHR are infringed. Despite their awkward language, many of the articles are important sources of legal protection for children today. Amongst these is Article 9 which guarantees the right to religious freedom. In a multicultural society such as our own, it is important for schools to remember its potential scope when considering the educational rights of minority groups. (Fortin, 2003: 342–58) Meanwhile, the Crick Report considered it essential for citizenship education to instil in pupils

> a sense of common citizenship, including a national identity that is secure enough to find a place for the plurality of nations, cultures, ethnic identities and religions long found in the United Kingdom.
>
> (1998: para 3.14)

These words suggest that a compromise must be found between the claims of minority groups to preserve all the elements of their cultural traditions, and those of assimilationists who expect minorities to be absorbed into the culture of the mainstream community. Poulter describes this compromise as a 'cultural pluralism within limits' (1998: 20–2). But it may be no easy task for schools to promote 'a sense of common citizenship' in communities which contain disparate ethnic and religious groups of children. They may also struggle to balance the rights of parents to bring up their children according to their own religious tenets against those of their children to develop their own views. Two recent cases demonstrate how these tensions may require resolution by the courts.

The first case, *R (SB) v Governors of Denbigh High School* [2006] UKHL 15, [2006] 2 WLR 719 demonstrates a pupil asserting her religious rights under Article 9 of the ECHR precisely as she would have done had she been an adult. Shabina Begum, a 15-year-old Muslim girl, complained that by refusing to allow her to wear the jilbab to school, her school had infringed her religious rights under the ECHR. Since she felt unable to attend school without wearing the jilbab, she also claimed that her rights under Article 2 of the First Protocol of the ECHR had been infringed. This states that 'No one shall be denied the right to education.' Her claim highlighted the potential conflict between a teenager's religious rights and the needs of a school and its wider community. The school itself and the religious leaders in the community were opposed to changing the school's uniform policy which allowed pupils to wear the shalwar kameeze but not the jilbab. The school maintained that allowing pupils to wear a variety of different clothing, including a religious symbol of a more extreme form of the Muslim faith, might encourage the formation of groups and cliques. Unlike the jilbab, the shalwar kameeze could be worn by a number of different faith groups, including Hindus and Sikhs.

Having lost at first instance and won in the Court of Appeal, the House of Lords found against Shabina that according to the majority, Shabina's religious rights had not been infringed because she had apparently chosen to attend the school knowing its uniform code and had complied with its rules for two years before objecting. There was also an alternative school which she could have attended wearing the jilbab. Baroness Hale of Richmond disagreed. In her view, the school's refusal to allow Shabina to wear a jilbab did infringe her rights under Article 9. She pointed out that Shabina's family had chosen her school for her when she was still only 11. As they grow older, children often form different views from those of their parents – this is part of growing up. Nevertheless, she too thought that Shabina's claim must fail. Article 9 does not provide an absolute right to religious freedom. It can be infringed as long as the interference is proportionate to its legitimate aim and a fair balance is struck between the competing interests of all concerned. Baroness Hale thought it justifiable for the school to interfere with Shabina's rights in the way they had done. In her view a school's task is

> ... to promote the ability of people of diverse races, religions and cultures to live together in harmony. ... A uniform dress code can play its role in smoothing over ethnic, religious and social divisions. But it does more than that. Like it or not, this is a society committed, in principle and in law, to equal freedom for men and women to choose how they will lead their lives within the law. Young girls from ethnic, cultural or religious minorities growing up here face particularly difficult choices: how far to adopt or to distance themselves from the dominant culture. A good school will enable and support them. This particular school is a good school. ...
>
> *R (SB) v Governors of Denbigh High School* [2006] UKHL 15
> [2006] 2 WLR 719 [97]

These words imply that schools should enable pupils to think for themselves and reject, if they wish, the more extreme dress codes of their religious belief. Nevertheless, one wonders whether the House of Lords' conclusion contributed greatly to Shabina Begum's understanding of the right to freedom of religion. She may have found it difficult to understand how the decision assisted the development of a tolerant attitude within the school. Whilst it demonstrates that young people must accept that their own rights may conflict with those of others in the wider community, it also demonstrates how difficult it is for schools to promote a 'cultural pluralism within limits,' on behalf of the State (Poulter, 1998).

When parents are introduced into the equation, matters may be further complicated. Parents may attempt to enforce their own rights under the ECHR, perhaps at the expense of their children's rights. The courts may find it difficult to find an appropriate balance if, for example, parents appeal to Article 9 to support their claims relating to their children. *R (on the application of Williamson and others) v Secretary of State for Education and Employment and others* [2005] UKHL 15, [2005] 2 All ER 1 which went to the House of Lords, demonstrated these tensions. It involved a group of fundamentalist Christians who strongly believed in using physical punishment as a form of discipline. They maintained that the Bible instructs parents to physically chastise their children and they pointed to the fact that current law allowed them to do so in their own homes (subject now to section 58 of the Children Act 2004). That being so, they objected to the fact that the teachers in the private school to which they all sent their children, could not discipline their children in this way on their behalf. The parents challenged the validity of section 548(1) of the Education Act 1996 which prevents all teachers in any school in this country, public or private, from using physical chastisement as a form of discipline, even if it is requested by the children's parents themselves. They unsuccessfully claimed that this prohibition infringed their own right to freedom of religion under Article 9 of the ECHR and that therefore the legislation should be repealed.

The reasoning of the House of Lords was similar to that discussed above in relation to Shabina Begum's claim. They considered that the parents' right to religion under Article 9 of the ECHR had indeed been infringed by the legislation banning physical punishment in schools, but that its breach could be justified to protect the rights and freedoms of *others* – the others here being the children involved. In their view, the legislative prohibition achieved a fair balance between the religious rights and freedoms of the parents and those of their children to be free of physical punishment.

In her decision, Baroness Hale of Richmond referred extensively to the provisions of the UNCRC to support her view that it was legitimate to limit parents' religious rights under Article 9. She pointed out that various provisions of the UNCRC, notably Article 19, protect children from all forms of violence and that the UN Committee on the Rights of the Child had welcomed the abolition of corporal punishment in all schools in England, Wales and Scotland. In the light of this international approval of the change in the law, she asked

> How can it not be a legitimate and proportionate limitation on the practice of parents' religious beliefs to heed such a recommendation from the bodies charged with monitoring our compliance with the obligations which we have undertaken to respect the dignity of the individual and the rights of children?
>
> *R (on the application of Williamson and others) v Secretary of State for Education and Employment and others* [2005] UKHL 15, [2005] 2 All ER 1, [84]

The outcome of the *Williamson* case was satisfactory, in that the House of Lords refused to accept that the parents' cause wholly favoured their children. Nevertheless, the case had an extraordinary and worrying feature. The courts at every level allowed the parents to present evidence about their children, as an anonymous group, without anyone considering it necessary to undertake an assessment of the children's actual position. They were referred to throughout as a group, with no individual identities. They were not separately represented and the courts knew nothing at all about them. In truth, they were effectively invisible. Instead, the lengthy judgments were devoted to an assessment of their parents' religious rights. Baroness Hale of Richmond described the situation well:

> My Lords, this is, and always has been, a case about children, their rights and the rights of their parents and teachers. Yet there has been no one here or in the courts below to speak on behalf of the children. ... The battle has been fought on ground selected by the adults. ...
>
> *R (on the application of Williamson and others) v Secretary of State for Education and Employment and others* [2005] UKHL 15, [2005] 2 All ER 1, [71]

Some might argue that there is no need for the courts to delve beneath the surface of apparently happy family units, as was the case here. There is no need for them to insist that parents' rights are not always entirely compatible with those of their children, as these parents had assumed. In this particular case, what point would there have been in consulting children who had probably, since birth, been indoctrinated by their parents? But as urged elsewhere, (Fortin, 2004: 264–5) the courts must then simply strive to ensure that the children's own position is fully assessed and their rights fully protected, whatever the children's own view of the situation. A court should not feel obliged to implement a child's choices if they conflict with his other long-term rights.

The *Williamson* case illustrates how easy it is for individual children to be forgotten in adult-orientated procedures, despite their being the focus of the litigation itself. It also highlights the complexity of situations involving an apparent conflict between the rights of parents and children. Some would say that it demonstrates the corrosive nature of rights language within the confines of family life. But, as Archard pointed out, this is not a reason to deny children their rights.

Conclusion

Teachers whose job it is to teach on the citizenship curriculum in schools today undertake a crucial role when they instruct children on their status as rights holders. It is not enough for active citizens to acquire a working knowledge of the contents of the UNCRC and the ECHR. Pupils should be encouraged to reflect on the true meaning of rights themselves. They should gain an appreciation of the way that overenthusiastic 'rights talk' can devalue the currency of rights. A critical analysis of their short- and long-term interests should also lead them to understand that some rights will inevitably conflict with others, and that the right to make choices, although valuable, may jeopardize other long-term gains. Without careful instruction on such issues, there is a danger that pupils will not fully appreciate the true value of being rights holders. Worse, they themselves may eventually join the ranks of sceptical adults when they emerge from their minor status.

References

Archard, D. (1993) *Children: Rights and Childhood*. London: Routledge.

Campbell, T. (1992) 'The rights of the minor', in P. Alston, S. Parker and J. Seymour (eds) *Children, Rights and the Law*, Oxford: Clarendon Press, pp. 1–23.

Crick, B. (1998) (Chairman) *Final Report of the Advisory Group on Citizenship: Education for Citizenship and the Teaching of Democracy in Schools*, Qualifications and Curriculum Authority.

Feinberg, J. (1980) *Justice and the Bounds of Liberty*. Princeton, NJ: Princeton University Press.

Fortin, J. (2003) *Children's Rights and the Developing Law*. Lexis Nexis Butterworths.

Fortin, J. (2004) 'Children's rights: are the courts now taking them more seriously?' [2004] 15 *Kings College Law Journal*, 253.

Fortin, J. (2006) 'Accommodating children's rights in a post Human Rights Act Era', *Modern Law Review*, 69(3): 299.

Fox Harding, L. (1997) *Perspectives in Child Care Policy*. London: Longman.

Franklin, B. (2002) 'Children's rights and media wrongs', in B. Franklin (ed.) *The New Handbook of Children's Rights: Comparative Policy and Practice*, London: Routledge, pp. 15–42.

Guggenheim, M. (2005) *What's Wrong with Children's Rights*. Cambridge, MA: Harvard University Press.

MacCormick, N. (1982) *Legal Rights and Social Democracy: Essays in Legal and Political Philosophy*. Oxford: Clarendon Press.

Minow, M. (1987) 'Interpreting rights: an essay for Robert Cover', *Yale Law Journal*, 96(8): 1860.

O'Brien Steinfels, M. (1982) 'Children's rights, parental rights, family privacy and family autonomy', in W. Gaylin and R. Macklin (eds) *Who Speaks for the Child?*, New York: Plenum Press.

Ofsted (2006) *Towards Consensus? Citizenship in Secondary Schools*, HMI 2666, Ofsted.

Poulter, S. (1998) *Ethnicity, Law and Human Rights: The English Experience*. London: OUP.

UNICEF (2004) *Citizens All? Children's Rights and Citizenship Education: An Endline Survey of Curriculum and Practice in a Sample of UK Schools.* UNICEF UK Citizenship Monitoring Project.

Wellman, C. (1999) *The Proliferation of Rights: Moral Progress or Empty Rhetoric?* Boulder, CO: Westview.

6

Children as 'Citizens' of the United Nations (UN)

Judith Ennew

Introduction

A political romance about children arose in the last two decades of the twentieth century, placing increasing pressure on the organizers of meetings about, or on behalf of, children to include 'children's voices' in the proceedings or lose any claim to credibility (Ennew, 2000). Children's presence now provides a generally spurious authenticity to adult-organized events of many kinds, particularly where these are high profile, international gatherings, even though children's actual roles are often extremely restricted (Hart, 1997).

This chapter examines children's presence in some global UN meetings since 1990, as well as examples of children's citizenship actions in UN's contexts. I ask what it might mean for children to be regarded as citizens of the UN, and note weaknesses of current notions of nationality and citizenship.

Citizens Rights and Human Rights

Although human rights are universal, their first practical expression was national, rather than international, in the legal entitlements of citizens in the constitutions of emerging nation-states (Henkin, 1979). Around the end of the eighteenth century, national boundaries sharpened as states defined both their own sovereignty and their suzerainty over subject nations. Simultaneously, the notion of 'nationality' became a legal status rather than a matter of inheritance. Novel state apparatuses were developed as tools of national governance. Chief among these were statistical categorizing and counting of citizens; a mode of inclusion/exclusion operating through mechanisms such as birth registration. This expedites the exclusion of children ('minors') from certain rights and powers while they still enjoy the status of legal inhabitants.

The catastrophic global war of 1914–18 began inter-nation attempts to co-operate in the name of peace. The ill-fated League of Nations espoused ideas of human rights derived from the turmoil of the Enlightenment, the French Revolution and the American War of Independence. Yet little of this concerned children as a group, despite the 1924 'Geneva Declaration on the Rights of the Child'. Nor was citizenship a major topic of debate other than with respect to universal suffrage, particularly extending votes to women. When the League's assets, aspirations and functions were taken over by the United Nations, after the 1939–45 war, a new era of human rights law began. As was the case with the League, the collaboration between the 'peoples' of the UN was rendered possible (and arguably necessary) by the existence of sovereign states. The UN lays down the human rights conditions for citizen membership of such a state, including access to decision-making mechanisms (such as voting) and certain other legal entitlements (such as entering into a contract or owning property). Living legally in a sovereign state (being a 'denizen') does not confer the right to franchise – a right denied to children along with certain other denizens, such as mentally-ill or impaired adults, prisoners and resident expatriates. Children are also excluded from trade-union membership, jury service, loans, marriage and contracts.

All categories of person can and do take citizenship actions, for example shouldering responsibilities or defending their own interests (Lister, 2006). Children's citizenship actions within a nation state may include producing wealth, advancing national development and dying for their country. Yet child worker-citizens and fighter-citizens are more likely to be regarded as victims than producers of national wealth or national heroes.

The UN has always recognized children's rights to protection, but has been slower to consider them as citizens, only recently paying partial attention to their political actions and potential as a global force. The rationale given for involving children in international events and meetings at which their rights and welfare are discussed is usually their 'right to give an opinion' on matters concerning their lives (Article 12 of the United Nations Convention on the Rights of the Child (UNCRC), 1989). However, their actual involvement in making decisions tends to be limited and they may have no formal place at the decision-making table. Indeed, as Geraldine Van Bueren argues, adult-controlled mechanisms are always likely to be required for children to represent their own opinions in their own right (Van Bueren, 1995). Children's participation is limited by adult control over not only the resources required for children to attend international events but also on the topics under discussion, the agenda and procedures of the meeting, the selection or election process and the selection of topics on which children are asked to give their opinions. In all of this, the adult role is, to say the least, ambiguous (Ratna and Reddy, 2002).

'Matters Affecting The Child': Children Attending UN Meetings

Children have been present at many meetings held under the UN's auspices. Varying numbers attended the 1993 Human Rights Conference in Vienna, the World·Summit on Social Development in Copenhagen in 1995, the First World Congress against the Commercial Sexual Exploitation in Stockholm in 1996 and the Second Congress in Yokohama, in 2001. They have also been involved in various ways in other meetings held by UN specialist agencies, such as the 'G8 Youth' events organized by UNICEF alongside G8 meetings in Scotland in 2005 and Russia in 2006. Working children also apparently represented their own interests to the International Labour Conference in 1998, under the auspices of the adult-organized Global March against Child Labour. The five global UN meetings I consider here are the 1990 World Summit for Children in New York (World Summit), the UN Conference on Environment and Development two years later in Rio de Janeiro (Earth Summit), the UN General Assembly Special Session on Children (Special Session) in 2002, the Regional Consultation for East Asia and the Pacific under the UN Secretary-General's Global Study on Violence against Children (Regional Consultation) in Bangkok in 2005, and the Committee on the Rights of the Child Day of General Discussion on Article 12 of the UNCRC, held in Geneva in 2006. Children's attendance at four of these meetings has been the subject of social science reports and/or evaluations. In addition, I was involved in developing the principles by which children became Delegates to the Regional Consultation and also attended the 2006 Day of General Discussion.

The World Summit for Children, New York, 1990

The World Summit for Children, which gathered an unprecedented number of national heads of state in New York, took place in the year following the adoption of the United Nations Convention on the Rights of the Child (UNCRC). The result was widespread publicity about the UNCRC and considerable growth in the numbers of signatures and ratifications, as well as international agreement on a number of promises about fulfillment of rights (mostly relating to health and education) before 2000.

The participation of children by giving their views in adult meetings where their lives were being discussed grew apace throughout the 1980s, in parallel to discussion of their right to 'participate'. The non-governmental sector was in the vanguard of this trend, but some UN departments and agencies included the views of limited numbers of young people in outcome documents. Nevertheless, even six months before the World Summit, the organizing committee decided children should not present their views (Woollcombe, 1998: 236). This was successfully challenged by non-governmental organizations with the result that, at the closure of the Summit, the chair of the committee that had opposed their inclusion said 'I address myself particularly to the children here' (Woollcoombe, 1998: 236).

Children's participation at the World Summit included a 'Children's Open Day' two days beforehand, consisting of songs, dances, national costumes and 'passionate appeals' on an open-air stage outside the UN building. Because the heads of state had not yet arrived, the children were, as David Woollcombe wrote later, 'literally singing for the birds' (1998: 236). Once the 71 leaders had materialized, two had a meeting with two selected children, in what seems to have been a far-from-satisfactory encounter:

> The kids were told to 'make it quick' as they were ushered in to see the two politicians, who were both exhausted after a long day of meetings. Nervous and

flustered, the children gabbled their presentation, pushed the papers over the table and left feeling angry and betrayed.

(1998: 237)

Once the Summit began, the children's role was restricted to decoration; in national dress, they led their own political leaders to the stage where Summit promises were signed. Then six of their number read the Summit Declaration in the six official UN languages. An extract from Woollcombe's diary provides a poignant description:

reading words they had no hand in writing, watched by two-dimensional portraits of the kinds of impoverished children which these words are designed to assist and by three-dimensional politicians who are entirely responsible for providing that assistance. Nothing could symbolize the powerlessness of children more accurately than this – and yet those children cry out the words with a passion!

(1998: 237)

UN Conference on Environment and Development, Rio de Janeiro, 1992

The Children's Forum at the 1992 Earth Summit in Rio de Janeiro grew out of the enthusiasm of a Norwegian teacher inspired by a meeting of children in Bergen in 1990 (Stephens, 1992). Unlike the World Summit, the organizers of the meeting in Rio de Janeiro intended to include children, although in practice their involvement in making or influencing decisions was as limited as it had been at the World Summit.

The Conference began when a replica Viking ship carrying children of different nationalities, arrived in Rio de Janeiro harbour. They had sailed from Norway via the east coasts of North and South America, collecting written messages from children in the ports it visited and bearing a UNICEF banner with a reminder about the World Summit 'Keep the Promise . . . ' (1992). Children were thus the bearers of a conspicuous adult proclamation, while their own messages remained muted. During the Earth Summit, children and young people were allotted special tents indicating their importance in proceedings, even though the activities tended to trivialize their presence. Sharon Stephens observed that:

The Children's Tent featured an extraordinary range of activities: storytellers; a series of 'hands-on' art workshops . . . puppet shows; 8 year olds from a Rio school presenting their own 'eco-rap' music; recycling workshops; improvisational theatre presentations, where children took roles as animals exposed to pollution and trees suffering from acid rain.

(1992)

These visible (and possibly adult-orchestrated) 'childish' activities contrasted with debates in the youth tent reflecting 'issues and values that many felt had been filtered out of the official Earth Summit negotiations' and challenging vested interests of transnational companies funding the Earth Summit (1992: 51). As had been the case in New York, the encounter between children and government leaders at the 'Children's Hearings' or 'Children's Appeal to World Leaders' was not a high priority for government representatives, who preferred to attend US President Bush's plenary speech, which was rescheduled to take place simultaneously. Stephens recorded that only government officials from four countries – USA, Norway, Germany and Brazil – attended the Children's Hearings.

The UN General Assembly Special Session on Children, 2002

The history of children's participation moved on and there was a palpable difference between their presence at the World and Earth Summits and the Special Session in 2002. Kofi Annan, then UN Secretary-General, wrote later that:

> For the first time, the General Assembly met to discuss exclusively children's issues; and for the first time, large numbers of children were included as official members of delegations, representing governments and non-governmental organizations.
>
> The children's presence transformed the atmosphere of the United Nations. Into our usually measured and diplomatic discussions, they introduced their passions, questions, fears, challenges, enthusiasm and optimism. They brought us their ideas, hopes and dreams.
>
> (Annan, 2002)

In the same UNICEF publication, however, an unnamed staff writer commented on the particular difficulties of bringing children to international events, and the danger that, in its worst manifestations, participation may be abusive (UNICEF, 2002). Children's citizenship of the UN is thus acknowledged to require a recognition of and provision for their vulner-abilities. A subsequent research assessment of the participation of children in the Special Session identified potential or actual violations of children's rights and report noted growing international concern in some circles about the wisdom involving children in international, adult meetings (Ennew et al., 2004). Researchers noted that children's exercise of inter-governmental citizenship is often expected to bear too great a democratic burden. Children who attended the Special Session could not be regarded as democratically elected representatives of children as a demographic group. They are usually hand-picked by adults or elected from small, unrepresentative groups. But this should not be used either to downgrade the value of their participation or to dismiss their opinions. The adults who attend UN meetings are equally unrepresentative of adults globally (Ennew et al., 2004).

Nevertheless, observers of children's participation in UN meetings were beginning to comment on the way children's 'views' are diluted and manipulated by the adults seeking their 'voices', through the expedient of deciding which topics should be discussed by children in regional forums organized to prepare them for global events. In the case of the Special

Session, children were provided with 10 topics to prioritize, rather than encouraged to select their own list of issues. In spite of this, there is a notable difference between the concerns expressed in outcome documents from adults and children (respectively *A world fit for* children and *A world fit for* 'us', compared in Ennew et al., 2004: 82–4). It is increasingly argued that children's citizenship rights would be better served through mechanisms encouraging representation of their views and concerns at community, local and national levels, which could then be forwarded to global events. This would mean a more democratic representation of children at UN meetings, without the need for their physical presence (Beers et al., 2006). Should this ever become the case, however, children's democratic representation in the UN could be argued to exceed by far that of adults.

East Asia and Pacific Regional Consultation: United Nations Secretary General's Global Study of Violence against Children, Bangkok, 2005

A long-term aim of the Steering Committee for the East Asia and the Pacific Regional Consultation in 2005, under the UN Secretary-General's Global Study on Violence against Children, was to use this meeting to promote local-level, institutionalized participation of children in decision making, as a foundation for their meaningful representation at regional and other international events. The immediate goal was to ensure that children's rights to participate were not achieved at the expense of other rights, by establishing a set of minimum, agreed, standards below which children's participation in the Regional Consultation would not be permitted. To ensure that both organizations and individuals could fully understand and adhere to these standards, a protocol (manual), containing all necessary working documents and procedures, provided step-by-step guidance (Veitch, 2005).

Both adult and Under-18 Delegates were systematically prepared for the children's participation. All delegates, whether over or under 18 years of age, received a background paper on children's participation and a copy of the child protection policy. Through consultations at national and local level, a total of 6,001 children in the region were consulted. Although this could be argued to be a small number compared with the billion plus children in the region, they provided recommendations and ideas for solutions. These fed in to the discussions of Under-18 Delegates at the Children's Forum, which took place during the two days immediately before the Regional Consultation. The results were a document outlining Under-18 Delegates' suggested solutions and recommendations to the problem of violence against children, and a Powerpoint™ presentation on the first morning of the Consultation. Both proved to be excellent tools for supporting Under-18 Delegates in working groups and for measuring the influence they had on the Outcome Statement from the Regional Consultation. In contrast to the Special Session outcome documents, just over half of the recommendations in this statement were related to the

Under-18 Delegates' recommendations in the document from the Children's Forum (UNICEF, 2005).

The process was not perfect, but the results of evaluation exercises carried out with both adult and Under-18 Delegates, as well as with members of the Steering Committee, show that the Regional Consultation ended with a general feeling of accomplishment. Under-18 Delegates generally stated that they felt they had participated throughout with equal status to adults, that they were listened to and their views respected and taken into account (Veitch, 2005).

Entitled to Speak, Participate and Decide – The Child's Right to be Heard, UNCRC Day of General Discussion, 2006

The objective of the Committee on the Rights of the Child Day of General Discussion, 15 September 2006, was to explore the meaning of UNCRC Article 12, and was related to a proposed General Comment on this topic. Days of General Discussion are public events undertaken regularly to receive and discuss opinions on specific rights from a wide range of participants. They can be attended by representatives of UN specialist agencies, NGOs and individuals, and can also receive written submissions from all these categories. On this occasion, interest was so high that attendance had to be restricted. Early discussions within the UN Committee on the Rights of the Child (UN Committee) were not unanimously in favour of children being present at this Day of Discussion because of the formality of the setting and previous experience of children becoming distressed by their participation. But NGOs and UNICEF brought about a change of attitude, organizing and paying for children's presence during the meeting, as well as at a preparatory meeting in which children were able to interact relatively informally, for a limited time, with eight members of the UN Committee.

The Day's Agenda consisted of an opening plenary session, with presentations by the UN Committee and UNICEF as well as children, followed by two parallel working groups on 'The child's right to be heard in judicial and administrative proceedings' and 'Children as active participants in society'. A final plenary session received reports from these working groups.

As with the UN Committee's previous experience, it proved difficult for children to adapt to UN procedures, which do not facilitate open discussion, even between adults skilled in expressing themselves in formal settings. A number of the participating children had clearly been accustomed to international meetings organized by NGOs in which each child was given time to bear witness – often to their individual experiences. Finding this would not be the case, some children became distressed and angry at the preparatory meeting. A planned joint children's statement was not presented to the opening plenary session, which was addressed by four individual children making personal, and often highly emotive, statements. In this case, as frequently happens, children were witnesses rather than representatives.

During the Day of Discussion, children and adults were not treated as equal participants. In the opening session, three adults were given 45 minutes to speak, while the four children were allotted a total of 15. Children were presented with attendance certificates, while adults were not; no explanation was given for this apparently patronizing distinction. Differences in attention were also notable. Children, who had generally listened to adult speeches impassively, sat up and appeared to take an interest when their peers began presenting. At the conclusions of children's speeches some adult UN Committee members applauded with what might be described as excessive enthusiasm. The Chair of Working Group 2 prioritized children's presentations in the afternoon, so that all children had a chance to speak and many adults were prevented from sharing their considerable experience. Working Group 1, on the other hand, was run as a 'discussion' under UN rules, so that both adults and children were able to make interventions.

One notable difference between this and some previous days of General Discussion was the almost total absence of UN specialist agencies, apart from UNICEF and the Human Rights Commission. One might have expected that the World Health Organization would be present to make a statement on children's consent to medical treatment, the International Labour Organization (ILO) to justify children's exclusion from trade unions, and the International Criminal Court to make an intervention in the working group on judicial and administrative proceedings.

The recommendations from this Day of Discussion, published two weeks later, quoted from an earlier General Comment that 'Listening to children should not be seen as an end in itself' but rather a way to improve and increase the interactions between governments and children (UN Committee on the Rights of the Child, 2003, quoted in 2006, para 13). The submission of alternative reports to the UN Committee from children and youth was recommended as 'a way of monitoring the implementation of the concluding observations at the national level' (para 57). The UN Committee stated that it is committed to explore ways of 'furthering participation of children in the work of the Committee, and in particular encourages more participation of children during pre-session country briefings with civil society representatives' (para 58). This tends to empha-size national, rather than UN, citizenship activity, particularly when combined with a strong recommendation that states parties 'move from an events based approach of the right to participation to systematic inclusion in policy matters in order to ensure that children can express their views and effectively participate in all matters affecting them' (para 27) (UN Committee on the Rights of the Child, 2006).

Children's Reports to the UN Committee

In addition to the presence of children in each of these events to discuss 'matters affecting the child' (Art.12.1 UNCRC) children can and do take citizenship action through reports made to the UN Committee under Article 44 UNCRC. Some go to Geneva as part of a state party delegation when the national reports to the UN Committee is being considered, others submit alternative reports, with the support of adult organizations. For example, the Indian National Movement of Working Children decided that preparing its own alternative report would be a way of 'pressurizing' the government to work within the UNCRC framework (Indian Movement, 2003: 3). The report of these worker citizens makes use of a UN mechanism primarily to target the national government with arguments for the institutionalization of children's active citizenship at national level:

> our report only covers the problems and issues of working children and is based on the areas and sectors that our member organizations represent. We do not claim to speak for all the children of India and we sincerely hope that children in other situations and circumstances and in different parts of India are also producing their own reports . . . This is also an issue that we feel the Government of India should help to facilitate. . . .
>
> (Indian Movement, 2003: 6)

Weibena Heesterman's comparison of UN Committee responses to children's alternative reports indicates that 'suggestions made in NGO reports may well be the same as those made by children and young people, while on occasion State Parties have also shown themselves disposed to initiate policies or take measures young people are likely to welcome' (2005: 373). 'Under such circumstances,' Heesterman comments, 'the most one can say is that young people's reports may well have tipped the scales' (2005: 373). She shows that UN Committee responses may be shocked responses to isolated reported cases of abuse, as in comments on a report from Japan, or dismissals of altruistic suggestions made by children, such as 'the requests made in the German and Belgian youth reports . . . to urge their respective Governments to levy taxes in order to safeguard the world's climate for the protection of future generations, or to counteract world poverty' (2005: 374). The UN Committee's response to the concern expressed by the Indian working children in their report that their families would suffer if they were forcibly removed from work without alternative support being made available, was effectively a *non sequitur*, which advised the Government of India to strengthen child labour legislation and ratify ILO Conventions 138 and 182 (Heesterman, 2005).

Is the Nation-State System the Best Basis for Human Rights?

'The peoples of the United Nations' ('United for a Better World') who drew up the Charter of the United Nations, based this on the principle of sovereign equality of all members (UN Charter Article 2: 10). Franchise within the UN is based on one member (state) one vote, in whatever context. Children have so far been excluded from Security Council meetings, although they did speak their own words in the General Assembly as part of the Special Session.

For some this process is insufficiently democratic, and it is arguable that a single vote for nations with widely-different-sized populations is at the least unrepresentative, while the fact that some nations have power of veto within some UN contexts tends to contradict the principle of sovereignty. In view of the complexity of issues and the huge size of the global population, one is tempted to agree with John Dunn's statement that it is impractical for citizens of modern states to take part in major decisions: 'they do not because they cannot' (Dunn, 1993: vi). Although the Committee for a Democratic UN is supported by elected bodies, such as the World Federation of United Nations Associations and the Parliamentary Assembly of the Council of Europe, its scope extends only to some dozen countries of the 192 Member States of the United Nations. A 'directly elected world parliament', the 'concept of global democracy' and 'representation of citizens in the international system' (www.uno-komitee.de) appear worthy ideals, but the envisaged discussion forum for parliamentarians would be unlikely to affect UN business. There seem to be no plans at this stage for including children's parliaments in this process, although the US-based organization 'Young General Assembly', which claims to be initiated and managed by people less than 18 years of age with 2.5 million members in 57 nations, has asked for a children's parliament to be included should such an international adult 'civil-society' parliament ever be established. Significantly perhaps, this suggestion was made in a submission to the 2006 Day of General Discussion (Young General Assembly, 2006).

The main problem with children's UN citizenship reflects a fundamental flaw in human rights based on UN structure, as well as the unequal power relations that recognize the sovereignty of some nation-states, while reducing other 'states' and 'nations' to clients. The Sioux Nation and the Karen State, for example, are linguistic rather than legal entities. The notion of the 'Peoples of the United Nations' takes no cognizance of the ethnic-minority 'nations' and 'states' that are subject to dominant, sovereign member states. This would matter less from a citizenship (indeed a rights) perspective if there were not such widespread discrimination within sovereign states against other 'peoples', who may not, for example in the case of refugees, be accorded so much as the status of legal denizens. International Human Rights Law makes repeated mention of the 'right to a nationality', for example UN Declaration article 15; 1966 Covenant on Civil and Political Rights article 24(3); UNCRC Articles 7 and 8. Yet many children have no such status and, like their parents, may die without ever being granted existence as citizens of states with access to human rights.

To give one example among many, Karen children born in 'temporary' refugee shelters in Thailand do not receive official birth certificates even if they are born in local hospitals. 'Temporary' in this phrase spans a period longer than the similarly temporary refugee camps for Palestinians, who likewise have no identity, and were not counted until the formation of a statistics office by the Palestinian Authority after 1993. Children in the camps may be given registration documents by the UN High Commission for Refugees but are not eligible to attend Thai schools, although they can attend 'primary school education tailored to suit their needs' within the camps (UN Committee on the Rights of the Child, 2005, para 307). The refusal of birth certification is the result of a confusion, common to many countries that equates a birth certificate with nationality. Thus children the world over live their lives without official existence.

Conclusion

The term 'United Nations citizen' is an oxymoron. While the UN is all we have at the moment, it is based on an international structure that privileges and prioritizes violations of rights through discrimination against certain 'peoples' as well as against denizen groups such as children. It has to be realized that the current global governance system of nation-states, with some posing as exemplars of a 'democracy' however they choose to define it – simply underscores the system of suzerainty that is at the basis of all inequalities. A glimmering of this shines through the Preamble to the Recommendations of the 2006 Day of General Discussion:

> *To speak, to participate, to have their views taken into account.* These three phases describe the sequence of the enjoyment of the right to participate from a functional point of view. The new and deeper meaning of this right is that it should establish *a new social contract.* One by which children are fully recognised as rights-holders who are not only entitled to receive protection but also have the right to participate in all matters affecting them, a right which can be considered as the symbol for their recognition as rights holders. This implies, in the long term, changes in political, social, institutional and cultural structures.
>
> (UN Committee on the Rights of the Child, 2006, emphases in the original)

In this sense, the answer to the question 'Do children become citizens of the United Nations when they participate in meetings and submit reports' is the same as Dunn's response about the democratic participation of adults: 'They do not because they cannot'.

References

Annan, K. (2002) 'Foreword', in UNICEF (2002) *The State of the World's Children 2003: Child Participation*, New York: UNICEF.

Beers, H. van, Chau, V.P., Ennew, J., Khan, P.Q., Long, T.T., Milne, B., Nguyet, T.T.A., and Son, V.T. (2006) 'Creating an enabling environment: capacity building in children's participation', *Save the Children Sweden, Viet Nam, 2000–2004*, Bangkok: Save the Children Sweden.

Dunn, J. (1993) 'Introduction', in J. Dunn (ed.) *Democracy: The Unfinished Journey 508 BC to AD 1993*, Oxford: Oxford University Press.

Ennew, J. (2000) 'How Can We Define Citizenship in Childhood?' Working Paper Series 10(2). Cambridge, MA: Harvard Center for Population and Development Studies.

Ennew, J., Hastadewi, Y. and Plateau, D.P. (2004) *Seen and Heard: Participation of Children and Young People in Southeast, East Asia and Pacific in Events and Forums Leading to and Following up on the United Nations General Assembly Special Session on Children, May 2002.* Bangkok: Save the Children Southeast, East Asia and the Pacific Region.

Hart, R. (1997) *Children's Participation: The Theory and Practice of Involving Young Citizens in Community Development and Environmental Care.* London and New York: Earthscan & UNICEF.

Heesterman, W. (2005) 'An assessment of the impact of youth submissions to the United Nations Committee on the Rights of the Child', *The International Journal of Children's Rights*, 13: 351–78.

Henkin, L. (1979) *The Rights of Man Today.* London: Stevens and Sons Limited.

Indian National Movement of Working Children (2003) 'The Alternative Report of the National Movement of Working Children', Submitted to the Committee on the Rights of the Child, July 2003.

Lister, R. (2006) 'Children and citizenship', *ChildRight* 223, February: 22–5.

Ratna, K. and Reddy, N. (2002) *A Journey in Children's Participation.* Bangalore: The Concerned for Working Children.

Steering Committee (2005) 'Minimum Standards', Steering Committee for the East Asia Pacific Regional Consultation for the UN Study on Violence Against Children.

Stephens, S. (1992) 'Children at the UN conference on environment and development: participants and media symbols', *Barn: Nytt fra forskning om barn I norge*, Nr. 2–3, 44–51.

UN Committee on the Rights of the Child (2003) General Comment No. 5 (2003) 'General Measures of Implementation of the Convention on the Rights of the Child', (Arts. 4, 42 and 44, para 6). Committee on the Rights of the Child, Thirty-fourth session, 19 September–3 October 2003, CRC/GC/2003/5, 27 November 2003.

UN Committee on the Rights of the Child (2005) *Consideration of Reports Submitted by States Parties under Article 44 of the Convention; Second Periodic Report of States Parties Due in 1999: Thailand. UNCRC/C/83/Add.15*, 31 May 2005.

UN Committee on the Rights of the Child (2006) *Day of General Discussion on the Right of the Child to be Heard*: Recommendations, Unedited version, Committee on the Rights of the Child, Forty-third session, 11–29 September, 2006. www.ohchr.org/english/bodies/crc/discussion.htm

UNICEF (2002) *The State of the World's Children 2003: Child Participation.* New York: UNICEF.

UNICEF (2005) *Report on the East Asia and Pacific Regional Consultation on Violence Against Children, Bangkok June 14 to 16, 2005.* Bangkok: UNICEF Regional Office for East Asia and the Pacific.

Van Bueren, G. (1995) *The International Law on the Rights of the Child.* Dordrecht: Martinus Nijhoff.

Veitch, H. (2005) *Evaluation Report on Children's Participation at the East Asia Pacific Regional Consultation for the UN Study on Violence Against Children.* Bangkok: UNVAC Regional Steering Committee.

Woollcombe, D. (1998) Children's conferences and councils', in V. Johnson, E. Ivan-Smith, G. Gordon, P. Pridmore and P. Scott (eds) *Stepping Forward: Children and Young People's Participation in the Development Process*, London: Intermediate Technology Publications, pp. 236–40.

Young General Assembly (2006) *Statement from the Young General Assembly on the 2006 General Discussion Day 'On the Rights of the Child to be Heard'*. Geneva, 15 September 2006. www.crin.org/docs/GDD_2006_Young_General_Assembly. DOC accessed 15 January 2007.

PART II

CONSTRUCTIONS OF CHILDHOOD AND CHILDREN'S EXPERIENCES

Introduction

The contributions in Part II explore some facets of the relationship between constructions of childhood, children's experiences and notions of the child as citizen. They thus provide knowledge on the de facto position of children, the rights they have or claim, the obligations they fulfil as well as what society expects from them. Within the children's rights arena, such issues are often addressed with the notion of the child's 'evolving capacity' (see Foreword by Jaap Doek and Introduction to Part I) which is variably defined. Rather than being solely a matter of age, capacity (or competence) depends also on experience and environment. In relation to this, contributions in Part II provide highly relevant analysis.

Different constructions of childhood attribute to children different characteristics, or emphasize certain characteristics whilst suppressing others. Thus, traditional images of children as dependent are associated with characteristics such as passiveness, vulnerability, immaturity and/or lack of competence (James and Prout, 1990). Some of the discourses on children's citizenship, particularly when associated with participation, seem instead to implicitly propose an image of 'little people' with their own rights, indeed stressing their independence. A further approach has stressed interdependence between children and adults, promoting a different model of children's citizenship (Cockburn, 1998).

As social science has 'deconstructed' the notion of childhood (James and Prout, 1990), it has become apparent not only that no single childhood exists but also that denial of the diversity of childhoods – in terms of age, gender as well as social, economic and cultural background – can have very negative consequences for a number of children whose experience, because it does not fit with dominant (and often idealized) images of childhood, is stigmatized or devalued. In light of such diversity, there is therefore an urgent need to question any assumptions. It is tempting to say that one of the lessons to be drawn from contributions in Part II is that it is necessary to challenge notions of children as either totally independent, or dependent or interdependent. Their relations to adults need to be replaced in their context and carefully examined rather than being defined on the basis of assumptions. Although this might appear evident at first, it however suggests how difficult it is to identify a common status or practice of citizenship for all children.

James, Curtis and Birch draw on theoretical developments over the last two decades which have scrutinized constructions of childhood that deny children rationality and agency. Their central thesis is that in England the image of children as dependent and in need of care, education and protection has led to legislation, policies and practices that have increased control over their daily activities. Increased protection leaves little space for social participation and thus active citizenship for children. Children's reactions to restraints on their autonomous activities might vary. In their study of children's perceptions of hospital spaces, child informants apply limits to their own active participation and free movement in the hospital. They thus seem precisely to conform to this representation of children as dependent, needing protection, care and supervision and to reject an image of independence during childhood.

Jones' contribution challenges assumptions about children's dependence on adults from a different perspective. Citizenship is approached here as 'participation in social and economic life' gained primarily through economic independence, which children do not enjoy. The notion of 'citizenship by proxy' demonstrates that parents, and not children, hold specific social rights. This is because of age-structured policies in which children are assumed to be dependent on parents at certain ages and independent at others, without consideration for the differential economic resources available in the family which make such dependence impossible (see also Clutton in Part III) and to the need for support that may arise later in life. Jones' contribution shows how age-structured approaches overlook the much differentiated situations and transitions to adulthood that young people experience. She suggests that an approach to citizenship in terms of rights and obligations between generations at societal, community and family levels is a more appropriate framework for policymaking. A life course perspective seems to be more apposite than assumptions of dependence or independence of children based on age criteria.

Alderson's contribution challenges the dominant image of young children as dependent on adults from another, complementary perspective. On the one hand, several compelling examples drawn from her research illustrate how children actively contribute to their families and communities rather than simply being passive and dependent on adults. Her research in neonatal units in England shows, for instance, how seeing premature babies as partners of professionals rather than passive recipients of care might improve services. On the other hand, the representation of children as 'naturally' dependent on their families is challenged in reference to its economic implications. Beside the denial of the economic value of children's contributions there is a more general occultation of the work of caring for them. However, it is a broader analysis that is introduced to explain the under-recognized limitation of citizenship of young children. Drawing on feminist and green economist contributions, she stresses the inappropriateness of the economic paradigm that renders any contribution that does not belong to the commercial or state-related economies invisible. By this means, unpaid house work, family or community mutual care – all central for early childhood – and other 'unregulated' economies are ignored.

Invernizzi's contribution describes children's experiences of work in Peru and Portugal, demonstrating that the child's work is not a simple reaction to adverse economic conditions and source of exploitation but has to be seen as a part of complex family strategies involving generation of income as well as practices of protection, socialization, autonomy and care for children. What is challenged here is the fundamentally positive character attributed to children's economic dependence on parents as it is embedded in discourses on the elimination of child labour. Families' strategies in relation to children's work might be very apposite in difficult economic contexts but also relate to different cultural and social constructions of childhood providing children with spaces of socialization, autonomy and self-determination. Her argument is that diverse practices towards and of children as well as different images of childhood have to be acknowledged as part of the debates on children's citizenship since they give a content to their 'informal' status within communities and to citizenship practice.

Since, within the children's rights discourse, *children's participation* has been seen as pivotal to the conceptualization of children's citizenship, this is a recurrent topic in several contributions. Those included in this part outline some issues that require scrutiny. A key issue put forward in James et al.'s contribution is the cultural politics of childhood that constrains possibilities for participation. The second issue of concern is, as observed by Morrow, the inability of many structures for children's participation, such as school councils, to provide spaces children see as empowering. Similar concerns are expressed by Ennew (Part I) in respect of participatory experience within UN-related events. Children's experiences might lead to disillusion rather than active involvement of young people, despite contrary adult intentions. Cynicism and disillusion may be among young people's reactions to societal control but, as shown by James et al., children might also conform to the image of children needing protection and supervision rather than requesting increased autonomy. Invernizzi and Liebel suggest that the spheres of autonomy children legitimately gain in their communities through work might be conversely made illegal through legislation and policies. However, Liebel (Part I) presents illustrations of experiences in southern countries where children have been able to progressively identify their own interests and negotiate solutions with authorities.

Elements of explanation for such variable experiences in relation to participation might be found adopted in different approaches. Liebel describes these experiences as a progressive educational process for children and adults anchored in children's everyday lives. The underlying paradigm of *protagonismo* is intended as 'the process in which the child integrates himself actively, expands [. . .] abilities and skills, critically identifies [. . .] problems and outlines possible solutions, reaches a higher degree of development and the ability to organise himself [/herself] in order to defend and develop his[/her] rights and to create a new world' (Liebel, 2001: 327). What is instead described by Morrow (and by Ennew in Part I) are experiences of involvement in adult-created structures or instances of decision-making.

A further important issue to be explored in the field of children's participation can be more precisely framed using the notions of dependence, independence or interdependence outlined above. Whereas general discourses and practices related to participation challenge the assumption of children being 'naturally' dependent on adults, experts have also challenged the image of children entirely independent in participative decision-making. This image has indeed been criticized as a Western concept of autonomy (for instance Alderson, 1998) although Morrow (in this volume) shows that scrutiny is equally required in the English context, where conceptualizations of participation might somehow have become 'too child focused' and overlook the way children and adults are interconnected. They do not necessarily correspond with children's requests for more interdependent or shared decision-making with adults. Her study shows how far levels of autonomy wished by children vary depending on the decision to be taken and the context. Participation might thus be seen as contextualized: different opinions, different decisions and different degrees of independence and interdependence of children have to be acknowledged.

Paradoxically, Invernizzi shows that children's views and decisions might be interpreted by adults as lack of discipline when it comes to the child deciding to work under age or leave school. As Morrow suggests, there is a need to read practices of resistance in an appropriate framework which includes consideration of autonomy and participation. Children's expressions of autonomy in their everyday lives can provide inspiration for thinking about and practising participation. Alderson's contribution provides interesting material for extending the notion of competence and participation to babies and very young children.

When considering chapters included in this section, it is the complexity and diversity of children's experiences that is underlined. Approaches to children's citizenship, in terms of practice particularly, have to deal with diverse spheres of autonomy for children and with interdependence with adults rather than simply relying on assumptions of children being either dependent on or independent from adults. Indeed a plea for a more inter-dependent model of citizenship has been proposed by Cockburn (1998) not only as a means of accommodating children but also to accommodate all different human beings. In this sense, James et al. (in this volume) suggest that 'children would be respected as autonomous and responsible social actors in their own right, valued for what they contribute to society as children' rather than assimilated as adults.

Such ideas seem to better reflect the children's practices and echo Lister's suggestion that children's citizenship can be better approached with a notion of 'differentiated universalism' (Part I). However, a great deal remains to be examined in order to reconcile data, social scientists provide on children's experiences and practices and on constructions of childhood with concepts of citizenship as a status as well as to other theoretical developments put forward in Part I. Even more complex is the task of relating these developments to examinations of policies and legislation provided in Part III. Contrasting analyses underline the need for interdisciplinary work in which consolidation of theoretical work would go hand in hand with research drawing on real children's lives in order to examine and rethink legislation and policies.

References

Alderson, P. (1998) 'Understanding wisdom and rights: assessing children's competence', in D.K. Behera (ed.) *Children and Childhood in our Contemporary Societies*, Delhi: Kamla-Raj, pp. 157–72.

Cockburn, T. (1998) 'Children and citizenship in Britain: a case for a socially interdependent model of citizenship', *Childhood*, 5(1): 99–117.

James, A. and Prout, A. ([1990] 1997) *Constructing and Deconstructing Childhood*. London: Falmer Press.

Liebel, M. (2001) 'Working children's protagonism, children's rights and the outline of a different childhood. A comparative reflection on the discourses in Latin America and the "First World"', in M. Liebel, B. Overwien and A. Recknagel (eds) *Working Children's Protagonism. Social Movements and Empowerment in Latin America, Africa and India*, Frankfurt/London: IKO, pp. 321–48.

7

Care and Control in the Construction of Children's Citizenship

Allison James, Penny Curtis and Joanna Birch

Introduction

The focus for this chapter is a thin red line. Red is for danger and the danger we explore here is one that is beginning to stalk contemporary English childhood and to impact upon children's everyday experiences. Masquerading as 'being in children's best interests' this thin red line poses a threat, however, not only to children's experiences as individuals, but it also sets a tighter boundary to childhood itself, separating children from adults in a number of profoundly important ways.

What, then, is this red line? In short, it is the conceptual line that exists between concepts of care and those of control, concepts that, as noted elsewhere (Hockey and James, 1993), shore up asymmetrical relations of power through the creation of dependencies of different kinds which, within Western, individualistic societies, have become 'naturalized' through 'reference to family-oriented social discourse . . . [and] the rootedness of the parent-child metaphor' (1993: 115). Thus, it is that the 'cared-for' may often find themselves at the mercy of the 'carers' who control them, a process often leading to the denial of citizenship rights through social exclusion. In the case of contemporary English childhood, as we show in this chapter, the caring–control that helps sustain children's dependency rests upon the tension that exists between children's rights to protection and those of participation. It is this tension, we argue, that is core to the ways in which children's citizenship is conceptualized and realized for children in their everyday lives.

As this chapter argues, although rights to protection and participation are enshrined by the United Nations Convention on the Rights of the Child (UNCRC) as key children's rights, in contemporary English society these are becoming increasingly incompatible, as calls for 'protection' – by adults on children's behalf – begin to work as forms of restraint on children's active social participation and to constrain their potential as citizens. Drawing upon research with children, carried out in hospital settings, we illustrate the ways in which contemporary representations of 'childhood' are actively repositioning children as both irresponsible and vulnerable, a representation that lessens their opportunities for active citizenship.[1]

The Social Construction of Children's (non) Citizenship

That children and adults are constituted through their difference from one another, and in this sense can be regarded as mutually defining categories, was remarked long ago by Jenks in his observation that 'the child . . . cannot be imagined except in relation to a conception of the adult (1996: 3). Like adults in so many ways, children are also significantly different, differences that are, largely, conceived through oppositions: small, rather than tall; sexually immature, rather than mature; and as now so often described in the literature, as becomings rather than beings (Lee, 2001). However, given their difference from adults, it is argued that children require different things in order that their becoming adult – their becoming like us – can take place and continue unimpaired. Thus, children ideally attend school, rather than work; watch cartoons rather than horror films; and they are expected to be content with their exclusion from many other aspects of the adult social world (James, Jenks and Prout, 1999: 37–58). Such social exclusion is by some regarded as being in their best interests since it is intended to be protective of their present lives and to therefore safeguard the future (see for example Elkind, 1981). Indeed, those children who do not experience such separations are often considered to have 'lost' their childhood (Winn, 1984; see Buckingham, 2000 for a critique). In this sense, then, children's difference from adults not only constitutes their very beingness but is also the justification for forms of social exclusion that will, it is said, ensure their eventual sameness!

At work here then is a system of classification that, as the anthropologist Mary Douglas (1966) argued, involves the social construction of conceptual boundaries that separate one thing from another, to create distinctive groups of belonging and, classically, to separate purity from danger, to distinguish the sacred from the profane. However, as she went on to show, through this act of separation or the remarking of difference, the boundary itself becomes a potent source of danger for – as a boundary – it is neither one thing nor the other. For Douglas this was exemplified by the fact that those animals, people or plants who elude easy social classification – those boundary sitters – often become the focus for special reverence, fear or repulsion. They are neither one thing nor another; they are matter out of place. It is, therefore, unsurprising that the idea of children's citizenship is considered to be problematic for, classically, full citizenship only belongs to adults. To confer children with equal citizenship rights would be to breach the boundaries that separate children from adults, the boundaries that help constitute their 'difference'.

Indeed, for Delanty (2000), citizenship is, in essence, about group membership. This makes boundary marking and processes of identification central to the idea of citizenship and, as outlined above, it is in the process of drawing up group boundaries for belonging that non-belongers are inevitably created. For the Greeks, indeed, these processes of exclusion, via the setting of boundaries, were a key component of their idea that citizenship is a privilege and that the citizen is a political being. Women, children and slaves were not entitled to be citizens; their minds being encumbered by the mundane world of things, they were not able to participate in the public world of politics. And though in Marshall's (1950) classic account, the institution of citizenship is held to alleviate such inequalities through the bestowal of full community membership and social, political and civil rights, exclusion still figures – children are citizens in potentia only. As Delanty reminds us, 'no account of citizenship can evade the fact that it was originally constructed in order to exclude and subordinate' (2000: 11).

Thus, as research in childhood studies has noted, not only do children lack political rights and indeed many other social and civic rights, but also a range of other social practices works to exclude them from the adult world. According to Roche, therefore, children are not citizens and they are 'often rendered silent and invisible by the attitudes and practices of adult society' (Roche, 1999: 476). But since children are denied political rights precisely because they are not adults, what Roche (1999: 480) describes as the "not-yet-fully-formedness" of the child' becomes an instance of 'naturalized' exclusion.

Indeed, it is often in precisely these terms that regimes of care, designed to protect children, are justified in their setting of limits to children's participation as social actors and agents. In this way, then, the adult-to-be that is 'the child' is denied full citizenship status through the imposition of 'care' regimes that control what children can do. As Roche describes,

the overwhelming imagery surrounding children and young people is negative; they either need to be better protected (better policed from the evils of the adult world) or better controlled (because of the failure of certain families to police properly their children).

(1999: 477)

On account of 'being a child', of being different from adults, children cannot participate as equal citizens and it is through the thin red line of protection that takes place as both care and control that this difference is both justified and sustained and children's dependency on adults confirmed.

However, according to Cockburn (1998), it is not an 'adult' type of citizenship that children need. Indeed, along with Roche, he argues that what is required is a new model of citizenship that can acknowledge and accommodate the difference between a child and an adult, rather than make it the basis for discrimination and exclusion. In the case of children such a model would be focused primarily on children's participation as active social and civil citizens. For Cockburn, this requires a fundamental rethink of what is meant by citizenship, by seeing children and adults as mutually dependent on one another through recognition of the essential interdependence of all human beings. Such a model would propose 'the antecedents of citizenship . . . not . . . [as] . . . something which people [such as children] need to qualify for but rather to be something pre-existing' (Cockburn, 1998: 113). In Cockburn's proposals, then, children's acquisition of citizenship is not visualized as incremental, as something children gain, bit by bit, as they grow up. Rather, children would be respected as autonomous and responsible social actors in their own right, valued for what they contribute to society *as children*.

Such a recasting of citizenship would, however, mean a thorough reconstruction of ideas of both 'childhood' and 'adulthood' for, as noted above, the conceptualization of children's difference is symbolized by their dependency upon adults and their need for care and control through protection. These are core to ideas of what children are. As Cockburn himself acknowledges:

> There is a need for a normative and ideological shift in viewing childhood not as a 'preparatory stage' but as a central component in society with an important and legitimate role to play in the continuation of that society . . . If social relations can produce dependent and devalued children, it can potentially produce the converse, that of children valued and respected.
>
> (1998: 114)

The Cultural Politics of Children's Citizenship

The UNCRC would seem to offer a powerful platform upon which children's citizenship might be constructed since the law is a key mechanism in what James and James have termed the cultural politics of childhood (James and James, 2004). As they show, in any society, the Law operates as one of the main regulatory devices that shape the space of childhood. It does this through developing social policies of different kinds; policies that seek to control the kinds of activities that children can do; the social and material environments they inhabit and the resources they have access to. In short – in and through the social policies of any society can be seen expressed a particular social construction of childhood. And, although this construction of childhood through law and policy has very material effects upon children's experiences, the different ways in which children respond to these regulatory experiences, can, nonetheless, lead to changes, as well as continuities, in particular constructions of childhood over time.

However, though the UNCRC represents a powerful international attempt to set out universal rights for all children through a particular envisioning of what 'childhood' should be, the ways in which the principles embedded within the UNCRC have been interpreted and subsequently translated as government policy have, for English children, not been especially progressive of their rights. Rather, the reverse. As the rights agenda has gained momentum, so have progressive governments created a wider net of social control, with 'an increasingly fine mesh [that] is permeating more areas of more children's lives than ever before' (James and James, 2001: 226). Whether in relation to education, health, crime or the family the kinds of actions that children might take towards realizing their rights as participative and active citizens are frequently countered by legislative controls that limit their effectiveness and reach. Thus, for example, though in relation to parental divorce children now have a right to be consulted about matters that concern them, exercising that right can prove difficult in a context where the overriding commitment is to the welfare principle that allows adults, rather than children, to decide what is in children's best interests (James, James and McNamee, 2004). Similarly, in relation to education, despite emphasis being placed on citizenship education within the curriculum, children's everyday experiences of school are those of an increasingly restrictive and prescriptive curriculum and a system of testing and classification that works against the expression of autonomous action by children themselves (see James and James, 2004).

As these examples show, therefore, the tension that exists between two of the more fundamental principles of the UNCRC – Articles 3 and 12, glossed here as being about rights to protection and rights of participation – are becoming in the English context increasingly incompatible and it is a tension that has significant consequences for children's citizenship status. For example, Article 3 says that States should 'undertake to ensure the child such protection and care as is necessary for his or her well-being'. However, defining what is necessary is far from easy. In an analysis of the recent policy developments around *Every Child Matters* (James and James, 2007: forthcoming) argue that far from being enabled to become reflexive and responsible individuals through the range of choices made available within the late-modern 'risk society' (Beck, 1992) children are being increasingly 'disabled'. This occurs through recourse to a developmental paradigm that casts children in need of protection *from* risk as they grow up. That is to say, by virtue of their supposed need for 'protection' *against* risk, children are not being permitted (or are less and less so) to make choices and take risks. 'Freed' from risk-taking, under the guise of being protected, this risk-free cultural environment turns out, however, to be one that is highly governed and controlling of children's participation. It is certainly not an environment that nurtures the reflexive individuality characterized as central to the modern risk society; neither is it conducive to active citizenship.

This desire to free children from experiencing risk is, however, not only just a UK phenomenon but has also wide humanitarian appeal. For example, as Hart has recently argued

agencies at all levels – from the transnational and governmental to the most local – are now engaged in the project of saving children as a distinct category of persons defined by age.

(2006: 6)

Focusing on the issue of child soldiers – an iconic group of children at risk and in need of saving – Hart cautions against the tide of moral panic that assumes all children are coerced into fighting against their will, an image core to the child-saving project. Citing work by Read (2001) he argues that a 'complex interplay of factors . . . result in young people's engagement in armed conflict' and that 'the experience of oppression or marginalization may be well understood even by the young and motivate them to risk their lives in combat' (2006: 6–7). That is to say, such children may choose to participate alongside adults, to be active citizens and fight for their future. As Hart argues, Western child-savers need to acknowledge such local values in programmes of demobilization so that children's very real grievances can be properly addressed, rather than remain buried under the guise of protection.

This example exemplifies rather dramatically the cultural politics of childhood that are at play in relation to children's citizenship under the guise of protection. It shows the ways in which particular ideas of child-hood and those of protection work hand-in-hand to set limits to adults' views about the kind of participation children *should* have in society. However, this process is not confined to war zones. As the next section explores, it is endemic in the English context and, rather worryingly, is a process that children themselves seem to take part in.

Children as Active Participants?

Article 12 of the UNCRC is one of the most-cited articles in relation to children's rights since it is here that children's active participation in matters that concern them is promoted. However, as many have already noted (Prout and Hallet, 2003), the rhetoric of participation is often louder than its practice and in any number of spheres of everyday life children's participation may be absent or simply tokenistic. Only rarely still are children's voices heard and their participation as active citizens encouraged.

But exactly why this is the case has yet to be fully teased out. The adherence to a strict developmental paradigm of children's growing competence may be one reason, as authors such as Alderson (1993) and James, James and McNamee (2004) have demonstrated. Indeed, for Hart (2006), this is what underpins the efforts of the child-savers, described above. However, here we wish to pursue another explanation: that an increasing focus on the need to protect children from risk is not only working to prevent children's access to different social arenas by setting limits or controls on their participation, but that children themselves may also be setting limits to their *own* participation because of the powerful risk-averse discourse that surrounds contemporary English childhood.

Evidence for this comes from our recent study into children's perceptions and experiences of hospital space. Designed as a project whose outcome would be to provide data from children about what they would see as a child-friendly space – rather than, as now, hospital space being designed in accordance with adults' prejudices about what they think children need – we asked children, in both outpatients' departments and on the wards, about what they like or dislike about various features of the hospital environ-ment. Taking place in three hospitals, the research covered the range from a well established children's hospital to a purpose-built children's unit in a district hospital and to a children's ward in a general hospital. As part of this project children aged between 4 and 16, who were visiting outpatients, were asked in a short interview to look at some photographs of different parts of the hospital – bed spaces, throughways, clinical areas, toilets and bathrooms and play spaces. They were asked to choose which photograph they liked best and to explain why. We also asked our informants if they thought children would be allowed in these spaces on their own. This was part of our quest to understand what a 'child-friendly' hospital environment might feel like, from a child's point of view – that is, what kind of space might children find empowering for their participation?

The answers they gave to the simple question about whether they would be allowed to be on their own astonished us and are highly revealing of a particular construction of children's potential as active participants. From 120 outpatient interviews, across all those three sites mentioned earlier, the answers children gave can be summed up as follows: children argue that children, as a category, require supervision in hospital spaces because they are both vulnerable and irresponsible. That is to say, children say that children need both care and control, a process that as argued above works to limit their active and independent participation as citizens.

Overwhelmingly, children thought that children would always need adult accompaniment in the different spaces of the hospital – usually mum or dad, or a member of the medical staff. In answer to the question – can you tell me if you think children are allowed in here on their own? – virtually all 120 children answered with a straight 'No'. This apparent need to have adult supervision applied across all spaces, including more private spaces such as the toilet and bathrooms and the cubicle and ward bed-spaces. Only very occasionally did a child say that children might, for example, be allowed to use a bathroom by themselves. Thus, for example, one 7-year-old girl said children would need supervision from their parents *'unless you need to go to the toilet'*, while a 7-year-old boy said:

No, but it depends, if you are over 3 or 4 because most doctors are around.

Here he suggests that because 'doctors are around' children over 4 could be on their own in a space without their parents.

A 12-year-old-girl, on the other hand, acknowledged that being on your own was, in any case, an unlikely occurrence. Looking at a photograph of the adolescent recreation room in one hospital, she articulated what children already know from their everyday life experiences – they are rarely left unsupervised:

Not really. They would have to have the staff sitting in.

Of the treatment room, the same girl said, yes, children might be allowed to be there on their own. However, this affirmation of the possibility for independent action, was immediately qualified by the necessity for prior adult permission

If you are older than 9 and they say it would be OK.

The catalogue of reasons why children think 'children' should not be allowed to be alone in a space is long and varied:

Might die
Might hurt themselves
Might bang themselves
Bang heads on table
Get lost
Fall from the bed
Under 10s would be with someone in case they drown
Might get locked in
Loads of electrical stuff
Might find medicines on the floor and eat them or drink them
No doors – might run off
Sharp things in cupboard
No in case someone slipped and cut their head open
Lots of needles might hurt yourself
Slip and fall
Trip up
Hot water
Fall over
Falling off the bed

Hospital spaces are, it would seem, full of dangers that pose risks to children and, indeed, when looking at the photographs, children readily scanned the environment *through* the frame of risk. They could see all kinds of potential dangers in the environments. One 12-year-old girl said of a cubicle room – '*The radiator. Children could burn themselves on that. Needs a guard*' – while a 12-year-old boy identified the sockets on the wall of the play room as a danger. A 14-year-old boy said children could not be on their own in the treatment room because '*You could jab yourself, get hurt*' and, noticing the shelf on the wall added: '*The shelf might fall*'. A 16-year-old girl, reasoning why children could not be in a bathroom alone, said '*because if you trip and fall over, I mean it says it's a wet area*'. And all of these identifiable environmental risks were in addition to the identification of stranger-danger, as articulated by one 4-year-old girl as '*No. the stranger might pinch them*' – and a 7-year-old girl arguing that: '*There might be bad people*'.

However, this reading of risk from the photographs reveals, we suggest, *adult* concerns about children's need for protection. That is to say, the children are articulating here the lessons which they have been taught about a particular kind of 'childhood' that results from the ways in which current social policy in England is engaging with children. Such a childhood is at risk, and under threat, with children seen as vulnerable to hidden dangers of all kinds (James and James, 2007). Electric sockets, sharp knives, hot water, slippery floors, medicines, needles and sharp edges are all identified as risks. Thus, one 12-year-old boy suggested that the bathroom would be improved if they '*put a box or something round that sink and pipes to make it safe for little kids*' and a 12-year-old girl, looking very closely at the picture of the ward advised the removal of the tiny little curtain hooks that were high up on the curtain rails *'because people could hurt themselves'*. And on the very rare occasion when one 10-year-old boy replied, 'yes' to our question as to whether children could be allowed in a bathroom on their own gave his reason as: *'it's all safe'*.

This representation by our informants of the vulnerability of children to risk is exacerbated, however, by their articulation of another common feature of the contemporary construction of English childhood: children as irresponsible. In this discourse, children are not just under threat, they also pose a threat and therefore need not only care but also control (Roche, 1999). During the interviews, children of all ages produced a catalogue of what children, left to their own devices, might do:

> *they could have needles and stab someone*
> *might grab something*
> *might break something*
> *might steal*
> *mess around and set something off*
> *press button*
> *fiddle with things*
> *touch things*
> *[ruin] expensive equipment*
> *make a noise*
> *pick something up & damage*
> *touch something & damage*
> *press the alarm*
> *Run off and go in a hospital room*
> *Mess it up*
> *No. they make a mess*
> *Mess about and knock stuff over*
> *Knock things over*

With rights come responsibilities and the denial of children's rights is often justified in terms of their lack of responsibility. This appears to be another lesson that children have learned about what children are. Thus, looking at a photograph of the recreation room one 14-year-old boy said:

> *No. [children can't be on their own] You never know. Some people might steal CDs . . . you need to know if you can rely on them.*

A 9 year old girl commenting on a photograph of the ward said:

> *No, definitely not. You wouldn't want someone to be on their own. They might run and make a loud noise when people need to sleep.*

Children as Citizens?

Listening to these children's representations of 'children' through this catalogue of constructions of 'the child' at risk, in need of care and of control provides ample support for Rose's (1989) contention that childhood is the most intensively governed period of the life course. As one manifestation of the contemporary cultural politics of English childhood, these representations of 'childhood' by children raise some important questions for children's citizenship. First, why should children and young people appear to hold such a negative view of children as a social category and, second, what consequences might this have for children's sense of self?

More detailed examination of the children's responses to our questions provides some answers. First, it is clear that in interpreting the hospital environment, which for some may be an unfamiliar one, children draw on their experiences of other settings, such as the school and the home. Thus, for example, two 4-year-old girls said children have *'got to sit on chairs'*, and that they *'need to hold hands'*, while a 7-year-old boy gave as his reasons why children couldn't be alone as follows: *'they'll mess about and won't listen and mess the room up or cry'*. A 10-year-old said that children might be allowed to be on their own *'if you are not naughty and splash and break things'* while an 8-year-old girl said children required supervision *'cos people could sneak in and they are not supposed to'*.

Such comments resound with echoes from the classroom where fiddling with things and making a mess are forbidden and frowned upon, while sitting still, holding hands and being sensible are positively rewarded:

> *Not on their own but may be older kids as long as there's a sign up that says be sensible. (12-year-old girl)*

Lessons learned at home and in the neighbourhood are also in evidence in, for example, the frequent mentions by children of expensive electrical equipment that might get broken, the need to be hygienic and keep well and the fear and danger involved in getting lost. A 14-year-old boy, echoing many a parental warning, said that children could not be alone

> *cos there's lots of expensive stuff . . . if you break it by accident, it's a waste of money*

A 9-year-old girl commented:

> *No, if they get glue on their fingers, they might put it in their mouth and they might drink something which has had someone else's mouth on it.*

And a 6-year-old girl said:

> *No, not without an adult. You want to be safe, not get lost and know where the family is.*

Thus, children are 'reading' the photographs by looking out for dangers in the environment, dangers that in other settings they have already been taught to recognize – and, indeed, to fear.

However, the data do also permit an alternative reading that offers a less grim picture. This appears in examples where children speak about themselves, rather than other children in general. In such examples, the children present themselves as independent and responsible actors – citizens in the making. And yet, it remains an incremental model of citizenship, embedded firmly in the dominant discourse of child development, rather than a new model of citizenship such as Cockburn (1998) proposes, discussed above. Thus, for example, having first identified a danger or risk, children and young people might qualify their statement by giving an age at which being on their own in that space might be possible for children. The age given is always the age which they themselves have recently passed:

> 12 year old: 'If you are older than 9 then it would be OK
> 10 year old: 'If they are like 10 or over, they could be trusted.
> 8 year old: If you are older than 6, but no, not on your own. There are lots of needles and stuff.
> 9 year old: If you are older, an adolescent or like over 8.
> 14 year old: If you are 10 or over, you are more responsible.
> 12 year old: If you are 7 or younger then you don't know what you are doing.

Thus, despite the dominance of the discourse of risk in children's own accounts that might seem to indicate that children concur with, and thus legitimate, the kinds of exclusionary barriers adults have increasingly placed around childhood under the guise of protection, this construction is of a 'child' who is younger and (therefore) less capable than themselves. Indeed, as noted elsewhere (James, 1993) such is the stigmatizing potential of the label 'child' that many of the older children and young people worked hard to distance themselves from the category of children altogether through, for example, the use of other terms such as 'people', 'little children', 'babies' and 'kids'. These were categories to which they did not see themselves belonging. There is, then, perhaps one small glimmer of light in a somewhat dark story of young people's own views of childhood – the potential that children have to act independently in relatively unfamiliar environments and to be active citizens.

Conclusion

That children can so readily articulate a version of childhood as a social space that is hedged around with danger and risk – albeit that they often do not see themselves as inhabiting it – should, we suggest, give pause for thought about the perils of the risk society and the import that this has for children's citizenship. It suggests that the greatest danger in the risk society is not that we fail to protect our children sufficiently but, rather, that, in caring too much, the controls that are put in place work to limit not only children's participation – in terms of the kinds of things they might do – but also their imagination about the kinds of people they are or might be. For this reason, close attention needs to be paid to the cultural politics of English childhood lest the thin red line that separates children from adults under the guise of protective care and control becomes any thicker.

Note

1 This research, entitled Space to Care was funded by the ESRC, 2005–7 ESRC Grant: RES-000-23-0765.

References

Alderson, P. (1993) *Children's Consent to Surgery*. Buckingham: Open University Press.

Beck, U. (1992) *Risk Society: Towards a New Modernity*. London: Sage.

Buckingham, D. (2000) *After the Death of Childhood*. Cambridge: Polity Press.

Cockburn, T. (1998) 'Children and citizenship in Britain', *Childhood*, 5(1): 99–117.

Delanty, G. (2000) *Citizenship in a Global Age*. Buckingham: Open University Press.

Douglas, M. (1966) *Purity and Danger*. London: Routledge and Kegan Paul.

Elkind, D. (1981) *The Hurried Child: Growing up Too Fast Too Soon*. Reading, MA: Addison Wesley.

Hallet, C. and Prout, A. (eds) (2003) *Hearing the Voices of Children: Social Policy for a New Century*. London: Routledge.

Hart, J. (2006) 'Saving children: what role for anthropology', *Anthropology Today*, 22(1): 5–8.

Hockey, J. and James, A. (1993) *Growing Up and Growing Old*. London: Sage.

James, A. (1993) *Childhood Identities*. Edinburgh: Edinburgh University Press.

James, A.L. and James, A. (2001) 'Tightening the net: children, community and control', *British Journal of Sociology*, 52(2): 211–28.

James, A.L. and James, A. (2004) *Constructing Childhood: Theory, Practice and Social Policy*. London: Palgrave.

James, A.L. and James, A. (2007) 'Changing childhood in England: reconstructing discourses of "risk" and "protection" in children's best interests', in A.L. James and A. James (eds) *European Childhoods: Cultures, Politics and Participation*. London: Palgrave.

James, A.L., James, A. and S. McNamee (2004) 'Turn down the volume? – not hearing children in family proceedings', *Child and Family Law Quarterly*, 16(2): 189–203.

James, A., Jenks, C. and Prout, A. (1999) *Theorising Childhood*. Cambridge: Polity Press.

Jenks, C. (1996) *Childhood*. London: Routledge.

Lee, N. (2001) *Childhood and Society*. Buckingham: Open University Press.

Marshall, T.H. (1950) *Citizenship and Social Change*. London: Pluto.

Roche, J. (1999) 'Children: rights, participation and citizenship', *Childhood*, 6(4): 475–93.

Rose, N. (1989) *Governing the Soul*. London: Routledge.

Winn, M. (1984) *Children without Childhood*. Harmondsworth: Penguin.

8

Youth, Citizenship and the Problem of Dependence

Gill Jones

Introduction: The Significance of 'Youth'

Most definitions of childhood, including the 1989 UN Convention on the Rights of the Child (UNCRC), include all those under the age of legal majority (generally 18), thus setting up an age threshold between childhood and adulthood. The aim is to redress the particular vulnerability of children which stems from their dependence on their parents or carers. There are two problems resulting from the use of an age threshold to denote this. The first is that children are presented as united in their dependence, whether they are able to be dependent or not. The second is that over-18s are not seen as in need of special protection.

As a sociologist who has specialized in research on young people's transitions between childhood and adulthood (focusing, though not exclusively, on the age range between 16 and 25), I would suggest that life transitions are far more complex, varied and (sometimes) extended than simple age thresholds would suggest. We no longer live in an age of linear progression from childhood to adulthood through rites of passage. Even the age of legal majority is losing its significance. The trend is clearly towards a continual extension of the period of economic dependence previously associated with childhood. Youth, in industrial and post-industrial societies, is a very complex, extended and *risky* period in the life course. Instead of ignoring this complexity we should address it.

This chapter is about the complex relationship between young people and citizenship. It explores citizenship as an element in the broader process of transition to adulthood, and considers the significance of age. My argument is based on the principle that citizenship (participation in social and economic life) is primarily achieved through economic independence.

Status versus Process?

Although the study of transitions to adulthood has been a major focus of youth studies in recent years, shaping two large national UK research programmes (Jones, 2002; Catan, 2004), there is unease in the world of childhood studies about focusing on life course processes, and debate about whether children should be seen as beings or becomings (Lee, 2001).

On the one side, it is argued that by emphasizing the processes, we lose sight of the children. The danger is that individuals are seen as 'cultural dupes' with experience and futures but without volition – a determinist viewpoint which denies the significance of individual agency.

The counter argument is perhaps illustrated through a case study. The care system in the UK has indeed focused on the here and now, and in overlooking the processes of becoming adult has let young people down (e.g. Stein and Wade, 2000). Care leavers are more likely to enter the labour market without qualifications, become unemployed, become homeless, become teenage parents and even become offenders. Much of the blame for this must lie with local authorities who, in focusing on the *here and now*, neglected future needs – hopefully this is now changing, with the development of life plans (SEU, 2003).

The point is that youth is a dynamic process. Youth is a period when young people are anticipating their adult lives as well as looking back at their childhoods. They do not suddenly become adult when they technically cease to be children. There is a complex transition from childhood to adulthood.

The sociology of childhood is a relatively new field of study. There is a long history, in contrast, in the sociology of youth, of debate about the relative significance of structure and process (see Jones and Wallace, 1992). The question is how young people 'fit' into society. Sociologists in the 1960s and 1970s debated over how young people were articulated with the social structure, whether as products of 'parent' social classes, or as a class in themselves – an 'age class'. This debate arose because of contemporary fears about generational conflict, at a time when there was widespread student rebellion on the one hand, and emerging working-class youth cultures (or sub-cultures) on the other. The upshot was recognition that temporal and social contexts were both critical in understanding social behaviour, and hence social change.

The Problem of Dependence

Some time ago, Claire Wallace and I wrote a book *Youth, Family and Citizenship* (1992) proposing a holistic approach, which would take account of life course *and* social contexts. We suggested that the concept of citizenship provided the opportunity to understand the processes of transition in youth. Drawing on the work of T.H. Marshall (1950), we saw citizenship as the relationship between the individual and the State, a relationship which involved rights and responsibilities on each side. In contrast to the UNCRC which centres on aspects of civil and political citizenship, most of our discussion was centred on the ways in which young people achieved social citizenship – evidenced by participation in social and economic life.

We argued that 'the family' – usually the parents – acted as a mediator between the child and the State. Thus, parents held citizenship rights on behalf of their children. As young people became adult, they gradually developed a direct relationship with the State, rather than one in which they were dependent on their parents for rights. According to this argument, children cannot be full citizens because of their status as dependants. The idea that parents hold parental rights in order to allow them to fulfil their parental obligations is supported by the Children Act 1989 in England and Wales. Similarly, Child Benefit, though paid to a parent, is intended as a means of combating *child* poverty. Can it then be equally suggested that parents hold their children's citizenship rights by proxy only in order to ensure that their children can indirectly access those rights? If this principle is established, we can move on to the key issue: that in families where parents do not fulfil this function, their children lack even indirect access to those rights. This is the most critical element of the problem of dependence.

It is because of the problem of dependence that the UNCRC is needed. While fundamental human rights are largely related to protection of the individual from abuses of the State, the UNCRC spells out that children need special care and assistance' because of their 'physical and mental immaturity'. The implication is that vulnerability is inherent in their status of dependence, and they need protection from abuses by their carers and the State.

The problem of dependence provides a framework for understanding inequalities in youth in which the ability to be dependent (and be supported) is an important dimension. Because there are inequalities of wealth within family households as well as between them, economic well-being or disadvantage in youth cannot be measured solely from statistics based on the family of origin. Though rights and responsibilities accrue, albeit unevenly, with age (Jones and Bell, 2000), access to them and the ability to exercise them depends on an individual's ability to mobilize personal resources (Barbalet, 1988). Young people's ability to acquire individual personal resources is limited, and they are increasingly dependent on family resources, over which they have no control. We find, for example, that – where family relationships are good, and where parents can afford to – parents will provide their children with economic support *for causes they believe in* (e.g. Jones et al., 2004, 2006). Just as Lister (1990) questioned whether women could ever achieve citizenship while they remain dependent on men, so young people cannot arguably be full citizens as long as they are dependent on their parents. Thus, though they may have nominal or partial rights, they do not necessarily have the means of accessing them. Whatever programmes of education and training 'choices' are theoretically available to them, their ability to capitalize on these depends on parental support. The dangers of assuming that young people can be dependent on their parents because they are below the age of legal majority are thus becoming clear. For many, the only hope of emancipation from parental control is through State welfare, which is gradually being withdrawn.

Polarized Transitions

UK research on young people's transitions over the last decade has shown emerging forms of inequality. At a time when postmodern interpretations were suggesting that social structures were breaking down, youth research has shown the continuing significance of structural inequalities of class, gender and ethnicity, and the continuing role of families in social reproduction.

Young people's experiences of transition to adulthood are seen as becoming polarized along social class lines. One the one hand are those on slow-track transitions through post-school learning which require continued dependence and family support, reflecting long-standing middle-class patterns. On the other hand are those, mainly of working-class origins, who reject, or cannot afford, such extended education-based transitions and seek their fortunes in the youth-labour market, with the risk of social exclusion if they fail (Bynner et al., 2002; Jones, 2002). There is also a less visible middle band of those (broadly reflecting the aspiring rather than actual middle class) who are trying to achieve middle-class, extended transitions with working-class patterns of economic support, and who are therefore at risk of joining the socially excluded groups (Jones et al., 2004). Divisions are thus increasing in the processes themselves. Within a broad trend towards the extension of economic dependence there is increasing divergence between those who can be dependent and those who cannot. Thus, the idea of a threshold age between those who are dependent and those who are not becomes even less defensible.

Generally speaking however, young people in the UK tend to become independent earlier than their peers elsewhere in the EU: they leave education and enter the labour market earlier; they are among the earliest home leavers; and they have high rates of teenage pregnancy (Iacovou and Berthoud, 2001). Furthermore, they have (in the past at least) mainly supported their own transitions to adulthood through earnings, rather than relying on the support of their parents or the State. This overall national picture is dominated by the working-class patterns of transition and family support, which are now subject to stress. The earlier transitions of working-class young people in the UK were economically underpinned by their own earnings. This is no longer feasible: the jobs which are available to unqualified school-leavers tend to be low paid, low grade and insecure. Many cannot turn to their parents for alternative support, as their parents are unlikely to have any expectation that they will fulfil an extended supportive role even if they had the resources. Young people on fast-track transitions to adulthood therefore face new risks, which seem to be specific to the UK in their configuration.

Some Caveats on Complex Transitions

Before moving on with my argument, I must pause to insert some additional complexities. Even taking into account variation in the timing and ordering of transitions, we still cannot think of transitions to adulthood as linear and unidirectional. First, children and young people under the age of 18 may be at different levels of dependence, and indeed some have to take responsibility for others (Dearden and Becker, 2000). Families operate systems of mutual obligation and interdependence which involve children as contributors to family systems as well as beneficiaries, in a reciprocal rather than dependent relationship (Jones and Wallace, 1992; Morrow and Richards, 1996). Second, it is important to recognize that (in)dependence is also multidimensional. Independence from parents can be achieved at different times and in different ways. It helps to think of transitions to adulthood as being along different but related strands (such as transitions into the labour market, or into independent homes, or into partnerships). They can be independent in one respect and dependent in another, for instance they may have independent incomes but still live in the parental home, and, furthermore, they can back track, for instance by returning to the parental home.

Parental Responsibility

The aim of the UNCRC is to protect children who are in a position of vulnerability, not to make them responsible for their own circumstances. Indeed it can be argued that the UNCRC expressly separates out children's rights, in order to ensure that it is adults who hold (and fulfil) the responsibilities.

Children's special need for protection reduces as they become emancipated from dependence on others. How far does the UNCRC take the issue of diminishing dependence on board? There is recognition in the UN Convention that childhood involves development: the evolving capacities of the child are recognized, as is variation by age, but the treatment of these concepts is very superficial. The UNCRC also indicates that parents have a primary function in ensuring that children are 'fully prepared to live an individual life in society', and that 'the family' should be afforded necessary protection and assistance to fulfil its responsibilities towards dependent children. It does not, however, comment on the ways in which parental care diminishes with the growing independence of the child.

The issue of how parental responsibility should in practice diminish with the increasing autonomy of the child has exercised minds in the UK for some time (Masson, 1995; Jones and Bell, 2000). Definitions of parental responsibility to care and maintain young people in the UK are unclear, and have certainly not kept pace with youth policies which have assumed that young people can remain dependent on their parents (Jones and Bell, 2000). There is very little in place to protect the 'new vulnerable'. Under the Children Act 1989, although parental responsibility continues until the age of 18, a parent may not be required to care for a child over the age of 16 years. Young people aged 16 and 17 are in a vulnerable situation. Those in education were deemed dependent, while those on training schemes were not, according to Child Benefit regulations and the Child Support Act 1991. At a time when education and training opportunities often run alongside employment, the validity of basing dependency status on education is questionable.

It is therefore not surprising that parents are confused about their legal responsibilities. In a recent study (Jones, 2004), over half of the parents interviewed thought their legal responsibilities to provide food and clothing, and housing for their children ended at 16 or 17 years, while most others thought that their legal responsibilities ended at 18 years. Most parents had no idea when their legal responsibilities to pay for their children's education ended, and 74 per cent thought they had no legal obligation to subsidize their children's low wages. Smith et al. (1998) similarly found that many parents of homeless young people in England saw their responsibilities ending at 18 years. Lack of clarity abut legal responsibilities may not be a problem in a caring family where parent–child relationships are good, but research shows clearly that some parents and adolescent children have such a poor relationship that the parents make use of their apparent right to evict their children at the age of 16 years. Many young people under the age of 18 have no-one to be dependent on.

This contrasts with other European countries. For young people elsewhere in Northern Europe the welfare state plays an important social protection role; while for those in Southern Europe the family is the main source of support (IARD, 2001; Holdsworth and Morgan, 2005; Jones, 2005a). In some countries, there is an age limit for parental responsibility (18 in Norway, 21 in the Netherlands, 26 in Italy, 27 in Germany); in others, responsibility ceases on completion of education or training (Austria, Hungary). Traditionally, in Southern European countries parental support is extended, especially towards students, and it is not unusual for 30-year-olds to live with their parents. The age of legal majority – mainly associated with civil and political citizenship – seems rarely to have a bearing on economic independence in Europe.

The Vulnerability of 16/17-Year-Olds

Age thresholds such as 18 signifying the end of childhood, inevitably set up a static, life-stage approach to individuals, rather than a more fluid and dynamic, life-course one. However, UK policymakers have gone further and introduced complex age-grading into welfare structures. In attempts to find ways of delivering welfare benefits and provisions to young people with different degrees of independence, policymakers have resorted to age-grading. In 1985, the Green Paper *The Reform of Social Security* reinforced existing age-banding on the dubious basis that

> It is clear that at the age of 18 the majority of claimants are not fully independent, and that the great majority of claimants above the age of 25 are.
>
> (Fowler report, Cmd 9518, 1985)

The social security legislation was based on a 'dependency assumption' (Harris, 1989) that young people under 18 can be dependent on their parents and do not need individual state welfare protection. Benefits were withdrawn from 16/17-year-olds in 1989 on the basis of this supposed dependence, but it became necessary to introduce Severe Hardship Payments in response to the many young people who lacked supportive parents and had been left destitute. Many commentators argue that the increase in youth homelessness following the 1989 Social Security Act was its direct consequence, but the lesson, that age is a very poor indicator of individual need, was largely ignored (Jones and Bell, 2000). Current youth policy structures (including Jobseekers Allowance and National Minimum Wage levels) contain many examples of age-grading, similarly based on assumptions about levels of dependence at different ages.

Policymakers still cannot determine whether 16/17-year-olds should be treated as dependants or not. Should benefits be paid to parents or to young people themselves? There have been anomalies. Thus, Child Benefit (CB) is payable to parents, but the more recently introduced Education Maintenance Allowances are payable directly to 16/17-year-olds to encourage them to stay in education.

It is only recently that their individual needs have become recognized again. The *Review of financial support for 16–19s* (HM Treasury, DfES and DWP, 2004) aimed to deal with some of the anomalies and ensure that all young people aged 16–19 had the support and incentives they need to participate in education and training. The report proposed a single coherent system of financial support for 16- to19-year-olds, giving more equal value to education, training and employment. It also tried to deal with the age/dependence problem. As a consequence, under-18s living in the parental home are treated as dependent unless they have full-time jobs. Support is paid direct to young people living independently or to their parents/carers if they are living with them. Parents are compensated through CB and Child Tax Credit (and CB is payable to parents in respect of 16–18-year-olds in unwaged training as well as those in education).

The review attempts to move away from age as an indicator of need. It takes account of various other proxy measures of independence, such as employment, income and household status (whether they have left the parental home). It still fails, however, to take account of the interdependence factor (that many young people who are living with their parents pay board money), or indeed recognize that many young people who have left home still receive financial support from their parents, especially among the middle class. Broadly, though, the review recognizes that age structures are not enough, and the social context in which needs arise must be recognized.

The Problem of Over-18s

Those of us who have been engaged in research on young people and those involved in working with young people (such as youth workers) are beginning to wonder what has hit us. Young people are disappearing from view. There was going to be a Young People's Unit in England; this went through various permutations until it emerged as the Children,

Young People and Families Unit, based in DfES. Youth – among under-18s, has been subsumed within childhood. Indeed current 'learning' (education and training) policies have effectively raised the school leaving age to 18. The result is a firmer dividing line in policy constructions at age 18 or 19. Just as the UNCRC concerns under-18s, so recent developments in the UK, including *Every Child Matters* in England, cut off at 18/19 years. This dividing line cuts right through most young people's transitions to adult-hood, and bears no relation to the 'lived experiences' of young people themselves. The consequence is that young adulthood is emerging as the conceptual means of identifying and addressing the needs of young people in the wider age range of 16–25 years.

I was recently involved in reviewing for the Social Exclusion Unit (SEU) the impact of government policies for socially excluded young people (Bynner et al., 2004). Our main recommendations were that policy struc-tures should be more supportive of transitions to adulthood, rather than ending at 19 years, and that policies should 'go with the flow' of young people's beliefs, rather than try to cut across them. The SEU (2005) picked up these themes with a report *Young Adults with Complex Needs* which attempted to develop policies to enable smooth transitions between youth and adult services. The point is that policies to support and enable smooth transitions to adulthood need to take account of the ways in which life course changes, such as leaving school, entering the labour market, forming an intimate partnership, having children, all involve changing socio-economic relationships and changing patterns of socio-economic responsibility. As young people begin in different ways to become independent of their parents, their needs and aspirations will reflect these changes in responsibility. Sometimes this can lead to 'second chances' such as returns to learning. Recognition in policy structures as independent adults must therefore also involve recognition in their social contexts (Jones, 2005b).

There has been research on young people's own perceptions of adulthood which suggests that age has become less significant to young people them-selves. In broad terms, adulthood means independence, specifically from parents, but this is measured in a range of ways. A generation ago, young people thought of adulthood in terms of work, the key to financial independence (Willis, 1984) and marriage, the key to home and family (Leonard, 1980). Recent studies suggest that young people initially think of independence in terms of autonomy, responsibility and maturity, but as they experience transition events such as setting up home, becoming a parent or gaining an adult income, they retrospectively begin to identify adulthood with these event markers (Jones, 2004; Holdsworth and Morgan, 2005).

A recent study of constructions of adulthood among 16- to 21-year-olds (Thomson et al., 2004) found perceptions of competence to be more sig-nificant than age or event markers, but that individualized constructions give way to relational ones, as young people 'settle down'. As young people begin to separate from their families of origin, their social networks change, and as a result they take on new responsibilities and can develop new competences and identities as workers or partners or parents or householders (Thomson et al., 2004; Jones, 2005b). These new competences are not always recognized by policy makers. Early entrants into the labour market are seen as having failed educationally, rather than as anxious to start work. Teenage mothers are treated as a target group for reintegration into education or employment, rather than as potentially good mothers. Unfortunately, most of the existing private, social obligations of children and young people are overlooked in the policy emphasis on visible 'active citizenship'. Going with the flow of cultural beliefs would mean recognizing existing class and ethnic patterns rather than imposing white middle-class ones. Policy incentives and disincentives designed for young adults need to take account of their social context, and in particular their economic relationships with their parents.

Conclusion: Towards a Generational Life Course Perspective

Anne-Marie Guillemard (2001) suggests that the welfare state, based on age thresholds, effectively standardized the life course into three phases, of education (childhood), work (adulthood) and rest (old age), thus accentuating the differences between these states rather than the relationships between them. Kohli (1987) calls this a 'tripartition' of the life course. What we see now is a de-standardization of the life course. The result, according to Guillemard, is a 'crisis of normativeness' in which people's lives have come adrift of policy structures. I have argued here that policy structures have always been adrift in the case of young people, and that 'youth' has never been successfully incorporated into policy thinking. The UNCRC is just another example.

A life course perspective involves more than understanding individual transitions to adulthood. It also means understanding intergenerational relations which form the framework for patterns of dependence and independence across the life course. Such an approach was advocated in the European Commission White Paper on Youth, which commented on the need for new social protection frameworks in the light of demographic change:

> This quantitative imbalance between old and young will bring about a qualitative change in relations between generations. The financial pressure on social welfare systems will be only one aspect of this challenge. Indeed, we will have not only to invent new mechanisms for solidarity between young people and their parents or even their grandparents, but above all to organise, to everyone's satisfaction, the transition between generations in societies undergoing profound change.
>
> (2001: 9)

Ultimately what we should be looking at is the changing relationships between generations at societal, community and family level. These intergenerational relationships change with demographic change, as fertility and infant mortality decrease and longevity increases. They also change over the life course as people move between dependence and independence, in complex patterns of intergenerational reciprocity. This agenda is in my view the most important agenda facing social science and social policy. It affects every manifestation of social cohesion, from parental responsibility, to perceptions of crime and social disorder, to willingness to pay taxes, to welfare and retirement pension rights.

It is becoming increasingly difficult to assign rights and responsibilities, define needs, formulate services or ascribe characteristics to a person according to their age – and this applies right across the life course. Just as we cannot assert that children are dependent or that young people are semi/quasi dependent, so we cannot ascribe dependence to the older generation, who are staying longer in employment. In order to understand the real complexity of contemporary lives we have to try to get beyond simplistic parcelling of the life course up into handy bite-sized packages. They may make policy-making easier, but they also make it less effective.

References

Barbalet, J.M. (1988) *Citizenship*. Milton Keynes: Open University Press.
Bynner, J., Elias, P., McKnight, A., Pan, H. and Pierre, G. (2002) *Young People's Changing Routes to Independence*. York: Joseph Rowntree Foundation.
Bynner, J., Londra, M. and Jones, G. (2004) *The Impact of Government Policy on Social Exclusion among Young People: A review of the Literature*. Social Exclusion Unit in the Breaking the Cycle series, ODPM – SEU.
Catan, L. (2004) *Changing Youth Transitions in the 21st Century: A Synthesis of Findings from the ESRC Research Programme Youth Citizenship and Social Change*. Brighton: TSA.
Dearden, C. and Becker, S. (2000) *Growing Up Caring: Vulnerability and Transition to Adulthood – Young Carers' Experiences*. Leicester: Youth Work Press and the Joseph Rowntree Foundation.
European Commission (2001) 'A New Impetus for European Youth', White Paper, COM(2001)681, Commission of the European Communities, Brussels, 21 November 2001.
Guillemard, A.-M. (2001) 'The Advent of a Flexible Life Course and the Reconfiguration of Welfare', Keynote Speech, COST A 13 Conference, *Social Policy, Marginalization and Citizenship*, Aalborg University, Denmark, November.
Harris, N.S. (1989) *Social Security for Young People*. Aldershot: Avebury.
HM Treasury, DfES and DWP (2004) *Supporting Young People to Achieve: Towards a New Deal for Skills*. Inter-departmental review of financial support for 16–19 year olds, London: HMSO.
Holdsworth, C. and Morgan, D. (2005) *Transitions in Context: Independence, Adulthood and Home*. Buckingham: Open University Press.
Iacovou, M. and Berthoud, R. (2001) *Young People's Lives: A Map of Europe*. Colchester: University of Essex, Institute for Social and Economic Research.
IARD (2001) 'Study on the State of Young People and Youth Policy in Europe', Report for the European Commission D.G. for Education and Culture. Contract n. 1999 – 1734/001–001.
Jones, G. (2002) *The Youth Divide: Diverging Paths to Adulthood*. York: Joseph Rowntree Foundation.

Jones, G. (2004) *The Parenting of Youth: Economic Dependence and Social Protection.* R000238379. End-of-award report to the ESRC.

Jones, G. (2005a) 'Social protection policies for young people: a cross-national comparison', in H. Bradley and J. van Hoof (eds) *Young People in Europe: Labour Markets and Citizenship*, Bristol: Policy Press, pp. 41–62.

Jones, G. (2005b) *Thinking and Behaviour of Young Adults 16–25: A Review.* Annex A, Report on Young Adults with Complex Needs, London: Social Exclusion Unit, ODPM.

Jones, G. and Bell, R. (2000) *Balancing Acts? Youth, Parenting and Public Policy.* York: York Publishing.

Jones, G. and Wallace, C. (1992) *Youth, Family and Citizenship.* Buckingham: Open University Press.

Jones, G., O'Sullivan, A. and Rouse, J. (2004) 'Because it's worth it? Education beliefs among young people and their parents in the UK', *Youth and Society*, 36(2): 203–26.

Jones, G., O'Sullivan, A. and Rouse, J. (2006) 'Young adults, partners and parents: individual agency and the problem of support', *Journal of Youth Studies*, 9(4): 375–92.

Kohli, M. (1987) 'Retirement and the moral economy: an historical interpretation of the German case', *Journal of Aging Studies*, 1(2): 125–44.

Lee, N.M. (2001) *Childhood and Society: Growing Up in an Age of Uncertainty.* Buckingham: Open University Press.

Leonard, D. (1980) *Sex and Generation: A Study of Courtship and Weddings.* London: Tavistock.

Lister, R. (1990) 'Women, economic dependency and citizenship', *Journal of Social Policy*, 19(4): 445–67.

Marshall, T.H. (1950) *Citizenship and Social Class and Other Essays.* Cambridge: Cambridge University Press.

Masson, J. (1995) 'The Children Act 1989 and young people: dependence and rights to independence', in J. Brannen and M. O'Brien (eds) *Childhood and Parenthood, Part 1: Parents and Children*, London: Institute of Education, University of London.

Morrow, V. and Richards, M. (1996) *Transitions to Adulthood: A Family Matter?* York: Joseph Rowntree Foundation.

Smith, J, Gilford, S. and O'Sullivan, A. (1998) *The Family Lives of Homeless Young People.* London: Family Policy Studies Centre.

Social Exclusion Unit (SEU) (2003) *A Better Education for Children in Care: The Issues* London: Social Exclusion Unit.

Social Exclusion Unit (SEU) (2005) *Transitions: Young Adults with Complex Needs.* SEU Final Report. London: ODPM.

Stein, M. and Wade, J. (2000) *Helping Care Leavers: Problems and Strategic Responses.* Department of Health, Quality Protects. http://66.102.11.104/ search?q=cache: hVN8Cg3RVv4J:www.doh.gov.uk/scg/leavingcare/getitright1.pdf+getitright 1&hl=en&ie=UTF-8

Thomson, R., Holland, J., McGrellis, S., Bell, R., Henderson, S. and Sharpe, S. (2004) 'Inventing adulthoods: a biographical approach to understanding youth citizenship', *The Sociological Review*, 52(2): 218–39.

UN (1989) *Convention on the Rights of the Child.* Office of the High Commission for Human Rights, United Nations.

Willis, P. (1984) 'Youth unemployment', *New Society*, 29 March, 5 April and 12 April.

9

When Does Citizenship Begin? Economics and Early Childhood

Priscilla Alderson

Introduction

Citizenship is considered in this chapter for its economic implications, and for young children's contributions to the economics of their household and communities, as well as their entitlements to use public services and amenities. 'Public' is taken to mean beyond the household or family, in small or larger neighbourhoods, cities or counties, nation-states, or global economic exchange. This review mainly considers children in England, although the patterns possibly apply to all countries, whatever stage of their history, from child workers to children as scholars, they presently occupy. The chapter aims to cover large issues albeit briefly.

There is not space to review here either how, in most times and places, even young children have been workers and contributors to their family economy, or how reluctant most States have been to intervene economically in the family to protect or provide for neglected or abused children (see Hardyment, 1984; Cooter, 1992; Hendrick, 2003). This reluctance persists despite neoliberal governments' increasing efforts to regulate children's and parents' behaviours (Rose, 1990).

Increasingly, young children are seen as economic dependents, burdens and costs (Zelizer, 1985), and childhood is seen in capitalist terms as the opportunity to invest now for future productivity and profit, and also for the future redemption of debts and correction of present failings towards imagined better societies (Qvortrup, 2005). New international concepts of children's citizenship and rights will be shown to complement children's seldom recognized contributions to their health, education and welfare services. The final section will review how alternative economic analyses open new ways of understanding the economics and citizenship of childhood.

New International Concepts of Children's Citizenship and Rights

Established in 1945, the United Nations (UN) aims to prevent war by promoting peace, justice and health through international diplomacy and action. Over-represented in poorer States, children particularly stand to benefit from the UN's efforts at redistributive justice. The UN Convention on the Rights of the Child (UNCRC, 1989) recognizes all children as citizens with economic rights and Article 24 covers richer countries supporting poorer ones in meeting higher attainable standards of care for children. The aspiration is that:

> Respecting the inherent worth and dignity and the inalienable rights of all members of the human family promotes social progress and better standards of life in larger freedoms, and lays foundations for justice and peace in the world.
> (UNCRC, 1989 preamble)

There are clear economic aspects of implementing the UNCRC provision rights to necessities such as education, health care, an adequate standard of living, nutritious food and clean drinking water, and also the protection rights from abuse, neglect, exploitation, cruel or degrading treatment and discrimination. Participation rights also have costs, respecting children's rights to life and survival, to due process of law, to an identity and nationality so that States, which register their children from birth, begin acknowledgement of obligations towards them. For the key economic right to work (Liebel, 2004; Liebel and Invernizzi this volume), the UNCRC sets conditions for protection from economic exploitation, from work that is hazardous or likely to interfere with the child's education, or to be harmful to the child's health or physical, mental, spiritual, moral or social development (Article 32). States should set a minimum working age or ages, and should regulate and enforce hours and conditions of employment. There is a contradiction when States refuse to recognize child workers aged less than a set minimum age, and therefore do not offer protections to improve the working conditions of the youngest workers (Mizen et al., 2001), who may be in most need of support. Just as feminists argue that much of their work is unpaid and unrecognized, so too is much children's work at home and school unrecognized and not even seen as 'work', but as 'learning or practising' supposedly mainly for the child's benefit. In narrowly defining work as 'paid employment' while vetoing slavery, the UNCRC overlooks how schooling involves very hard, unpaid and enforced work and very long hours for many children.

The key concepts of children as citizens in Article 12, with their rights to form and express views, to be consulted 'in all matters that affect' them, and for due account to be taken of their views, are sometimes criticized as potentially undermining children's protection and provision rights and best interests, if children resist adults' decisions about their welfare. However, no human rights are absolute, but are conditional upon national law and security, public order, health and morals, and avoidance of harm to third parties. Children's rights are further qualified by concerns to respect the child's best interests and parents' rights and responsibilities. The UNCRC only goes as far as children influencing matters that affect them, not being the main or sole decider. English law goes further, by recognizing the child's right to decide (*Gillick v. Wisbech & Norfolk AHA* 1985), but the Gillick/Fraser ruling is also limited. Children's decisions have to satisfy adults that they are competently made, informed, wise, and in the child's best interests. Article 12 tends to be classed as a civil and not an economic right. However, the next sections consider economic implications of Article 12.

Child Citizens and Public Services

During recent decades, people using public services have been treated less as active citizens than as passive consumers to whom services are 'delivered'. In practice, however, effective (and cost-effective) education and healthcare depend on the child's active cooperation and partnership when adults learn from children's 'views', as the following two examples illustrate.

During research about disabled children's views about their schools, I met 'Susan' (Alderson and Goodey, 1998: 119–20). When 4 years old, Susan insisted on moving from her local reception class, where she felt 'smothered and mothered', to be a weekly boarder at a special school. She is blind though, like many children at that school, she is exceptionally far-sighted about life and values. Susan recalled how, 'Mum had to drag me screaming down the [school] drive because I didn't want to go home.' By 10 years of age, Susan was determined to be the first person in her family to go to university. She thought carefully about her secondary-school choices and visited several schools to look round them. One was too rigid and unfriendly, she thought. Her local schools were not academic enough, but if she left her boarding school the LEA would force her to attend one of these. Yet she felt 'stifled' at her present school in a small class, and wanted a change. 'It's a really, really difficult decision,' she said. She decided to board at her present school and during the day to attend a nearby public school (on a very large split campus), sharing a liaison teacher with two other visually impaired students. 'It would be a struggle but I would get the hang of it,' she decided. Her father wrote a report explaining the decision for the LEA who approved Susan's choice. A year later she was very pleased with her decision, academically and socially. In some ways, Susan was the only person who could make a really informed decision that took account of her experiences, values and plans. She is academically successful, but during our research we found girls and boys with average abilities and with learning difficulties, who talked about their considerable insight into their own and their families' and friends' needs and interests, and how education services could help them most effectively, as well as how services were unhelpful. Their understanding correlated less with their age or assessed intelligence than with their experience.

In the second example, during an ethnographic study of four neonatal intensive care units (NICU), I observed 'John' and interviewed his mother and staff caring for him (Alderson et al., 2005). (Altogether, we interviewed 40 senior staff and the parents of 80 babies.) The four NICUs differed markedly in the attention that was paid to learning from the babies. John was born 14 weeks early, and he was in the most 'baby-led' unit with great efforts made to keep the lighting and noise low. John looked relaxed and contented in a soft fabric 'nest' that, like the uterus, helped him to maintain a foetal curved position, limbs gathered together and hands close to his face, so that he could soothe himself by sucking his fingers or stroking his face. In some other NICU, babies' limbs hang over loose loops of rough towelling and they try to gather their limbs together. The babies' subtle behaviours can be 'read' as their 'language' expressing their views and preferences (Brazelton and Nugent, 1995; Murray and Andrews, 2000). Using Als's (1999) detailed observation programme, a staff member had written John's care plan, showing his 'strengths and sensitivities' (not deficits), and identifying 'goals and recommendations' for care. The plan, written 6 weeks after his birth when he still needed some mechanical support with breathing, presents John as a major agent in his own health care. His 'competencies' included:

- initiating breathing movements much of the time;
- smooth well organised movements to protect and calm himself;
- making efforts to open his eyes in response to his mother's voice;
- using strategies such as grasping and holding on, taking his hands to his face, putting his feet and hands together to calm himself;

Goals: From the observations today it appears that John's next steps are

- consistent efforts to breathe on his own;
- more time in restful sleep (and other goals);

Recommendations to help John 'achieve his goals' included, continuing to:

- work gently with John, respond to his signs of discomfort by pausing, soothing him with still hands and letting him settle before proceeding (and other recommendations);

Consider:

- if it would be possible to position his bed where it is less light and busy;
- using bedding tucked around him and a stronger ridge around his feet to help him to find boundaries to push on and to help him contain some big tiring movements.

Three weeks later, John had made so much progress that the plans changed, for example, to 'continue to offer his dummy if it looks as if he might want to suck and let him choose if he wishes to take it into his mouth' and ways to encourage John to breastfeed in his strenuous efforts to coordinate breathing, sucking and swallowing.

Approaches to promote babies' own agency (Als, 1999) are important economically. The adults can help the babies to sleep more deeply and so to gain strength to breathe, feed, grow, resist infections and become well enough to leave the NICU earlier, and thus to reduce costs (Goldson, 1999;

Symington and Pinelli, 2006). Care for a long-stay baby may cost over £1 million. Effective health care involves adults working in partnership with individual children and learning from their embodied knowledge, as we also found with young children who have diabetes, a condition that can have serious and expensive complications (Alderson et al., 2006). Knowledge uniquely gained from closely observing and listening to individual children, and trying out different care techniques with them, can also be generalized to inform public services in order to benefit many other babies and children. Within these child–adult partnership approaches, respect for Article 12 is integral to cost-effective protection and provision for children as citizens.

The English Children's Agenda and Child Poverty

This section reviews economic aspects of children's citizenship in the English Government's Children's Agenda *Every Child Matters* (Treasury, 2003) and the 2004 Children Act (which covers England, and also Wales in non-devolved matters only). The Government's goals are primarily economic: to reduce child poverty primarily by increasing parental employment, to produce highly qualified, high-earning future workers, and to prevent costs of future crime and dependence (Treasury, 2003: 5–6). The dominant authors of the Childcare Bill (2005) are the Treasury followed by the Department for Education and Skills (DfES) (meaning employable workers), Department for Work and Pensions and Department for Trade and Industry. In the Children's Agenda, every child is implicitly positioned as a threat to social cohesion and prosperity, at risk of not fulfilling personal potential, of becoming a criminal and of being abused. Victoria Climbé's name echoes through the documents, as a prototype of need, although from among 11 million children she was one of the 50 to 100 children per annum who die from abuse or neglect (Treasury, 2003: 15). Victoria was known to several children's services, and buck-passing might have contributed to her misfortunes. The potential for buck-passing will greatly increase when all children's services must be coordinated through intrusive, time consuming, controversial and highly expensive electronic databases of every child and family (see www.arch.org.uk for research and debate about the database and Children's Agenda).

The Government's policies to 'end child poverty' include specific early-years interventions. A frequent quote in policy reports to support expanding pre-school interventions is from the US High/Scope Perry longitudinal study, which claimed that for every dollar spent on part-time pre-school interventions 7 dollars could be saved later. However, the three studies usually cited originated during the two decades from 1960s to 1970s with African–American children. They are 'not generalisable outside the US' and are inevitably 'suggestive estimates', partly because the cost calculations include 'highly controversial crime victim compensation figures' and very high imprisonment rates and costs among black youths (Penn et al., 2006: 27). The reports say little about the quality and processes of the interventions, and they ignore the young children's well-being and views. Penn et al. (2006: 28–9) conclude that the studies' findings are too tentative to support firm government policies, and that early childhood interventions alone cannot compensate for socio-economic inequalities in income, healthcare, schools, housing and local environments. Yet instead of adopting redistributive policies, the Government continues to plan numerous targeted and assessed interventions for young children.

The Government claims to have consulted adults and children when planning the Children's Agenda, but children's influences are not clear, unless in the Agenda's unexceptionable five aims: to be healthy, stay safe, enjoy and achieve, make a positive contribution and achieve economic well-being. There is no mention of time with family and friends, fun and free leisure time, which are usually children's priorities. The Agenda aims to establish 3,500 children's centres based mainly in schools by 2010 for children aged 0–14 years. Extended schools will open from 8.00 A.M. to 6.00 P.M., 50 hours a week throughout the year, longer than European working hours for adults, in order for the 'childcare market' to meet all local needs for fully employable parents. Most of the related government funding will support new and refurbished buildings and over 35 layers of planning, inspection, regulation and consultancy agencies (Treasury, 2001). It is unclear how flexible tailored care for each child is compatible with these elaborate structures geared to setting cost-effective testable targets. The Agenda will greatly expand the market in training and employing qualified policymakers and practitioners, and the new Children's Workforce Development Council is one response to concerns that England has far too few skilled and qualified childcare and education staff.

Child poverty in Britain has been rising since 1979. Although 750,000 to 850,000 children have been 'lifted out' of poverty since 1997, progress has slowed and it is expected to become harder for children living in households with under 60 per cent of the median income adjusted for composition of households (JRF, 2006). In inner London, child poverty rates rose to 54 per cent, 700,000 children by 2004; 70,000 of them were in temporary accommodation for homeless families (ECP- ALG, 2005). Current neoliberal economics assumes that lightly regulated markets increase the national wealth and allow wealth to 'trickle down' throughout society. Despite being the wealthiest State in Europe, Britain is the least equal one (ESRC, 2005) and has among the worst child poverty records, 21st out of 24 (JRF, 2006). London had a 23 per cent increase in its billionaire residents in the year up to April 2005. The top 1,000 richest people in Britain in 2005 owned £249,615 billion, whereas in 1997 they owned £98.99 billion. The share of the national wealth for the poorest 50 per cent of British people was 10 per cent in 1986 and fell to 5 per cent by 2002. Meanwhile, the cost of buying a home in London (especially high for young families as first-time buyers) doubled between 1996 and 2001 (Ingram, 2005). Many young families carry decades of debts and interest on student loans for higher education that was free for older people in Britain. The Children's Agenda expects working parents to pay for childcare until children are 14-years-old, whereas in some Nordic countries, the strain on the family budget is far less when children look after themselves after school hours from around 8 years of age.

Current policies are transferring costs from present onto younger generations. The 'prudent' government is rebuilding and refurbishing schools and hospitals at unprecedented rates, but avoids showing the true costs in its budgets. Instead it relies on private companies to build and rent out the premises and services within them. In use-now pay-later Public–Private Partnership (PPP) contracts, today's new buildings are paid for, many times over with interest, in the next 30, 40 or 60 years (Pollock, 2004). PPP policies encourage firms to provide cheaper-to-build and expensive-to-run-and-repair premises, as well as less ecological ones. The trademark atrium entrances, several stories high, absorb vast heating costs. Even if schools or hospitals have to close, PPP contracts ensure that private companies continue to be paid as if the buildings were fully used. PPP policies imply that it will be easier for future generations to pay for our costs as well as their own. However, global warming and dwindling oil supplies are likely to multiply future costs of living.

Many researchers and voluntary organizations call for increased parental employment, tax credits and benefits for families. They deplore the high costs of childcare and housing, and the very low salaries that many parents earn (e.g. O'Neill, 1998; Piachaud, 2001; Hirsh and Millar, 2004; Bradshaw and Mayhew, 2005; ECP-ALG, 2005; Platt, 2005; JRF, 2006; Pantazis, 2006). Although some debate the complications of defining and assessing poverty, social capital and social exclusion (Fine, 2001; Morrow, 2004; Mayhew et al., 2005; Pantazis et al., 2006), there are broad tendencies to support the government's concepts of economics in terms of monetary profit–loss, wealth and poverty, income and earning and spending power or potential. A widespread consensus associates childhood poverty with the supposedly adverse outcomes of teenage pregnancy, 'workless' households, and 'lone' parenting. The latter phrases deny all the important work performed within households, and that 'lone' parents live with their children.

Modern economies bring not only great material benefits for many children, but also serious problems. Economists, governments and the World Bank tend to assume that economic problems can be solved within the same economic paradigm and policies that produce poverty and inequality (Henderson, 1993; Wall, 2005). The paradigm identifies wealth with money; aims to increase income and expenditure through trade and growing productivity; measures poverty relative to higher income households and States in ever-escalating spirals of income and expenditure, and invests in intensive education, regulation and surveillance to produce future high-earning adults. However, clearer understanding of childhood poverty's causes and solutions may be found in alternative economic paradigms, reviewed in the next section.

Alternative Economic Paradigms

Figure 9.1 shows feminist economists' distinctions between the mainly male-dominated formal economy, and women's mainly unregulated, unrecognized and unrewarded work (Henderson, 1993; Mies, 1999). Children's even less visible activities also largely belong to the lower rows. Feminists regard the commercial sector as absorbing and then discarding workers, unconcerned with the previous costs of childcare and education, the continuing costs of care at home, and the subsequent costs of caring for rejected, old, sick or disabled workers. Feminists argue that far from the top commercial layer generating all wealth and support for society, commerce depends on all other layers.

Green economists show the formal economy exploiting nature as an 'externality'. Nature is preferably a free resource (land, air, water, minerals, forests) except for the labour required to process natural resources, and is also a free dump for unwanted 'outputs' – pollution and rubbish. Neoliberal economics increasingly threatens the finite planet by plundering and polluting nature in driving for infinite growth, consumption and profit, (Kennett and Heinemann, 2006). Placing nature on the lowest rung of the economies parallels perceptions of childhood on the first rung of society and as partly a natural state and one that renews societies. Absorbing children into commercial contexts tends to transfer them away from natural settings into buildings and vehicles (Katz, 2004, 2005).

Green and other critical economists challenge mainstream economics' claims to be a 'hard' mathematical science, supposedly dealing with time-less, value-free concepts. Instead, they argue that economics is socially constructed, heavily value laden and destructive, and that economics falsely identifies human psychology with competitive greed. Greens do not see money as the measure of all things, but as a volatile unreliable indicator and predictor, often of priceless natural and human resources. Although Gross Domestic Products (GDPs) measure economic growth and success in goods, they are also inflated by 'bads': the costs of crime,

Formal regulated economy – the System
Private commercial sector, corporations, the market
Government, public tax-funded sector, state services
Unregulated economies – the Lifeworld
Informal and underground economies
Unpaid housework and subsistence work
Family and communal reciprocity, voluntary work, self-help/support groups
Free associations, amateur arts and sports, faith groups, protest groups
Nature

Figure 9.1 *The Economies of the System and the Lifeworld.*

prisons, illness, disasters, accidents, waste and pollution. A US annual Index of Social Health measured the 'bads' of infant mortality, child abuse and poverty, teenage suicides, drug use, mental illness and high-school dropout rates. During 1977–94, as the GDP steadily rose, so too did these reported problems (Douthwaite, 1999). A healthy GDP does not necessarily equate with a healthy nation.

Alternative green economics proposals advocate: holistic respect for the interconnectedness of all things; moral and aesthetic values, and social solidarity; favouring simple, peaceful, harmonious ways of living rather than stressful competitive and violent ways; creating rather than consuming; promoting sustainable local trade instead of exploitative, wasteful global trade (Hamilton, 2003; Wall, 2005). Similarly, some childhood researchers suggest that instead of imposing Western values on children living in subsistence communities (Katz, 2004; Gupta, 2005; Penn, 2005) we have much to learn from them about ways of sharing the planet among over 6 billion people. Feminist and green economic paradigms indicate that we need clearer distinctions between types of poverty: between destitution (to be prevented and relieved urgently) and the frugal thrift in which people in most times and places have lived and which social justice requires we will all be forced to readopt sooner or later (Mies, 1999; Mayer, 2000; Hillman and Fawcett, 2004).

In Figure 9.1, the feminist tiers have been adapted to fit Habermas's (1987) concepts of the 'System' and the 'Lifeworld'. The neoliberal System (commerce, government and law, the power elite) colonizes and absorbs the Lifeworld (personal and civic life). This process also involves turning social and political issues (such as childcare and education) into ones of technical expertise. Neoliberalism further involves disorganized, deregulated global capitalism: the withdrawal of practical material support for citizens by the welfare state, accompanied by invasion of State and economic power (the System) into controlling both public and private life (the Lifeworld). The current Children's Agenda illustrates such policies. Habermas considers that people are treated less as active determining citizens, than as passive clients of State services and consumers guided by the mass media. He believes that the encroaching System results in fewer shared meanings and understandings, social bonds and integration, with increased feelings of helplessness, alienation and demoralization. Many areas of public life, schools and universities, charities and churches, and childhood itself are being drawn up into the top two layers to become more tightly regulated businesses. Extended children's centres, which confine children into one institution all week for 'wrap around care' under constant adult surveillance, isolating them into narrow age groups and away from all adults who are not paid carers or teachers, are likely to reduce children's status from contributing citizens into economic units whose performance gauges the school's cost-effectiveness. This could increase the social exclusion of the youngest generations (Mayall, 2002; Zeiher, 2003), which the Children's Agenda is supposed to counteract.

Conclusion

This review of children's under-recognized citizenship and economic contributions to their families and communities suggests that concepts of 'delivering' health care and education services misunderstand the crucial contributions that children can make within more cost-effective public services. Despite its unprecedented concern with private family life, the government continues historical traditions in mainly preferring self-reliance (parental paid employment) to direct material support for children. The multi-billion pound Children's Agenda mainly funds buildings, databases, committees and other infrastructures and not direct care of children. Alternative feminist and green economics point out gaps and problems in current mainstream economics, that have powerful implications for childhood, which so far have been little debated. There are risks that the System's over-concentration on monetary wealth and poverty and on children's future earning potential could turn children into hostages to the future, and paradoxically impoverish their present Lifeworld, restricting their citizenship, their enjoyments and relationships, freedoms and rights during their early years.

References

Alderson, P. and Goodey, C. (1998) *Enabling Education*. London: Tufnell Press.

Alderson, P., Hawthorne, J. and Killen, M. (2005) 'The participation rights of premature babies', *International Journal of Children's Rights*, 13: 31–50.

Alderson, P., Sutcliffe, K. and Curtis, K. (2006) 'Children as partners with adults in their medical care', *Archives of Disease in Childhood*, 91: 300–05.

Als, H. (1999) 'Reading the premature infant', in E. Goldson (ed.) *Developmental Interventions in the Neonatal Intensive Care Nursery*, New York: Oxford University Press, pp. 18–85.

Bradshaw, J and Mayhew E. (eds.) (2005) *The Well-being of Children in the UK*, 2nd edition. London: Save the Children. http://www.york.ac.uk/inst/spru/wellbeing.html, accessed 25 May 2007.

Brazelton, T.B. and Nugent, J.K. (1995) *Neonatal Behavioral Assessment Scale*, 3rd edition. Clinics in Developmental Medicine no. 137, London: MacKeith Press/CUP.

Children Act 2004. London: Stationery Office.

Cooter, R. (1992) *In the Name of the Child: Health and Welfare 1880–1940*. London: Routledge.

Douthwaite, R. (1999) 'The need to end economic growth', in M. Scott Cato and M. Kennett (eds) *Green Economics*, Aberystwyth: Green Audit Books, pp. 27–35.

ECP and ALG – End Child Poverty and Association of London Government (2005) *Not One of London's Children Lives in Poverty, 700,000 Do*. London: ECP, ALG.

ESRC (2005) www.esrcsocietytoday.ac.uk, accessed 28 December 2005.

Fine, B. (2001) *Social Capital versus Social Theory: Political Economy and Social Science at the Turn of the Millennium*. London: Routledge.

Goldson, E. (ed.) (1999) *Developmental Interventions in the Neonatal Intensive Care Nursery*. New York: Oxford University Press.

Gupta, P. (2005) 'India', in H. Penn (ed.) *Unequal Childhoods*, London: Routledge Falmer, pp. 119–41.

Habermas, J. (1987) *The Theory of Communicative Action, Vol. 2: Lifeworld and System: A Critique of Functionalist Reason.* Cambridge: Polity Press.

Hamilton, C. (2003) *Growth Fetish.* London: Pluto.

Hardyment, C. (1984) *Dream Babies – Child Care from Locke to Spock.* Oxford: Oxford University Press.

Henderson, H. (1993) *Paradigms in Progress: Life Beyond Economics.* London: Adamantine.

Hendrick, H. (2003) *Child Welfare: Historical Dimensions, Contemporary Debate.* Bristol: Policy Press.

Hillman, M. and Fawcett, T. (2004) *How We Can Save the Planet.* Harmondsworth: Penguin.

Hirsch, D. and Millar, J. (2004) *Labour's Welfare Reform: Progress to Date.* York: Joseph Rowntree Foundation.

Ingram, M. (2005) 'Labour policies make London a haven for the super-rich', *World Socialist* Website, www.wsws.org/articles/2005/apr2005/lond-a23.shtml, accessed 20 December 2005.

James, A. and James, A. (2001) 'Tightening the net: children community and control', *British Journal of Sociology*, 52(2): 211–28.

Joseph Rowntree Foundation (JRF) (2006) *What Will it Take to End Child Poverty?* York: JRF.

Katz, C. (2004) *Growing up Global: Economic Restructuring and Children's Everyday Lives.* Minneapolis, MN: University of Minnesota.

Katz, C. (2005) 'The terrors of hyper-vigilance', in J. Qvortrup (ed.) *Studies in Modern Childhood*, Basingstoke: Palgrave, pp. 99–114.

Kennett, M. and Heinemann, V. (eds) (2006) *International Journal of Green Economics*, volume 1/2.

Liebel, M. (2004) *A Will of Their Own: Cross-cultural Perspectives on Working Children.* London: Zed Books.

Mayall, B. and Zeiher, H. (eds) (2003) *Childhood in Generational Perspective.* London: Institute of Education.

Mayer, A. (2000) *Contraction and Convergence: The Global Solution to Climate Change.* Totnes: Green Books.

Mayhew, E., Uprichard, E., Beresford, B, Ridge, T. and Bradshaw, J. (2005) *Children and Childhood in the United Kingdom.* European Childhood Economics Survey, COST A19, pp. 403–56.

Mies, M. and Bennholdt-Thomsen, V. (1999) *The Subsistence Perspective.* London: Zed Books.

Mizen, P., Pole, C. and Bolton, A. (2001) *Hidden Hands: International Perspectives on Children's Work and Labour.* London: Routledge.

Morrow, V. (2004) 'Children's "social capital": implications of health and well-being', *Health Education*, 104(4): 211–25.

Murray, L. and Andrews, H. (2000) *The Social Baby.* Richmond: Children's Project Publishing.

O'Neill, J. (1998) *The Market: Ethics, Knowledge and Politics.* London: Routledge.

Pantazis, C., Gordon, D. and Levitas, R. (2006) *Poverty and Social Exclusion in Britain: The Millennium Survey.* Bristol: Policy.

Penn, H. (2005) *Unequal Childhoods: Young Children's Lives in Poorer Countries.* London: Routledge Falmer.

Penn, H., Burton, V., Lloyd, E., Mugford, M., Potter, S. and Sayeed, Z. (2006) *Early Years: What is Known about the Long-term Economic Impact of Centre-based Early Childhood Interventions?* London: EPPI-Centre, SSRU, Institute of Education.

Piachaud, D. (2001) 'Child poverty, opportunities and quality of life', *The Political Quarterly*, 72(4): 446–53.

Platt, L. (2005) *Discovering Child Poverty: The Creation of a Policy Agenda from 1800 to the Present*. Bristol: Policy.

Pollock, A. (2004) *NHS plc*. London: Verso.

Qvortrup, J. (ed.) (2005) *Studies in Modern Childhood*. Basingstoke: Palgrave.

Rose, N. (1990) *Governing the Soul*. London: Routledge, pp. 99–114.

Symington, A., and Pinelli, J. (2006) 'Developmental care for promoting development and preventing morbidity in preterm infants', *Cochrane Database Systematic Reviews*, (2). Art. No: CD001814. DOI: 10.1002/14651858. CD001814.pub2

Treasury (2003) *Every Child Matters*. London: Stationery Office.

Treasury, Department for Education and Skills, Department for Work and Pensions and Department for Trade and Industry (2005) *Childcare Bill*. London: Stationery Office.

United Nations (1989) *Convention on the Rights of the Child*. New York: UNICEF.

Wall, D. (2005) *Babylon and Beyond*. London: Pluto Press.

Zelizer, V. (1985) *Pricing the Priceless Child: The Changing Social Value of Children*. New York: Basic Books.

10

Dilemmas in Children's Participation in England

Virginia Morrow

Introduction

Recent social policy formulations in England have utilized a number of rather ill-defined concepts. Since 1997, the New Labour Government has enabled social policy and social research to focus attention on social context, examining the quality of relationships within specific areas or neighbourhoods, using the concept of social capital. World events following 9/11 and 7/7 have also led to an emphasis on what it means to be a UK citizen, ideas of belonging and identity, and community cohesion. Unconnected to this, the implementation of the United Nations Convention on the Rights of the Child (UNCRC), particularly Article 12, has increased participation activities with children in England. This chapter explores the meanings of these concepts and the implications for children's participation and citizenship (Children are defined here as all those under the age of 18, as per UNCRC).

Social Capital, Community Cohesion and Citizenship

Social capital is a nebulous term, derived from the work of US political scientist Robert Putnam (1993), but has become globally pervasive. Definitions included trust, social networks of cooperation and reciprocity, civic engagement and strong community identity. 'Building social capital' is one aim of the strategy for improving deprived inner-city areas (NRU, 2003; see Morrow 2005). 'Social capital' remains an elusive concept, although it is a useful tool for social policy research, because it asks questions about the quality of social relationships within specific neighbourhoods in the here-and-now (Morrow, 1999a). However, it was never intended to include children as active citizens, who are by definition excluded from civic participation because of their age. Further, much existing research on 'social capital' does not adequately define 'community', and tends to assume that children's 'social capital' is derived simply from their parents'/carers' social capital, for example, 'bonding social capital is important in health for children, families and the elderly' (NRU, 2003). This is too limited: children in middle childhood spend much of their time in their neighbourhoods, close to their homes, playing out in the street, many older children have part-time jobs or undertake marginal economic activities, are members of organizations and clubs, and they also come into contact with local services, and spend time in school – and schools can be important sources of identity and belonging in their own right (Morrow, 1999a; 2005).

Many elements of social capital overlap with the concept of community cohesion. Community cohesion has come to the fore in recent policy formulations, following a government inquiry into 'riots' in the north of England in 2001, where groups of young Muslim men were involved in disturbances (Home Office, 2002). A cohesive community is defined as one where there is 'a common vision and a sense of belonging for all; diversity is appreciated and positively valued; those from different backgrounds have similar life opportunities; and strong positive relationships are developed between people from differing backgrounds, in workplaces, schools, and neighbourhoods' (Home Office, 2002).

Recently too attention has been paid to the concept of citizenship. A literal definition of citizen is 'an inhabitant of a city', and thus must include children. However, citizenship also involves 'having rights and duties of a citizen, and conduct in relation to these duties'. In other words, 'citizenship' contains an active, behavioural element (Chambers Concise 20th Century Dictionary). 'Citizenship education' has been introduced into the National Curriculum in England, implying that 'citizenship' is something that children need to be taught, which they do not already possess (see also Lockyer, this volume).

Links between 'social capital' and 'citizenship' are often made in policy documents, for example, the Office of National Statistics suggests that 'the main aspects [of social capital] are *citizenship*, neighbourliness, trust and shared values, community involvement, volunteering, social networks and civic participation' (ONS n.d.). An extract from a speech made by the former Home Secretary, David Blunkett, in 2002, is indicative of the rhetoric used:

> we must think about building social capital in the wider context of citizenship. The two weave together. Those who volunteer in their communities tend to be more likely to vote. Conversely, those who have a sense of citizenship tend to work with others to improve their communities.
>
> (Blunkett, 2002)

How do these debates relate to children? The Home Office, for example, recognizes that children are crucial to 'community' life, highlighting 'intergenerational tensions', the 'disengagement of young people from the local decision-making process', and 'inadequate provision of youth facilities and services' are identified as problems, yet the solution is seen as enabling young people 'to contribute fully to the development of cohesive communities and to have their own, distinctive voice' (Home Office, 2002). A number of criticisms can be made of this: we must question whether children were ever 'engaged' in the first place; second, there are structural reasons for inadequate youth facilities and services related to the privatization of leisure and cuts in spending; and third, the suggestion that young people must be 'enabled to contribute' is not only patronizing, it ignores the fact that many young people already 'contribute' to their communities in various ways, but their contributions are invisible because they are not measured or valued. Further, the proposed indicators of community cohesion were largely adult-oriented, and the only indicator that related directly to children being the percentage of pupils achieving five or more GCSEs at A*-C. Presumably this was based on an assumption that areas with high levels of community cohesion have higher educational outcomes, but it gives an indication of how children are conceptualized in these debates to which I return later in this chapter.

Participation

Unrelated to this wave of work on community cohesion and social capital has been a large amount of participation work with children that has been undertaken in UK by a range of organizations, including voluntary and public sector bodies, over the past decade; this has been reviewed by Kirby et al. (2003) who found some examples of positive change, particularly at small-scale, local level. This (and other academic research) has shown that young children can engage with notions of rights, decision-making, and being listened to; that children would like to have a say in decisions and to be heard; and that children can see decision-making from others' points of view (Morrow, 1999b). Yet, in general, research has found that children's participation is limited. However, it is worth examining what is meant by participation in this context.

As many authors have noted, the concept of participation is not straightforward, even in relation to adults: for example, 'participation has proven difficult not only to define, but to practically initiate and sustain' (Zakus and Lysack, 1998: 7). Most work on children's participation draws upon Roger Hart's (1992) adaptation of Arnstein's (1969) 'ladder of citizen participation', and this has been unquestionably useful, because citizen participation does indeed have various levels and meanings. However, there is a danger of abstracting children's participation as an end in itself and thus losing sight of the way in which children and adults are interconnected, and the ways in which adult structures and institutions constrain children. In other words, there is a danger of children's participation becoming, oddly, too 'child-focused', and it might be helpful to return to basic questions about what children's participation means in the context of hierarchical structures in which their lives are conducted. Boyden and Ennew note that there are two definitions of participation, participation in the sense of 'taking part in', or being present, and participation in the sense of 'knowing that one's actions are taken note of and may be acted upon' (1997: 33). Chambers Concise 20th Century Dictionary also has two definitions: the first is 'having a share in, taking part in' (others have referred to this as *'passive participation'*). The second definition includes 'worker participation', defined as 'the involvement of employees at all levels in the decision-making of a company' – *'active participation'*. These two aspects of participation are interlinked, and it is difficult to achieve the second without the first. This would lead us to explore to what extent children feel they participate in (= are part of, by default) their neighbourhood, community or school, and how this relates to the extent to which they feel they 'actively' participate, that is, have a say in decision-making in their neighbourhoods or institutions. These communities and institutions are, of course, established by and controlled by adults. A further point is that participation in both senses is assumed to be 'a good thing' that leads to increased self-efficacy, which in turn leads to an increased awareness of choices, which contribute to improved 'well-being'. However, this may be problematic for children, given that they are excluded from one of the key markers of citizenship, the right to vote.

Empirical Example – Children's 'Social Capital'

The chapter draws on data from an empirical research project to explore some of these issues. The research was conducted for the Health Education Authority in the late 1990s, to explore the relevance of Putnam's (1993) concept of 'social capital' in relation to children. The premise was that the 'social capital' in a community affects well-being. The research was conducted in two schools in relatively deprived wards in a town in SE England (disguised as 'Springtown'; children chose their own pseudonyms; the site was chosen to match another HEA study on adults and social capital). One ward (West Ward) consisted of 'suburban sprawl', with post-war housing and factories; the second (Hill Ward) consisted of a mixture of industrial development, and Victorian, inter-war and post-war housing development. The sample comprised 101 boys and girls in two age bands: 12–13 and 14–15-year olds, and a sizeable proportion were from minority ethnic groups. The project used qualitative research methods and structured activities to explore young people's subjective experiences, the nature of their social networks, and their experiences of participation in decision-making in schools and neighbourhoods (see Morrow 2001a; findings Morrow, 2001b). The chapter draws upon children's discussions about 'being listened to' in relation to school and neighbourhood.

Participation in School

Schools are not under statutory obligation to run 'school councils' (a group of teachers and pupils representative of various year groups in the school), but School 1 had one, and a range of topics were discussed. Many children were not satisfied the way it was run, as an extract from a discussion with Year-8 pupils demonstrates:

> Harry: . . . I'm the class rep, on the school council, they can pass information on to me, . . . we say these things in the year meetings, and then that gets passed onto the school meetings, and then it goes to the senior teachers, and we have said stuff and it has worked.

Researcher: . . . What about the rest of you, do you agree?

Kellie: no, not really, what I think they should do, is just get all the school reps together, and all the classes, and all speak about it all together. The teachers don't tell us much, they just tell us about a couple of things and then that's it, over for about another 4 weeks . . .

In a discussion with a group of Year-10s, even the two representatives did not feel the school council worked well:

Dave: its a good way for people to voice their opinions, but it doesn't really happen, like, the most say you'll get is what trip you wanna go on

Amy: . . . I asked the head teacher to have more vegetarian meals, that was about six months ago, and nothing's happened. So he's saying he thinks all the people should stay in school for school dinners so we don't get in trouble down the shops, but what are we supposed to eat?

And another group of Year-10s, Mike commented:

I think we get played like fools, cos we have council meetings, ok, I'm a council rep, but I say this stuff, but they don't listen to me, they think I'm just a laugh, . . . they ask us what we want, then they say no, we can't have it, what's the point of asking us?

In a survey of civil rights in schools, Alderson (1999) found cynicism or anger about 'token councils' which suggests that these experiences are fairly widespread. On the other hand, in School 2, there was no school council, and pupils had no forum in which to voice their suggestions, and children felt there should be one. As one girl said: 'Teachers are always telling us to speak up for ourselves'.

Children 'participate' in school, in the sense of 'being there', but to what extent do they feel they have a share in it, and what does it mean to them? From their point of view, the experience of school was ambivalent – there are positive and negative aspects. First, many children described how schooling and the acquisition of educational qualifications was extremely important to them, and second, school was an important place to be with friends. Both elements are shown in the following extract:

Dave: people do moan about school, but when they go they know they will learn stuff, they will have a bit of fun and they do meet their friends, so it's not all that bad.

Amy: yeah, if they've got all these ambitions . . . to get a good career, they can't do it without going to school.

Dave: because even the people who say that they don't care about their grades . . . , they always long to get good grades . . .

Homework was often included in lists of activities outside school, and some young people mentioned how their neighbourhoods may be quiet, which is 'boring', but also 'good for getting homework done'. The importance of school as a site of social interaction also emerged in other forms of data. Photos showed school students walking to school in pairs or groups and then clustered in the playground. Kerry, 14, wrote about how: 'In school when I am not in my lessons I hang around with my best friend and my friend. ... We normally just walk around having girly chats'.

However, some aspects of school life, such as the non-democratic nature of school, the content of school work, and the relationships between teachers and pupils, may constitute negative experiences for some young people. As one 14-year-old boy put it: 'None of the teachers really build up our confidence or anything'. Others spoke of how the teachers' 'favourites' were usually 'boffins' or 'brain-boxes' and some young people seemed to express an awareness that only one form of knowledge, that is academic knowledge as measured in exam results, was valued. One boy said 'I hate being told what grade the teachers expect of you, its very high expectations.' These comments suggest that active participation needs to be understood in the context of relationships within school. The quality of these relationships may affect the extent to which children are likely to 'participate'. However, adults working in schools may also feel they have little opportunity to 'participate' in decisions.

Civic Participation

Local authorities are under no obligation to consult with young people about provision of services and facilities, though some local authorities do have a Youth Forum or Youth Council. However, children were aware that they had not been directly consulted in decisions about changes in their neighbourhoods. Some children described their neighbourhood environments as satisfactory, but others expressed a strong sense of exclusion from the social life of the neighbourhood. Their concerns focused on the following issues: traffic (not being able to cross the road safely); some children from minority ethnic groups described racial harassment – for example, one boy described how he doesn't play outside his block of flats: 'if I've got nothing to do I play inside with my own computer (not) outside as usually people are quite racist to me, . . . that's why I don't like my area much'; safety in local parks (dog mess, needles, drugs, also assaults), and outside the shops; rapists and 'gangsters' on the streets.

Some Year-10 students described how they felt mistrusted by the adults in their neighbourhoods. One discussion hinged around the issue of being regarded with suspicion in shops:

Amy: it's horrible, cos you walk into a shop, you've got no bag on you, you're looking quite smart, and you've got all these security guards watching you like a hawk, / . . . /

Olanda: they stereotype us. / . . . /

Many young people commented that there wasn't enough to do in the area for their age group. In England, leisure activities have been increasingly privatized. Children needed money for transport into town, and then more money for entry into leisure facilities. 'Hanging about' is often the only activity available that does not involve spending money, but this presents a dilemma: on the one hand, their parents are not willing to allow them out on their own, yet the fact that they go out in groups makes them look threatening. This context of mistrust, which children are acutely aware of, is likely to have an effect of their capacity to 'actively participate' in their neighbourhoods.

In discussions about decision-making in neighbourhoods, most children felt their needs had been ascertained through their parents. Amy (age 15) said: 'they send, like, questionnaires to our parents, but its not our parents who want to go to the Youth Club, its us. So they should ask us'. A group of Year-8s had the following discussion:

Them: no . . . they don't ask the kids,

Agnes: its adults saying "oh lets have a bingo hall," what are we gonna go and do?

Gavin: since we can't vote and stuff, they don't think that we're that smart, because they think parents have got all the experience, / . . . /

Agnes: they've just put a bowling thing up, . . . but they haven't asked us, they haven't said to us do you want this, do you want that, *we should get a say in it*

One girl commented that she felt they should have a say in the community, 'because what happens does affect us as well as the adults and they don't seem to think about that when they're making decisions'. This led to some direct action in the past:

Mike (age 15): cos I remember, I was living in my old house . . . there was the woods like over to the side, and they knocked it down to build more houses, and we didn't [want that] we used to play there and have our like tree houses, dens and things, but they didn't ask us. We tried slashing their tyres and things like that, nicking keys, and stuff but it didn't work. *We was young then*, so . . . [laughter]

In adult terms, Mike's description would quite likely be seen as vandalism, or at best an act of resistance. However, from his point of view, one might suggest that it is the only form of 'participation' available to him.

The town council had recently started a 'Youth Forum', but children were not aware of it:

Gemma: No-one knows about it, if there is one

Tamisha: I think there should be one, but

Miranda: but they'd choose the people who do all the best in school, . . . and they're not average people, are they?

These comments suggest that participation, in the sense of being actively involved in decisions that affect them in their neighbourhoods, appears to be virtually non-existent for these children. This links clearly to children's 'citizenship' because even where supposedly democratic structures such as school councils are in place, children did not seem to feel they were experiencing 'participation' through them, and the exclusion they appear to feel is likely to limit their sense of self-efficacy. One problem facing this age group is that they may have no consistent channels through which to communicate, or to convert their energy into a positive resource for their neighbourhoods. Miranda's comment, above, suggests that she is aware of the limits of democratic participation, and this has implications for citizenship – both in terms of actual involvement in childhood, and future participation in adulthood. Again, however, children's participation needs to be understood in the context of adults' participation (whether parents, neighbours, youth workers, shop workers) around them.

Discussion

What do these examples tell us about participation and citizenship? From the point of view of children, participation by default, is limited. They did not seem to feel they shared in community life, whether in their schools or neighbourhoods. Their participation in the sense of being actively involved in decisions that affect them, was also very limited. In terms of civic participation, this is not really surprising given that they are positioned outside of democratic structures by their very nature as children, in that they do not attain the right to full adult citizenship, at least in terms of voting rights, until the age of 18. However, even where supposedly participatory structures such as school councils operate, school students do not appear to be experiencing 'active participation' through them. Their experiences of both these aspects of participation (or lack of it) may have implications for their perceptions of democratic institutions later, and this begs the question of whether a 'healthy scepticism' is learnt early in life. A sense of participation could be fostered early on by including young people in decision-making processes, whether in schools or neighbourhoods, but it seems that many (adult) structures and practices need to change before this can happen effectively.

In many popular (media) discussions of children's rights and 'participation', absolute decision-making dominates. Yet children do not appear to be asking for adults to relinquish their power. Rather, they want to 'have a say' in, but not necessarily make, the decisions themselves, and further, 'it depends on what is being decided'. They are asking for inclusion and participation and are aware of their exclusion and lack of participation, and appeared to be concerned with the mundane problem of being accorded little respect, and having little opportunity to simply have a say and contribute to discussions. These concerns need to be addressed before attempts at effective participation can be made. Children's views also reflect what has been termed a 'social' model of citizenship that emphasizes 'the ways in which people are connected to each other, rather than being viewed as acting as individualised, autonomous, rational beings separate from each other' (Cockburn, 1998: 100).

Ultimately the extent to which children are 'listened to' will vary from micro-level (within families) to the meso-level (within institutions such as schools and in their neighbourhoods), and is likely to be affected by individual characteristics. As Roche suggests, 'there is no single voice of childhood' (Roche, 1996: 36). *How* children participate, then, needs to be understood in the socio-cultural context of those particular children, though it would be a mistake to overemphasize the differences between minority children and white children – they are all 'children' and subject to status markers set by the adult world. Children use the language of participation and inclusion, encapsulated by the phrase used by many of them, *'we* should be able to *have a say'*. This emphasizes their embeddedness in sets of social relations, whether familial, institutional or within their neighbourhoods. However, at the same time, they are aware that, as children, they are effectively denied a range of rights that adults take for granted. This awareness is likely to become problematic as children get older. A more nuanced approach to participation, rights and citizenship is needed, which is less based upon a categorical distinction between adults and children. We should also be aware that children may not welcome 'participation' in the adult sense of the word, and we need a broader definition of citizenship, based on relationships between people, because functionalist definitions are too limited and fail to account for what happens in practice when adults consult with children.

This suggests that if we want to expand children's active participation, we have to approach the issue of participation holistically. In other words, we need to look at both aspects of 'participation', and see how constrained young people are within their existing structures and settings (their 'passive participation') and how these constraints may affect willingness or capacity to participate, before attempts can be made to enhance their 'active participation'. We also need to explore the broader context and try to understand whether (even) adults in deprived or disempowered communities 'participate' in any effective sense. This links to the community cohesion agenda outlined at the beginning of the chapter. Government appears to want (or even requires) children to participate, but on the other hand, only on the government's terms. The documentation on community cohesion simultaneously constructs children as the problem to be solved, *and* as the solution to the problem, but this raises a question of ethics: as Ennew notes in her discussion of conceptualizations of citizenship in childhood,

> It is not fair to expect the powerless to assume responsibility for transforming the
> hierarchical structures in which their lack of power is inscribed. Indeed, to do this,

is to blame them for their situation, and reproduces the same inequalities in political and economic structures, while reinforcing the economic structures that produce and maintain inequalities. In this respect, participation is a kind of conjuring trick.

(2000: 5)

Conclusions

I have suggested first that the concept and practice of 'participation' for children is not straightforward and needs to be not only clearly defined, but also seen critically; second, that social context is crucial in understanding how, why, or indeed, whether children 'participate'. Third, adult models of childhood, institutional structures and adult practices towards children – in other words, how children are conceptualized, viewed and treated – are key to understanding children's participation (see also Ennew, this volume). An examination of these models and practices may be the next stage in promoting effective children's participation. In other words, there is a need to explore the extent to which 'participation' can be on adult terms only, and to what extent 'participation' is redefined as 'resistance' when children try to change things or express their views in ways that adults find problematic.

The past 15 years have seen a rapid growth in research and consultation with children in the UK. However, there is an increasing awareness that 'children and young people have been giving the same key messages to decision makers for several years, and . . . despite this there is little evidence of . . . an impact on the development of strategic plans' (Donnelly, 2003 writing in the context of Liverpool, but widely applicable). Kirby et al. (2003) suggest that there is still work to be done in ensuring that participation is effective in bringing about change, and that it is sustained. It makes sense to build upon what has been done, not least because there may be a danger of 'consultation overload' – asking children similar questions, over and over again, without any sign of change, sends a negative message to them about the limits of participatory democracy. This is a question of politics and ethics that needs addressing. Kirby et al., recognize this when they suggest that organizations need to change (2003: 144), but this begs the question of precisely *how* change in organizations can be brought about, and *which* organizations need to change. Policy priorities may clash with participatory agendas, and this needs to be unpicked. Practitioners and researchers now need to locate the barriers to effective participation for children. Ignoring that there are barriers, and not paying attention to context, is likely to lead to frustration and disappointment. There is overwhelming evidence now from many sources, participatory projects, research reports, evaluations, and audits, that children are responsive, creative and measured in responding to calls for their views. The challenge now is not only to get adults to listen, but to act upon what they hear. This might be how active participation and (active) citizenship for children can be connected.

Acknowledgements

The author would like to thank the children and the schools who participated in the research described here, and acknowledges funding from the Health Education Authority.

References

Alderson, P. (1999) 'Civil rights in schools', ESRC Children 5–16, *Research Briefing No. 1*, ESRC, Swindon.

Arnstein, S. (1969) 'Eight rungs on the latter of citizen participation', *Journal of American Institute of Planners*, 35(4): 216–24.

Blunkett, D. (2002) *How Government Can Help Build Social Capital*. Speech to PIU Seminar, www.homeoffice.gov.uk/docs/piuspeech.html, accessed 6 December 2004.

Boyden, J. and Ennew, J. (1997) *Children in Focus – A Manual for Participatory Research with Children*. Stockholm: Radda Barnen.

Cockburn, T. (1998) 'Children and citizenship in Britain', *Childhood*, 5(1): 99–117.

Donnelly, E. (2003) *Consulting Children and Young People in Liverpool*. Liverpool City Council.

Ennew, J. (2000) *How Can We Define Citizenship in Childhood?* Working Chapter Series, 109(12), Harvard Centre for Population and Development Studies, Harvard School of Public Health.

Hart, R. (1992) *Children's Participation: From Tokensim to Citizenship*. Florence: International Child Development Centre.

Home Office (2002) *Building Cohesive Communities*. London: TSO, www.communities.gov.uk, accessed 23 May 2007.

Kirby, P., Lanyon, C., Cronin, K., and Sinclair, R. (2003) *Building a Culture of Participation*. London: DfES.

Morrow, V. (1999a) 'Conceptualising social capital in relation to the well-being of children and young people: a critical review', *The Sociological Review*, 47(4): 744–65.

Morrow, V. (1999b) ' "We are people too." Children's perspectives on rights and decision-making in England', *International Journal of Children's Rights*, 7(3): 149–70.

Morrow, V. (2001a) 'Using qualitative methods to elicit young people's perspectives on their environments', *Health Education Research: Theory and Practice*, 16(3): 255–68.

Morrow, V. (2001b) *Networks and Neighbourhoods: Children's and Young People's Perspectives*. London: Health Development Agency.

Morrow, V. (2005) 'Social capital, community involvement and community cohesion in England: a space for children and young people', *Journal of Social Sciences*, 9: 57–69.

NRU (Neighbourhood Renewal Unit) (2003) *Renewal.net Toolkit: How to Build Social Capital*, www.renewal.net, accessed 24 May 2007.

Office of National Statistics, (n.d.) www.statistics.gov.uk/socialcapital/website, accessed 6 December 2004.

Putnam, R.D. (1993) *Making Democracy Work. Civic Traditions in Modern Italy*. Princeton, NJ: Princeton University Press.

Roche, J. (1996) 'The politics of children's rights', in J. Brannen and M. O'Brien (eds) *Children in Families. Research and Policy*, London: Falmer Press.

Zakus, J.D.L. and Lysack, C.L. (1998) 'Revisiting community participation', *Health Policy and Planning*, 13(1): 1–12.

11

Everyday Lives of Working Children and Notions of Citizenship

Antonella Invernizzi

Introduction

The broad issue addressed in this chapter is 'how can working children be considered citizens?' During the last decade a great deal has been learned about widespread use of child labour and the many forms of exploitation, hazard and abuse child labourers around the world face. One could thus put forth the idea that promoting working children's citizenship is principally about implementing relevant Articles from the United Nations Convention on the Rights of the Child (UNCRC, 1989) and particularly protecting children from exploitation and work that is detrimental to their development or undermines education.

In this chapter it is instead suggested that it might be useful to begin with young people's everyday lives rather than international instruments. This exercise allows identification of some contradictions in the field that indicate the latter approach might be far too simplistic. The last section of this chapter will then return to the initial question and outline some ways children's citizenship may be understood.

The Meaning of Children's Work in Everyday Lives of Children and Adults

This section briefly presents aspects of the meaning working children and their parents attach to work and their experiences. These views have been analysed through two distinct pieces of research; one in Lima (Peru) and the other in the Algarve (Portugal).[1] In Lima it focused on everyday lives of street working children and their families. In the Algarve a broader category of economic activities was examined including work in farms, shops, restaurant and other family businesses, construction, tourism and catering as well as care of family members such as young children, disabled parents or the elderly.

As a matter of fact, children's work means different things not only in different societies but also to different children and adults in one setting. Research thus attempted to identify a set of dimensions sufficiently broad to account for the diversity. The central hypothesis proposes that work simultaneously relates to at least four interdependent dimensions: survival, socialization, autonomy and exploitation.

In extreme poverty children's work clearly related to the survival of the family or less frequently the survival of the child living on his/her own. An economic slant on survival is nevertheless largely insufficient for understanding involvement of children in work as many of the processes observed relate to cultural practices and social networks. For instance, one cannot understand why some young girls are sent out to the street in Lima whereby others are kept at home despite need for income without reference to diverse cultural practices and gender issues. Some families implicitly refer to a representation of gender rooted in urban middle-class experience and thus see the street as a morally polluting environment for girls, made up of very inappropriate sexual conduct. Married women are likewise kept out of those spaces since their presence there damages the honour of the male head of the family who should also ideally be the sole breadwinner. In contrast some migrants from rural areas in the Andes hold very different views. Not only does the street seem a very acceptable place for women to have businesses (sometimes very successfully) but girls and boys are also given considerably more autonomy and everybody is expected to contribute in one way or another for the well-being of the family. Moral facets of sexuality are also described in a different manner by migrants from the Andes; for instance, abstinence before marriage does not appear to be a strict requirement for girls and their sexual behaviour does not necessarily damage the honour of the male head of the family. Furthermore, like their mothers, migrant girls enjoy greater autonomy in economic and spatial terms than middle-class girls.

Those qualities clearly concern the socialization of children, especially the latter. The issue can be broken down into different questions. What is seen as appropriate child- rearing practice? What do children and adults describe as appropriate ways of preparing children for adulthood? What do children learn through work? How does school experience relate to socialization?

In short, both in Portugal and Peru research found that children's work fulfils important functions of socialization which appear to be 'rational' in the specific economic and social situations where children live. School is very expensive in Peru which poorest families simply cannot afford. In both countries research reveals a great distance between local culture and one embedded in school curricula, factors that contribute to explaining children's poor results arising amongst disadvantaged sectors of the population. In both countries high rates of repetition and dropping out can be viewed as indicators of problems within the education system. Although the situation has dramatically improved in Portugal over the last decade, dropping out towards the end of compulsory school is still very high and seems to relate to lack of opportunities for professional training which undermines pupils' incentive to complete school. In this context some young people and families see early involvement in work providing informal professional training; the formal process being unaffordable or unavailable. Informants often state that opportunities for social mobility heavily depend on qualifications. However, they suggest that early involvement in work is an equally important, often as the only strategy available in order to avoid worst forms of poverty and exclusion.

In Peru, a further key issue in terms of socialization is the high level of autonomy some families seem to promote. These practices appear to simultaneously find explanations in cultural practices and very harsh socio-economic conditions. On the one hand, anthropologists who study socialization in the rural Andes postulate that children's independence is very highly valued in the community. For instance, children as young as five or six might be expected to have their own animals, tend them or cultivate their own fields. Independent learning through experience is also highly encouraged, which does not always fit with the learning style imposed in school. It is not therefore surprising that migrants in Lima sometimes encourage their children to have small businesses in the streets at a very early age as a means of boosting income as well as learning about people, environment and business. On the other hand, the most disadvantaged informants stated that this high level of independence might be essential for guaranteeing the survival of the child. Should parents die, become ill or disabled the child's skills would at least ensure that she/he is able to generate sufficient money for daily meals. These examples illustrate the importance of that context when examining what children actually learn through work and why.

The third dimension of the meaning of children's work in everyday life relates precisely to the same autonomy or self-determination that is positively valued in itself as part of normal childhood experience. In the case of the economic independence of migrant children mentioned above it happens, for instance, that some children ask for their own business in circumstances where it may be far more lucrative if they helped the mother at her pitch. However, mothers who participated in the research did not deny the opportunity of independence to children and often accepted their decision.

Indeed in their work or because of their work young people make a number of decisions: they might decide to work or not to, in what to work, make decisions on using income, leisure time, clothes and other purchases. Some decide how to manage and organize their work. Data also indicate a number of more 'controversial' decisions whereby young people sometimes decide to economically support families instead of going to school or learn to work instead. In Peru some children were able to decide where to live, with whom and thus move out of the family home. All these decisions reflect their aspiration to be in control of some aspects of their lives. Parents sometimes disagree with those decisions. A few adults in the Algarve opposed the child's intention of leaving school and getting a job. They said they finally capitulated to accepting the adolescent's determination and finally contacted the employer and kept an eye on working conditions.

One could argue that the decision to leave compulsory school before completion is 'wrong'. When looking at problems in the education system rates of repetition and economic difficulties some young people face, it nevertheless becomes difficult to argue that it is the 'wrong' decision. Rather, one must conclude that there is no single 'right' decision but many possible ones depending on the young person and her/his circumstances. This is an important issue in the debate on children's participation referring to Article 12 of the UNCRC that asserts the right of the child to express her/his opinion and have that taken into account in matters affecting them.

Paradoxically, the young person attempting to be in control of her/his own life might be deemed incompetent because the decision to leaving school is against what is assumed to be in her/his best interest. However, this appears to be too simplistic.

Exploitation, abuse and hazard (the fourth dimension put forth above) are far from being absent from these experiences. Children's work in the streets of Lima or family businesses or farms in Portugal can be strenuous, carried out over long hours, undermine study and may present different hazards. Interviews with young people in Portugal clearly indicate that work is particularly overburdening when associated with dramatic family changes that require their income or a greater contribution to specific tasks. Young people mentioned events such as parents splitting up or divorcing, unemployment, illness, death or disability of one. However, assessment of these risks faces many challenges in practice. Among them is the fact that, for instance, some hazards do not come with work-related tasks but are part of the child's living environment. This might be heavy traffic in the streets of Lima or dangerous implements on farms in Portugal. Another problem is that what is dangerous or strenuous for an inexperienced child appears to be acceptable for one who is used to the task. Indeed the majority of children in Lima are able to deal relatively well with heavy traffic.

However, the most important issue to emphasize here is that work performed by children might be judged detrimental in some respects but an insight into everyday practice might lead one to conclude that it is beneficial in others and indeed might be a means of protecting children from worse forms of exploitation and the worst hazards. Some mothers who participated in the study in Lima indicated that despite governmental economic support for their trade, conditional on leaving children at home, they continued to take children to the street. In their view, leaving them at home all day would have caused more difficulties. They said that children would perhaps have wandered around rather than gone to school, spend the money on video game rather than buy or cook a lunch. Some mothers saw girls 'at risk' if left alone in the very poor neighbourhoods. Some were able to enrol children in schools in the city centre that are of higher standard than ones available in very poor neighbourhoods. They also argued that in the street they could check if children did their homework after school and more generally keep an eye on them. Surprisingly, in Portugal a few parents also argued that taking children with them to work during holidays and weekends was a means of ensuring better supervision. Increased supervision or increased family income might thus be advantages although this will not always exclude risks or economic exploitation.

In other terms, exploitation, abuse and hazards need to be read within the specific situation of children and in the light of efforts families make to protect and socialize children rather than simply in terms of deficiencies. Indeed, many successful efforts and strategies should be considered as well as problematic ones.

Research with working children worldwide drew together accounts about children's suffering, risks, frustration, abuse exploitation and tiredness but also provided evidence of positive aspects of children's work. As McKechnie and Hobbes proposed, children's work is a matter of advantages and disadvantages (IWGCL, 1998).

Adult and children's accounts of good or bad work seem to refer to an implicit balance of both advantages and disadvantages that seem to explain why many of them present a rather positive assessment of children's work despite general condemnation. Examined in the light of the four dimensions presented above, one can gauge how far children and adult's views are important for policymaking and planning appropriate interventions. They give an insight on strategies developed in very difficult socio-economic contexts where what matters is assuring the survival of the child, family or family business, providing a meaningful socialization, protecting the child from abuse, hazard and exploitation as far as possible and at the same time providing her/him with a level of autonomy and self-control as it is not only necessary for survival but also how it is viewed as appropriate in different cultures and communities.

The Meaning of Child Labour in International Instruments: UNCRC and ILO Conventions 138 and 182

International campaigns and media have largely publicized the worst experiences of child labour worldwide. The notion of child labour is different to that of children's work in that it almost entirely refers to aspects of work detrimental for children. Child labour, in that sense, is primarily what should be eliminated. However, hot debates took and take place about what constitutes labour and work with a broad grey area of economic activities on which there is no consensus.

From a formal point of view, the two key instruments of the International Labour Organisation (ILO) have given substance to the notion of child labour. The first is ILO Convention 138 (1973) concerning the Minimum Age for Admission to Employment. In brief, Article 2 states that the minimum age for employment should not be less than the age of completion of compulsory school and not less than 15 years. Age 14 is however accepted for countries in which economic conditions and lack of provision for education justify exceptions. Complementarily, Article 3 states a higher age (18) for admission to hazardous economic activities and lower age (13 or 12) for light work. Light work is specified as that which is not likely to be harmful to health or development of children and does not undermine school attendance and pupils' performance at school.

A first feature of this instrument is its intention to regulate employment rather than address the overall problem of children's work. The second feature is that age is the key criterion for deciding what child labour is, combined with characteristics of tasks (hazardous or light work). Ennew, Myers and Plateau replace this way of approaching child labour in a more general discourse they call 'labour market discourse'. Child labour is described here 'primarily as the participation of children in what "should be" exclusively adult labor markets'(Ennew et al., 2003: 4).

In many respects, most children's work observed in both Lima and the Algarve should be considered child labour through this perspective. First, because any work performed by children under 12 years, even if light, appears to be unlawful. Second, most of it involves some detrimental, strenuous, hazardous features or might interfere with school. It cannot technically be considered light work and one could argue that young people under 15 should be excluded.

However, the original focus of this convention was on employment and thus many economic activities in family setting might theoretically be assessed against other criteria. This has indeed been a criticism of Convention 138: it might lead to entirely overlooking abuse and exploitation of children outside of formal employment.

It is probably this kind of consideration that led some governments to broader definitions of children's work. In fact, Portuguese legislation forbids any work under age of 16 or before conclusion of compulsory school. More precisely, young people are allowed to work earlier (i.e. ages 14 or 15) if they complete nine years of compulsory school; if not, even those older than 16 years are expected to give precedence to school (PEETI, 2000). Unlike other European countries, the Portuguese government apparently rejected the option of permitting light work for young people. In practice, thus, even part-time work in family settings described in the first part of the chapter is illegal in Portugal.

The second key ILO instrument is Convention 182 (1999) concerning the Worst Forms of Child Labour which precisely identifies work that have to be eliminated immediately. Beside slavery, forced labour, trafficking and sale of children, prostitution, pornography and illicit activities, Article 3 includes as worst forms: *'work which, by its nature or the circumstances in which it is carried out, is likely to harms the health, safety or morals of children'*.

Again, when considering the difficulties working children face, it is impossible to maintain that harm to health or safety is entirely absent from economic activities observed in Lima or the Algarve. However, it is difficult to discriminate harm to health and safety that relates to work from the one that relates to poor living conditions. Even more difficult to assess is the issue of the morals of children as that definition varies from one context to another. We have seen above how different groups provide differential assessments of risks working girls face in the streets of Lima. Some will conclude street work harms the morals of girls whereby others will suggest that under certain conditions this is an acceptable way of increasing incomes, socializing girls and providing them with acceptable levels of independence. Rather than being objective, definitions of the worst forms of child labour accordingly rely on cultural considerations.

Broadly speaking, features of ILO's notions of child labour above relate to what Ennew et al. (2003) have called the 'human capital discourse' on child labour as put forth by many international organizations and governments. Child labour appears to be the 'result of underdevelopment' and is understood as 'activities and working conditions that undermine the development of health, knowledge and skills, which children require to contribute later as adults to national economic development and their own prosperity' (Ennew et al., 2003: 4).

The underlying assumption is evident: detrimental work that impedes children gaining important skills and knowledge and undermines their health ends up prolonging poverty and disadvantage into their future lives. However, this way of thinking also assumes that national economic development goes hand in hand with the prosperity of the most deprived groups. This assumption does not take into account discrimination, oppression as well as lack of appropriate educational opportunities and professional training that most disadvantaged groups face. This way of considering child labour also overlooks the strategies communities, parents and children are developing in order to keep out of the worst forms of poverty and exclusion which might include children's work. Prohibition of child labour and worst forms of child labour defined in this way aim at promoting future prosperity but might fail to address poverty and the lack of opportunity working children are presently experiencing.

ILO conventions thus conceive children's work solely in terms of potentially detrimental facets. An important number of aspects of children's work that are essential for working in partnership with the communities are missing and particularly advantages of work such as those described earlier.

Some organizations have indeed developed a different approach to child labour, which Ennew et al. call the 'social responsibility discourse'. They see child labour as 'a problem of "social exclusion" leading to work that exploits, alienates and oppresses children and separates them from society's normal protections and opportunities' (Ennew et al., 2003: 5). Following this line, mobilization is required rather than prohibition of work, as proposed by working children's movements (see Liebel in this volume).

A fourth discourse identified by Ennew et al. is the 'child-rights oriented' discourse, which describes child labour as 'work that is detrimental for children involved'. Scrutiny of work therefore needs to include analysis of situations and should ideally take into account views and experiences of children in order to assess 'conditions that impair children's growth and well-being and violate their rights' (Ennew et al., 2003: 5). The main reference is the UNCRC, beside other human rights instruments.

Article 32 of the UNCRC is the most evident reference, stating 'the right of the child to be protected from economic exploitation and from performing any work that is likely to be hazardous or to interfere with the child's education, or to be harmful to the child's health or physical, mental, spiritual, moral or social development'.

However, this is clearly not sufficient. First, because the best interest of the child should have primary consideration (Art. 3) and it could conflict with policies that, for instance, prioritize the economic development of countries or regulation of the labour market rather than the child's well-being as discussed above. Second, the fact that best interest relates to many other aspects of the young person's life, as shown in the first part of this chapter. The 'child-rights oriented' discourse is thus holistic. A number of other rights of the child should, therefore, be considered and one should at least include the right to life, survival and development (Art. 6), health (Art. 24) and education (Arts. 28, 29). Furthermore substantial consideration should be given to so-called participatory articles and, at least, the right of children to express their views and have them taken into account (Art. 12) which in the arena of child labour policymaking has often been an issue for collectives of working children (Art. 15). A further challenge comes from the input parents and communities might have in protecting children and promoting their best interest, framed as *'respect for the responsibilities, rights and duties of parents, family and communities who provide direction and guidance in the exercise of the child's rights'* (Art. 5). The list of rights is not exhaustive but sufficient to illustrate the relevance of a holistic approach.

In practice, however, ILO notions of child labour and the rather narrow age-related criteria are strongly embedded in the UN Convention. The second part of Article 12 indeed refers to other international instruments and particularly to the duty of governments to implement legislations of minimum age for admission to employment. The key issue here is, there-fore, about different and conflicting philosophies underpinning ILO and human rights instruments (Ennew et al., 2003), which have an impact on how their rights are promoted and citizenship might be conceived.

Ways of Understanding Working Children's Citizenship

What are the implications of the above analysis when thinking about working children's citizenship?

The first consideration is about the important gap between informants' (children and adults) discourse on children's work and the meaning of work embedded within international instruments. ILO conventions, in particular, only see work as potentially detrimental and exclude consideration of potentially positive outcomes. This approach does not permit building on existing survival strategies, cultural practices and relying on resources existing in specific socio-cultural contexts. This might potentially exclude communities and undermine their efforts to protect working children whilst also ensuring other aspects relating to their best interest (socialization, survival, autonomy, etc.). Limited space in this chapter does not allow reference to literature dealing with child rights approach to children's work and precisely to the growing evidence of the potentially detrimental outcome of simplistic means of elimination of child labour.

If simplistic approaches to child labour can be detrimental for children, simplistic concepts of children's citizenship, for instance the one that would solely refer to the rights of children to be protected from exploitation and hazardous or harmful work, might also prejudice children's interests. This recalls Ruth Lister's (2003) proposition that any notion of citizenship might have 'inclusionary' as well as 'exclusionary' powers. In her terms the 'janus-faced nature of citizenship operates simultaneously as a mechanism of both inclusion and exclusion and also a language of both discipline and resistance' (Lister, 2003: 4–5). Discourses that deny the positive as well as indispensable aspects of children's work, solidarity and struggle to survive might thus unintentionally amount to speaking the language of discipline and exclusion.

The second consideration is therefore about who decides which rights and duties children should have. Examples above are among the many that emphasize how important it is to include children and their communities in the definition of not only child labour but any definition of their rights and, thus, children's citizenship. How can children's citizenship thus be defined?

Looking back at the overall exercise attempted here and accepting the risk of oversimplifying, it could be argued that at least four points of entry are possible for examination of potential working children's citizenship. They could be placed at the extreme poles of two continuums, the first referring to citizenship as a status and the second to citizenship in practice or active citizenship (see Lister in this volume).

At one pole of the first continuum we would place a formal approach to citizenship: for instance, rights and obligations children should have, based on international and national instruments (UNCRC, ILO, national legislation). Here one could optimistically suggest that we would be able to identify a set of questions and indicators for monitoring implementation and promotion of working children rights. However, as seen above, a further debate would be required because of conflicting philosophies and content of these instruments.

At the other extreme of the continuum one could instead consider that children are *de facto* members of communities and have informal status; that is informal rights and duties allocated to them. As stated above, there is much distance between the extremes of these two poles whereby work might precisely be one of the duties allocated in communities, whereas duty to go to school, a key issue in international instruments, would for different reasons have secondary place. This is part of the many different views on and experiences of childhood.

A second continuum would consider the issue of 'active citizenship' or citizenship in practice. The theory of citizenship as Lister states has moved to include more dynamic aspects relating to struggles by individuals.

Referring to Gough's (1992) work, she suggests that 'citizenship is also pivotal to the definition and interpretation of needs and to the struggle for their realisation and conversion in rights' (2003: 7). At one extreme on this continuum we would place formal organizations that attempt to defend the rights of children. Among them, various forms of children's participation and, for instance, working children's movements and organizations referred to by Liebel (in this volume). One of the characteristics of the vast majority of organizations promoting children's participation is that adults are generally formally excluded and should theoretically become 'facilitators'.

On the other extreme, we would have 'active citizenship' defined as the struggle by children in everyday life, aiming to improve their well-being, satisfy needs and improve position within their social environment. As members of their communities children sometimes struggle against exploitative and abusive adults but very often work hard with adults not only against exploitation but more generally for improved living conditions. Children contribute to other peoples' well-being within differing spheres of autonomy allowing them to make key decisions. Some of their decisions as well as some tasks they carry out are not the ones governments, policymakers and other adults want them to make. They may be illegal or not seen as being in their best interest, such as the decision to leave school to work in order to help the family. However, they are seen as efforts to defend their interests and expression of their active citizenship.

These examples seem to be an appropriate illustration of the 'contested' character of any notion of citizenship Lister (2003) refers to. The argument proposed here is that an understanding of children's everyday practices, values and intentions as well as of adults in their communities are essential in the task of conceiving what children's citizenship might be. They provide indispensable knowledge on the informal status and active citizenship of children and adults living in very difficult circumstances.

Conclusion

By contrasting everyday practices of working children and their families with legal instruments the great distance between the way children's problems are defined and tackled becomes apparent. It is easy to conclude that no legal instrument can be technically deemed to be fundamentally good for promoting children's rights and citizenship. Any instrument should be carefully examined instead as the standard put forward might clash with the multiplicity of children's experiences, related socio-economic conditions and cultural practices and have negative and unexpected outcomes for children.

Indeed, this illustrates how diverse and controversial understandings of children's citizenship can be. The way forward is perhaps to suggest that the content of the notion of children's citizenship should be part of a debate that gives voice to all different actors involved. It would have to refer to formal status as well as informal membership of children, to practical children's participation promoted by organizations as well as to informal practices by adults and children in everyday lives.

Note

1 Both used a variety of qualitative methods including semi-participant observation, repeated interviews with children, parents and professionals and group discussion. Methods and research findings are presented in Invernizzi, 2001, 2003 (Peru) and 2005, 2007 (Portugal). The research in Portugal was funded by the Swiss National Science Foundation.

References

Ennew, J., Myers, W. and Plateau, D. (2003) 'The Meaning, Nature and Scope of Child Labor', Draft for the Colloquium on *Combating Abusive Child Labor*, Iowa.

Invernizzi, A. (2001) *La vie quotidienne des enfants travailleurs*. Paris: L'Harmattan.

Invernizzi, A. (2003) 'Street-working children and adolescents in Lima: work as an agent of socialization', *Childhood*, 10(4): 319–41.

Invernizzi, A. (2005) 'Perspectives on children's work in the Algarve (Portugal) and their implication for social policy', *Critical Social Policy*, 25(2): 198–222.

Invernizzi, A. (2007) 'Children's work in Portugal. An exploration of children's motivations, family organisation and views on socialisation', *International Journal of Children's Rights*, forthcoming.

IWGCL (1998) 'Working Children: Reconsidering the Debates', Report prepared by J. McKechnie and S. Hobbs, Amsterdam: IWGCL.

Lister, R. (2003) *Citizenship. Feminist Perspective*. Basingstoke: Palgrave.

PEETI (2000) *Guide of Legislation and Resources on Child Labour*. Lisbon: Ministry of Labour and Solidarity.

PART III

HOW POLICY AND LAW THINK ABOUT CHILDREN'S CITIZENSHIP

Introduction

Contributions to Part II have illustrated the way in which constructions of childhood influence both the theory and practice of citizenship insofar as applied to children. In the Introduction to Part II it was argued that assumptions underlying constructions of children – such as their dependence, independence, interdependence or indeed any other 'characteristic' – need to be challenged and that more attention needs to be paid to the realities and diversities of children's lives, experiences and practices. If accounting for this diversity makes it difficult to find a 'simple' meaning of children's citizenship, this supports the suggestion that in citizenship theory the development of an approach of 'differential universalism' (Lister in this volume) appears better to accommodate children as well as human beings in general.

The recent notion of the 'citizen child', underpinned by the UN Convention on the Rights of the Child (UNCRC) (Doek, Foreword to this volume), is likewise not free from conceptual difficulties. Just as the meaning of adult citizenship is variable, so is that of children's citizenship. As illustrated in earlier chapters, it is far from the case that the UNCRC provides a conclusion to any quest for an agreed understanding of what it means to be a 'child citizen'. The UNCRC does not address the responsibilities inherent in the notion of children's citizenship (Milne, Fortin, Lockyer in this volume) nor does it (nor, perhaps, as an instrument of international law, can it) reflect the great diversity of practices of citizenship (Lister, Liebel, Invernizzi in this volume). Rather, the UNCRC is an instrument affirming the universal status of children as rights holders in relation to government at local, national and international level, and promoting certain structures and conditions for giving effect to the rights it enshrines. It thus supplies some essential ingredients or 'building blocks' (Lister, this volume) of citizenship but not others.

In Part III, contributors explore further the nature of different constructions of childhood and the way in which they influence or underpin policy, legislation and practice. It is pertinent here to consider, amongst others, the UNCRC's own 'construct' of children and childhood, in which the child is a legal subject and rights holder from birth, without discrimination, whose agency is to be recognized and whose participation (however defined) is to be encouraged and nurtured in accordance with the her/his evolving capacity. The ultimate goal is of ensuring the full and harmonious development of the child (see Doek, Foreword and Introduction to Part I). When examining specific polices, legislation and practice, authors in Part III refer to one or another of these key features of the UNCRC.

Piper, building on King and Piper (1995), develops the theme of 'constructed' children within the theoretical framework of autopoiesis. Applying this theorization, she notes that law as a system, in common with other systems, may be regarded as 'thinking' about children (or indeed any other group or subject) in a certain way. The legal system requires constructions, or 'semantic artefacts' of such subjects in order to enable it to perform its allotted functions. Children may thus be constructed, for example, as threat to social order, as consumer citizen or as future unit of production. Piper argues that all of these particular 'semantic artefacts' are evident in the current English policy *Youth Matters*, and that this produces particular associated notions of responsibility and irresponsibility. Thus, policy responses will be directed at developing children's capacity to behave as responsible consumer/producer/ contributor citizens and at punishing irresponsibility, cast as anti-social behaviour. Alternative semantic artefacts – the child as rights holder or as citizen in the here and now – are absent from this view, because it is unnecessary and even incompatible with the relevant policy imperative. Piper's analysis points not only to the great distance between English policy (*Youth Matters*) and a concept of the child as citizen now but also provides insight on the mechanisms by which, one could argue, some of the UNCRC-related duties of the state appear to be circumvented. The fundamental notion of non-discrimination in respect of children's rights to a full and harmonious development, and thus their rights to relevant provision, seem to be eluded by movements between artefacts of the child as a threat, as citizen consumer and as investment for the future. Rather than being the subject of a right, assistance might, for instance, become conditional on the child fulfilling a number of obligations or 'paying off' as an adult the investment made by the state.

This theorization, emanating from the disciplines of law and philosophy, has much in common with the analysis made by sociologists of childhood, notably James et al. (1998). As Piper explains, the different conceptions may constitute the 'external knowledge' for law as a system. However, as she demonstrates, law's role in relation to large areas of decision-making affecting children is very limited. Furthermore, the functions conferred on law in relation to such decisions are such that the dominant set of knowledge relates not to the child in any particular view but to economic considerations and the rationing of public resources. The result is that *any* view of the child is suppressed. This resonates with Fortin's remarks in Part I about the *Williamson* case, in which the relationship under scrutiny, as discussed by all except one member of the House of Lords, Baroness Hale, was that of the parents and the school – a relationship in which the children appeared to have no part to play in their own right.

In her analysis of EU policy on children and citizenship, Stalford notes in effect a further 'semantic artefact': children as adjuncts to the economic status of their parents. This broadly conforms to the analysis of established UK approaches as discussed by Jones in Part II and by Clutton in this Part, in which children may claim citizenship only 'by proxy'. However, Stalford identifies a nascent shift in the EU position, which she associates amongst other things with the influence of international recognition of children's rights, exemplified in the UNCRC. This shift is reflected, albeit in limited circumstances, both in legislation and in case law emanating from the EU. The EU may yet formally absorb children's rights in its constitutional framework, if the Charter of Fundamental Rights is eventually adopted as part of a reformed EU constitutional framework.

Consistent with Doek's presentation of the citizen child, the shift in position is properly to be seen as one which moves away from the child as 'citizen becoming' to 'citizen now'. Clutton reinforces the importance of this for excluded children: 'the presentation of children and young people as "citizens in the making" who must claim citizenship "by proxy" serves to exclude those children and young people who grow up in marginalized families or who are removed or expelled from family units'. The UNCRC's insistence on the status of children as rights holders in their own right might be interpreted as supportive of this move away from citizenship only 'by proxy'. Clutton explores the extent to which the UNCRC has been a driver of policy in this direction within the UK. She describes the different conceptual approaches that have been adopted in England, Wales, Scotland and Northern Ireland in constructing post-devolution policy on children and young people and suggests that the Welsh model, in contrast to the other three, presents children and young people as rights bearers within 'the modern social contract of citizenship', based squarely on an attempt to implement the UNCRC in domestic policy to the extent permitted by devolved powers. Whilst still largely reflected at a level that could be cast as political rhetoric, this model is the basis for national and local strategies which have the potential to produce a different construction, or 'semantic artefact', of children. Its implementation deserves attention over the coming years.

If the UNCRC can be used to promote policies more conducive to children's citizenship, can it also provide a mechanism for enforcement of the concomitant rights? Fortin, in Part I, refers to the UNCRC's lack of teeth – that is, the lack of a judicial enforcement process in either a domestic or international forum. The reporting and monitoring process is easy to dismiss as 'merely' political and administrative and therefore likely to be ineffective in bringing about significant change. However, such a dismissal overlooks the potential of political and administrative processes.

While relatively inept at enforcement of the rights of individuals, these processes may be more effective than judicial processes in influencing policy and practice (Williams, 2007). It is therefore pertinent to examine the potential of the UNCRC in this regard and this is taken up in the final chapter in this volume. Croke and Williams suggest that the UNCRC should be read as imposing a form of 'trusteeship' of (at least a version of) children's citizenship. They examine the monitoring process as a means of oversight of implementation of the obligations of the 'trust' by member States. This is not a direct, individual enforcement mechanism, although the *indirect* effect of the UNCRC in promoting the establishment of Children's Commissioners, should not be forgotten: such Commissioners may (though do not always) provide an avenue for individual complaint, negotiation and (limited) redress where children's rights are engaged. Only time will tell whether the UNCRC may help bring about significant change in the way law and policy think about children and citizenship: as Croke and Williams acknowledge, much depends on political and structural support for the detailed work necessary to operationalize children's rights.

References

James, A., Jenks, C. and Prout, A. (1998) *Theorizing Childhood*. Cambridge: Polity Press.

King, M. and Piper, C. (1995), *How the Law thinks About Children* (2nd Edition), Aldershot, Arena.

Williams, J. (2007) 'Incorporating children's rights: the divergence in law and policy', *Legal Studies*, 27(2): 261–87.

12

Will Law Think about Children? Reflections on *Youth Matters*

Christine Piper

Introduction

Youth Matters, a consultation paper published by the DfES in 2005, and its sequel, *Youth Matters: Next Steps* (DfES, 2006a), promise more opportunities for all teenagers and more support for those 'at risk of poor outcomes'. Chapters 3 and 5 of *Youth Matters* were headed, respectively, 'Empowering Young People' and 'Young People as Citizens: Making a Contribution' and three of the four key challenges stated relate to children as current citizens. The government aims to engage and empower young people in the provision of services, to encourage volunteering within the community, and to provide better information and advice so that young people can make informed choices (DfES, 2005: para 12; see also para 16 and Chapter 2).

Next Steps also set out the 'system changes' (DfES, 2006a: para 8.1) needed to deliver these proposals and to ensure that all 13 to 18-year-olds, as well as all other children, achieve the five outcomes – to be healthy, stay safe, enjoy and achieve, make a positive contribution and achieve economic well-being' – which were specified in *Every Child Matters* (DfES, 2003: para 1.3). The Children Act 2004 has incorporated proposals from *Every Child Matters*, with Children's Services in England and Wales dealt with in Parts 2 and 3 respectively. Some of those provisions have already been implemented and will be used to put in place the proposals from *Youth Matters* and *Youth Matters: Next Steps*.

This, and any further relevant legislation, will constitute the texts which require legal interpretation by courts when called upon to judicially review the operation of statutory provisions in practice and to adjudicate disputes. It is in this context that this part of the book and the title of this chapter refer to law 'thinking about' children.

Law as a System which Thinks

To conceive of law in this way is to draw crucially on the work of Luhmann on social systems and also that of Teubner on law as a self-referential, closed system of communications (see, for example, Luhmann, 1986, 2004; Teubner, 1988, 1989 and 1993). Using the biological notion of autopoiesis or self-reproduction, social systems such as science, law, politics, religion, education and economics can be seen as networks which – using only their own procedures – generate knowledge about the world and establish what is 'true' (King and Piper, 1995: 22–4). Such truths may, however, be accepted as true only for the social system which generated them. On the other hand, the truths of authoritative systems, as science now is, may be reconstructed within the procedures of other social systems. There is, for example, analysis of the way law has reconstructed child welfare science to fulfil its functions (Monk, 2000, 2005; Piper, 2000; King and King, 2006).

The truths of a system such as law may, nevertheless, be accepted by other systems simply because those systems accord law the role of establishing truth within certain parameters. Those parameters are set by law's function in society: to stabilize expectations (Luhmann, 1982), to provide certainly of outcome in disputes, to impose norms and to reduce the complex to a clear legal/illegal distinction.

Law is, then, very important for other systems, notably politics, as a means whereby contentious problems are recast and resolved and, thereby, neutralized (King and Piper, 1995: 29). Law cannot ignore the external environment in the procedures by which it achieves these outcomes but it must 'code' that external knowledge (1995: 25); it must think about it in ways which 'fit' the truths already established by law's communications and it must 'appear as capable of achieving all its ambitions' (King, 2006: 43). Further, what law constructs through its internal communications cannot be the 'real' adults or children of the social world but, rather, what have been referred to as semantic artefacts. Law constructs as many artefacts as are needed for its various 'programmes' – the areas of law in which it operates. Consequently, there are several children to be found in legal communications, each with a fragment of the characteristics of 'real' children. The number of such children is limited only by the number of different 'jobs' law is required to perform.

In relation to *Youth Matters*, therefore, two questions result from this analytical approach. First, what semantic artefacts of children and young people have been used in the political communications inherent in these policy documents? Second, will law be required – or be able – to think about children in this way?

Children in *Youth Matters*

In politics, particular images of children are constructed to support and 'sell' policy changes and so, if necessary, politics as a system of communications reconstructs knowledge about children from, for example, science, religion or economics, in order to produce acceptable images. As we have seen, *Youth Matters* contains conceptualizations of children and young people as citizens but they exist alongside political constructs of victim, threat and investment which have been important for a long time (Hendrick, 1994: 1; Hendrick, 2005: 31–2). Further, whilst all these constructs of young people show continuities with 'old' images there are significant variations which have implications for the 'child as citizen' agenda.

The Child as Victim

In *Youth Matters* the government's stated vision 'is to see services integrated around young people's needs' (DfES, 2005: para 11). The Government's response, at the end of 2005, to the Audit Commission's 2004 Report on Youth Justice also constructs the child as victim in its policy aim to 'shift services towards prevention and early intervention in an integrated way, across services, before children reach crisis point' (YJB, 2004: para 6.2). However, the child as victim construct is hard to find in most of the recent political documents relating to children who offend or behave anti-socially, or, indeed, in documents about 'youth' generally. *Youth Matters* is no exception. Other semantic artefacts have proved politically more useful.

The Child as Threat

The child as (potential) offender and threat is clearly visible in *Youth Matters*:

> A minority of young people can get involved in behaviour that is a serious problem for the wider community, including anti-social behaviour and crime. The Government is clear that when this happens we need to respond firmly.
>
> (DfES, 2005: Executive summary, para 7)

The Youth Justice System and the courts will deal firmly with such minors: there will be no excuses for young offenders and those engaging in anti-social behaviour. A version of the child as threat – one modified by social inclusion policies to provide opportunities – also appears in *Youth Matters*. The child who has wasted chances is a threat who must be disciplined as noted by Ruth Kelly, then Education Secretary, in the Preface to *Youth Matters*:

> It is wrong that young people who do not respect the opportunities they are given, by committing crimes or behaving anti-socially, should benefit from the same opportunities as the law-abiding majority. So we will put appropriate measures in place to ensure they do not.
>
> (DfES, 2005: 1)

At one level this simply means that benefits would be withdrawn. For example, the 'topping up' subsidy of opportunity cards for disadvantaged 13 to 16-year-olds would be withheld 'from young people engaging in unacceptable and anti-social behaviours' (DfES, 2005: 6). At another level it justifies the introduction of new court orders. For example, the use in England and Wales of anti-social behaviour orders for 10 to 17-year-olds increased from a total of 185 imposed in 2001, to 515 in 2003 and 1077 in 2004 (Home Office, 2005).

A further version constructs the child as a threat simply on the basis of risk factors being present in the life of the child who then becomes liable to a level of control which would not otherwise be justifiable to an electorate. As Goldson notes, 'Children face judgement . . . not only on what they *have done*, but what they *might* do, who *they are* or who they are *thought to be*' (Goldson, 2005: 263–4). It is within the context of these sets of images that we need to examine the meanings given to the child as citizen in *Youth Matters*.

The Child as Current Citizen

The Government, which puts great emphasis on its citizenship policies for young people, announced in March 2006 that funding of £ 115 million would be available over two years through the Youth Opportunity Fund and the Youth Capital Fund (amounting to around £ 500,000 for an average local authority). This is ring-fenced money for which young people can bid to improve facilities and activities in their neighbourhood.

> We must empower these young people to take responsibility for shaping the facilities and services they need. And, because for too long too little has been invested in youth services – we must show we have listened to young people – and will continue to do so – by making the investments they are calling for.
>
> (Gordon Brown quoted in DfES, 2006b)

What we seem to have here, and in the following statement by Beverley Hughes, Minister for Children, is the young person as consumer-citizen.

> Never before has a Government put so much responsibility into the hands of young people to let them decide what activities or facilities they need, whether it is a youth café or establishing better sports or art facilities.
>
> (in DfES, 2006b)

Other aspects of the citizenship agenda are in hand. The Russell Commission (see Russell Commission, 2005) and the charity 'V' launched in 2006 aim to encourage more volunteering and the setting up of peer-mentoring schemes for young people to encourage not only more support for the 'mentee' but also more responsibility in the mentor (DfES, 2006: 19). However, volunteering is also part of the Respect Agenda (see Home Office, 2003) whose overall aim is 'tacking anti-social behaviour'. The Respect Action Plan (Respect Task Force, 2006) therefore sets proposals for intervention and empowerment for young people alongside a more punitive policy strand (Rogers, 2006: 18–19).

These images of children and young people as threats suggest that several meanings are being accorded to citizenship. There is the responsible exercise of choice, including consumer choices, which encourages the development of the child's maturity – if given in a graded and supportive way – as well as access to more appropriate services. There is also, as we saw in relation to the child as threat, a concept of responsibility which imports culpability – an absolute standard with punitive outcomes.

What is missing is the child citizen as rights' holder. Proposals in *Youth Matters* have been influenced by the political need to respond to those articles of the United Nations Convention on the Rights of the Child (UNCRC) which impose on States Parties duties to give or allow minors access to information and consult with them (UNCRC, Articles 12, 13 and 17), and which seek to ensure all organizations concerned with children and young people work towards what is best for them (Article 3). The current images of young people do not, however, appear to support processes by which minors can enforce rights to consultation and services.

Article 27 of the UNCRC states that governments must recognize the child's right to an adequate standard of living for the child's development but for that to be effective a child or young person (or their representative) would need the right to challenge the relevant authority in cases of default. This does not seem to be on the political agenda although the Commission on Families and the Wellbeing of Children has called for a legal entitlement to universal services for parents (see Rogers, 2006: 24). Rather, the Government resisted pressure to include a duty to promote rights in the functions of the Children's Commissioner (England) in Section 2(2) of the Children Act 2004 and specifically excluded the ability to review serious cases of individual children (see Williams, 2005: 45–7).

The Child as Future Productive Citizen

It is, however, the child as future productive citizen – the 'citizen-worker-in-becoming' (Lister, 2005: 455) – that appears as most influential in *Youth Matters*. By shaping the child as future citizen, investment to make it more likely that the child will become a productive and law-abiding adult is justified and justifiable. Such 'preventative' investments can be presented as reducing future expenditure on, notably, the penal system, social security payments and the health service. So targeted investment 'in the potential of every single child in our country' (Brown, 2002) is now explicit government policy. *Youth Matters* refers to investment in youth facilities and support services (2005: paras 18, 31, 63; Chapters 3 and 4 especially) but it states that a major aim of the investment is to reduce crime (2005: para 65) and being assessed as at risk of 'getting into trouble' is crucial for access to targeted support (2005: para 32 and chapter 6).

However, the investment agenda requires a 'pay-off' and the fear is of a bad investment in the child. In this context the risk is that the investment may not prevent offending, unemployment or teenage pregnancy: if the benefits do not accrue or are not likely to materialize, then continued investment would not be economic (Lister, 2005: 455–6). Consequently, the dominant image of the child changes to justify withdrawal of investment: it becomes the child as threat who can be disciplined and punished for not using opportunities properly.

Implementing Youth Policy

The children to be found in *Youth Matters* are political artefacts which law could reconstruct into legal communications but the child as citizen with rights would continue to be overshadowed by other constructs. However, there are two reasons why law may not even need to reconstitute this external knowledge.

First, semantic artefacts already constructed by legal communications may well suffice: law may not think about children in any new way but be able to function with existing images. Those constructs already identified in the operation of family, child, criminal and education law, such as the child as victim, as a bundle of needs, as an offender, or as product, would be drawn on to fulfil functions in relation to new legislation.

Second, law may not need to 'rethink' children and young people because it may never be asked to adjudicate on the meaning of new legislation or review its operation. There would be no work for law if the necessary decisions, reviews and monitoring could be made within other systems: law as a social system would then be bypassed and its authority diminished. This might occur if, for example, decisions – with subsequent funding – on the selection of geographical areas, target groups and priority risks and needs are made within the procedures of other systems without there being any recourse to law. Here economics, organizing its communications around management concepts, or politics, making decisions on calculations of power and control, are the obvious substitutes for law. If such were the case, then the function of the legislation would simply be to set up a system onto which the guidance, inspection, targets, monitoring and money are pinned.

New Powers and Duties

We need then to consider in more detail what law might be called upon to do in relation to the legislative consequences of *Youth Matters* and its 'parent' paper, *Every Child Matters* (DfES, 2003). Sections 10/11 and 25/28 of the Children Act 2004 impose new duties on Children's Services Authorities, in England and Wales respectively, who must promote co-operation with `each of the authority's relevant partners' 'with a view to improving the well-being of children in the authority's area'. This duty relates to specific aspects of well-being which mirror the five outcomes in *Every Child Matters*:

(a) physical and mental health and emotional well-being;
(b) protection from harm and neglect;
(c) education, training and recreation;
(d) the contribution made by them to society;
(e) social and economic well-being.

Partners to this venture 'must co-operate with the authority in the making of arrangements under this section' (sections 10(5) and 25(5) respectively) and they must ensure that:

(a) their functions are discharged having regard to the need to safeguard and promote the welfare of children; and
(b) any services provided by another person pursuant to arrangements made by the person or body in the discharge of their functions are provided having regard to that need.

(ss11(2) and 28(2))

To these ends a children's services authority and any of their relevant partners may '(a) provide staff, goods, services, accommodation or other resources; (b) establish and maintain a pooled fund' (Sections 10(6) and 26(6)).

The Education and Inspection Act 2006, section 6, also imposes duties on local education authorities (LEAs) in England whereby the LEA must secure for the under 13s 'adequate facilities for recreation and social and physical training', and, for persons aged 13 to 19 must, 'so far as reasonably practicable', secure access to 'sufficient' educational and recreational leisure-time activities. These must be aimed at 'the improvement of their well-being', defined by reference to the five outcomes as incorporated in the Children Act 2004. The LEA must consult with young people in making plans for recreational facilities and must publicize those facilities although only parents may complain to the new Her Majesty's Inspector (HMI) about the running of a school (Section 160; see Thomas, 2006: 19).

So, in these legislative contexts, what will law be asked to do and how will law think about 'users' who are also minors? Providers and users of the services overseen by Children's Trusts might require clarification of the scope and nature of the duties, whether they have been carried out in accordance with guidance and with the proper exercise of discretion, whether co-operation with other agencies has been sufficient, and whether implementation has been rights compliant. A review of the responses by law to the nearest equivalent to these sections – section 17 of the Children Act 1989 – gives little cause for optimism.

Decisions for Law: The Children Act 1989

Section 17 imposes a general duty on every local authority 'to safeguard and promote the welfare of children within their area who are in need' by providing 'a range and level of services appropriate to those children's needs'. Section 17(10) defines 'in need' and Schedule 2 Part 1 provides specific duties and powers relevant to the general duty. These provisions are drawn such that a wide discretion is given to the local authority. Consequently, law has been called upon to adjudicate on several issues relating to the exercise of this discretion, notably in relation to rights of 'appeal' against the local authority's assessment and outcomes. However, the judges in *R v Birmingham CC ex p A* [1997] 2FLR 841 (see Williams, 1998), restricted access to the courts by confirming that the section 26 complaints procedure should normally be used before an application can be made for judicial review (see Williams, 2002).

A series of cases – *R(G) v London Borough of Barnet; R(W) v London Borough of Lambeth; R(A) v London Borough of Lambeth* [2003] UKHL 57, [2004] 1 FLR 454 – also failed to establish a 'duty' to assess (see Cowan, 2004) and also decided against the argument that the general duty in section 17 becomes one owed to a specific child once that child has been assessed as in need (see Masson, 2006: 235–9). Further, notwithstanding the decision in *Z v UK* [2001] 2 FLR 612 ECtHR, the jurisprudence of the European Court of Human Rights (ECtHR) has had relatively little effect on the interpretation of section 17 (see Bainham, 2005: 461–4).

Not surprisingly, the conclusion of those who have summarized the case law in this area is that the local authority is only marginally accountable in relation to the provision of children's services (Murphy, 2003: 103; Masson, 2006) and so very little is left for law to adjudicate.

Law's Thinking about Children

In the cases reviewed above, the courts have either refused adjudication (as in relation to breach of statutory duty), limited the scope of applications based, for example, on negligence, or construed duties in ways which mean that they cannot give an individual child rights to use the law to seek a remedy. Most often the child is invisible. As Jane Fortin similarly comments in relation to the *Williamson* case in her chapter, 'courts knew nothing about [the children]'. Further, the knowledge that law is reconstructing in these cases is most certainly not the child welfare science that has become so important an element in child protection and parental dispute cases. Rather, where necessary, political precepts about the need to ration the use of public money and economic truths about the importance of selecting, apportioning and monitoring resources are reconstructed within law. This economic discourse, as Priscilla Alderson also notes in this volume, is one that rarely constructs children as anything other than a unit of consumption or future production.

On this analysis law will rarely think about children and young people in relation to the new services proposed for young people in *Youth Matters*. Law is unlikely, if asked to adjudicate, to release resources to combat exclusion and to insist on individual children being given more opportunities. Yet, at the same time, law continues to think about the child as offender and as threat: most young offenders – 'youths' (see Piper, 2001) – now have only two chances before they are prosecuted and dealt with in a youth court. Law may also be asked to adjudicate where young people fail to take up the opportunities they are offered under the proposals in *Youth Matters*. That document states very clearly that young people who engage in criminal or anti-social behaviour are to be excluded from the benefits and opportunities on offer.

The Side-Lining of Law

It would appear that law has proved ineffective in securing more resources for children and young people and has not constructed any clear image of the child as a citizen with rights and to whom duties are specifically owed. Some of the reasons for this lie in the fact that law by its very nature is constrained in its use. First, legal provisions are implemented at the level of the individual person or authority. Where there is a general duty to a group of children law reconstructs political and economic information, rather than child welfare knowledge, to give authority to its decisions. These external truths may marginalize the needs of children and reduce the scope of law's functions. Second, law operates in a compartmentalized way and there can rarely be a crossing to another area of law where the use of law just might release resources.

In some contexts the side-lining of law in settling family affairs and disputes about children may be a good rather than a bad thing. The concern in the context of support and services for children and young people is that they are then at the mercy of contingent political and economic constructs of minors. Maybe there is, nevertheless, some leeway here. Law makes decisions on matters referred to it and, as necessary, it reconstructs authoritative truths from elsewhere. It also has, in effect, its own margin of appreciation in how it analyses rights. Perhaps then the rights discourse itself needs to become more authoritative in society and be used more authoritatively. How might this be done?

Law's Use of Children's Rights

The two main Convention sources of rights relevant to children in the UK are very different and provide different opportunities for implementation such that the image of the young person as a rights holder can be a political or legal construct. The European Convention on Human Rights (ECHR) generates legal communications and gives access to the courts but the impact has been relatively small. In family law the courts are seemingly reluctant to articulate children's interests as rights (Harris-Short, 2005; Fortin, 2006) and, in adjudicating on service provision, as we have seen, law has faced the challenge of an external authoritative management 'system' and its response has, in effect, removed the image of the child with needs.

The other Convention – the UNCRC – has so far been largely irrelevant to the operations of law because it was established as a political statement of intent and the methods of redress and promotion are themselves within that system. The UN Committee, political pressure, review officers, commissioners and ombudspersons are the tools, using political and economic processes, by which this latter Convention is overseen. For example, a 'champion' for children is considered to be very important in promoting new legislation and monitoring the practice of public bodies dealing with children and all parts of the UK do now have a Children's Commissioner (Williams, 2005: 52).

However, judges, within the intrinsic limitations of law outlined above could use both Conventions more positively and, indeed, are doing so. As well as directly adjudicating on ECHR rights they may reconstruct the principles of the UNCRC within legal communications, as did Thorpe LJ in *Mabon v Mabon and others* [2005] EWCA Civ 634 when he referred to the 'obligations' imposed by Article 12. In *The Queen (On the Application of the Howard League for Penal Reform) v. The Secretary of State for the Home Department, Department of Health* [2002] EWHC 2497 (Admin), Munby J similarly referred very broadly to 'human rights law' when deciding that the duties of a local authority under the Children Act 1989 applied to children in prison service establishments.

Conclusion

To give children and young people more 'voice' and more services, this 'rethinking' by law would need to be substantial. Yet decisions in recent education law cases such as *Abdul Hakim Ali v Headteacher and Governors of Lord Grey School* [2006] UKHL 14 have continued to narrow rather than broaden the possible uses of Law (see also Fortin, in this volume). Further, the legislation stemming from *Every Child Matters* and *Youth Matters* gives few rights but, instead, establishes several review bodies such as the new Office for Standards in Education, Children's Services and Skills and the new HMI set up by the Education and Inspection Act 2006. This new HMI has its remit set and its effectiveness overseen by a new Crown office: a system which largely bypasses law.

In all these developments the communications being used are those produced within politics and economics. Their reconstruction within law is what is determining legal outcomes which are not best promoting the welfare and citizenship of children and young people. However, Fortin (2006: 302) has argued that, whilst there is 'judicial myopia' regarding children's Convention rights, the courts could legitimately do much more within the legitimate jurisprudential approaches of law. I hope she is right.

References

Bainham, A. (2005) *Children: The Modern Law* (3rd edn). Bristol: Family Law.

Brown, G. (2002) 'Budget statement', *House of Commons, Hansard*, April 17.

Cowan, D. (2004) 'On need and gatekeeping', *CFLQ*, 16(3): 331–8.

DfES (2003) *Every Child Matters*, Cm 5860, London: Stationery Office.

DfES (2005) *Youth Matters*, Cm 6629. London: Stationery Office.

DfES (2006a) *Youth Matters: Next Steps, Something to Do, Somewhere to Go, Someone to Talk to*. London: DfES.

DfES (2006b) '£115M funds will go direct to young people for the first time – Hughes', *Press Notice 2006/0025*, London: DfES, 8 March.

Fortin, J. (2006) 'Accommodating children's rights in a post Human Rights Act era', *MLR*, 69: 299–326.

Goldson, B. (2005) 'Taking liberties: policy and the punitive turn', in H. Hendrick (ed.) *Child Welfare and Social Policy, An Essential Reader*, University of Bristol: Policy Press.

Harris-Short, S. (2005) 'Family law and the Human Rights Act 1998: judicial restraint or revolution?' *CFLQ*, 17(3): 329–61.

Hendrick, H. (1994) *Child Welfare: England 1972–1989*. London: Routledge.

Hendrick, H. (2005) 'Children and social policies', in H. Hendrick (ed.) *Child Welfare and Social Policy, An essential Reader*, University of Bristol: Policy Press.

Home Office (2003) *Respect and Responsibility – Taking a Stand against Anti-social Behaviour*, Cm 5778. London: Stationery Office.

Home Office (2005) Statistics on ASBO, Table 2A, compiled by Research and Statistics/Office for Criminal Justice Reform. London: Home Office.

King, M. (2006) 'What's the use of Luhmann's Theory?' in M. King and C. Thornhill (eds) *Luhmann in Law and Politics: Critical Approaches and Applications*, Oxford: Hart Publishing.

King, M. and King, D. (2006) 'How the law defines the special educational needs of autistic children', *Child and Family Law Quarterly*, 18(1): 23–42.

King, M. and Piper, C. (1995) *How the Law Thinks About Children* (2nd edn). Arena: Aldershot.

Luhmann, N. (1982) *The Differentiation of Society*. New York: Columbia University Press.

Luhmann, N. (1986) 'The autopoiesis of social systems', in F. Geyer and J. van der Zouwen (eds) *Sociocybernetic Paradoxes: Observation, Control and Evolution of Self-steering Systems*, London and Beverly Hills, CA: Sage.

Luhmann, N. (2004) *Law as a Social System*. Oxford: Oxford University Press.

Masson, J. (2006) 'The Climbie inquiry: context and critique', *Journal of Law and Society*, 33(2): 221–43.

McNeill, P. (2001) 'Curriculum 2000 – What HE Applicants may offer in 2002', *SPA [Social Policy Association] Matters*, (February/March): 4–5.

Monk, D. (2000) 'Theorizing education law and childhood: constructing the ideal pupil', *British Journal of Sociology of Education*, 21(3): 355–70.

Monk, D. (2005) '(Re)constructing the head teacher: legal narratives and the politics of school exclusions', *Journal of Law and Society*, 32(3): 399–423.

Murphy, J. (2003) 'Children in need: the limits of local authority accountability', *Legal Studies*, 23(1): 103.

Piper, C. (2000) 'Assumptions about children's best interests', *Journal of Social Welfare and Family Law*, 22(3): 261–76.

Piper, C. (2001) 'Who are these youths? Language in the service of policy', *Youth Justice*, 1(2): 30–9.

Respect Task Force (2006) *Respect Action Plan*. London: Home Office.

Rogers, C. (2006) *Implementation of Every Child Matters Green Paper*. London: National Parenting Institute.

Russell Commission (2005) *A National Framework for Youth Action and Engagement*. London: Stationery Office.

Teubner, G. (ed.) (1988) *Law as an Autopoietic System*. Oxford: Blackwell.

Teubner, G. (1989) 'How the law thinks: towards a constructivist epistemology of law', *Law and Society Review*, 23(5): 727–56.

Teubner, G. (1993) *Law as an Autopoietic System*. Oxford: Oxford University Press.

Thomas, J. (2006) 'Education and Inspection Bill 2006', *Childright*, 225: 15–19.

Williams, C. (1998) '*R v Birmingham City Council ex parte A* – an unsuitable case for judicial review?' *CFLQ*, 10(1): 89–99.

Williams, C. (2002) 'The practical operation of the Children Act complaints procedure', *CFLQ*, 14(1): 25–43.

Williams, J. (2005) 'Effective government structures for children? The UK's four children's commissioners' *CFLQ*, 17(1): 37–53.

Youth Justice Board (YJB) (2004) *Government Response to the Audit Commission Report – Youth Justice (2004): A Review of the Reformed Youth Justice System*. London: Youth Justice Board.

13

The Relevance of European Union Citizenship to Children

Helen Stalford

Introduction

There is now a vast literature critiquing the nature and scope of citizenship which, over the past 20 years or so has been subject to intense scrutiny by the children's rights movement. Similarly, EU citizenship has, since its inception in 1992 (by the Treaty on European Union), provided academic fodder for legal and political commentators who have progressed from exposing the exclusive and artificial nature of the concept (Weiler, 1998), towards commending its success in endowing politically active and geographically mobile EU nationals with a range of important social and civic rights (Fries and Shaw, 1998; O'Leary, 1999; Castro Oliveira, 2002; Barnard, 2005). In contrast with the development of mainstream citizenship debates, there has been very little effort to consider the relevance of EU citizenship to children (Ackers and Stalford, 2004). This is primarily due to the long-standing absence of any explicit children's rights agenda at EU level; children did not form part of the original vision of the European Union when it was first established in 1956 as a vehicle for promoting economic and political cohesion between the Member States because of their intrinsic economic and political incapacity. The routine disregard for children's rights issues by the EU institutions continued throughout the latter part of the twentieth century in spite of the development of a more robust EU human rights and social agenda. The late 1990s marked a sea change in relation to children's rights, however, mainly because it coincided with the integration of targeted, albeit modest children's rights provisions into the constitutional fabric of the European Union. This came about partly as a result of the 1997 Treaty of Amsterdam which incorporated new measures into the Treaty establishing the European Community (EC Treaty) prohibiting discrimination on grounds of age (Article 13 EC), and into the Treaty on European Union providing a new basis for intergovernmental co-operation to tackle offences against children (Article 29 TEU). This was closely followed by the introduction of the Charter of Fundamental Rights of the European Union which included, for the first time, explicit children's rights provision (McGlynn, 2002; Cullen, 2004; Stalford, 2005). These developments, in turn, responded to a growing awareness of the impact of EU laws and policies on children which had been highlighted by a more robust campaign by children's rights lobbying groups (Lansdown, 2002).

While these constitutional changes are by no means insignificant, some of the most dramatic steps to enhance children's rights in the European Union have been orchestrated by the EU judiciary, primarily in its interpretation of EU citizenship. Taking as a starting point the formal, legal definition of EU citizenship, the discussion in this chapter explores the characteristics of EU citizenship, examining in particular the extent to which it accommodates children's rights and interests. The ultimate aim of this analysis is to evaluate whether EU citizenship reproduces the inequalities inherent in nation-based citizenship exposed by other contributors to this collection or, conversely, whether it provides new opportunities to engage children in a more meaningful way in the political, civil and social processes of the European Union.

The Definition and Scope of EU Citizenship

EU citizenship is formally (albeit vaguely) defined by Article 17 of the EC Treaty as follows:

1. . . . Every person holding the nationality of a Member State shall be a citizen of the Union. Citizenship of the Union shall complement and not replace national citizenship.
2. Citizens of the Union shall enjoy the rights conferred by this Treaty and shall be subject to the duties imposed thereby.

The first part of this definition denotes EU citizenship as a status, conferred exclusively and automatically on those who hold the nationality of one of the 27 Member States. The second part of the definition also denotes citizenship as a practice whereby individuals are afforded a discrete set of rights (and subject to a defined set of responsibilities) which are set out in the remaining text of the Treaty and in the expansive secondary legislation that elaborates on the Treaty provisions. Articles 18–22, in particular, set out some specific citizenship rights, namely the right to move freely between the Member States of the European Union, as well as some limited voting and other political rights.

Aside from this formal definition, EU citizenship is a judicial construct; all legislative acts elaborating on the provisions of the EC Treaty are open to the scrutiny of the European Court of Justice (ECJ) and this is no less so of the citizenship provisions enshrined in Articles 17–22. Indeed, Article 18, which associates EU citizenship with free movement, coupled with the body of secondary legislation that defines the substance and scope of these mobility rights (notably Regulation 1612/68 OJ L257/2, partially amended by Directive 2004/38 OJ L158/77), have generated an extensive case load for the ECJ over the past decade, leading to increasingly expansive judicial interpretations of the mobility-related entitlement available to EU citizens. Consequently, EU citizenship has been widely exploited by individuals to gain access to a panoply of residence, civil and social welfare rights in other Member States on the same basis as nationals (Harris, 2000; Van der Mei, 2003). To what extent, then, is this model of citizenship compatible with children's rights, and has judicial activism in this context served to enhance children's lives in any meaningful way?

Is EU Citizenship Compatible with Children's Rights?

The formalized definition of EU citizenship outlined above stands in stark contrast to the more abstract notion of nation-based citizenship which is typically associated with Marshall's classical triad of civil, political and social rights (Marshall, 1950) and with notions of equality, inclusion and participation in a community (Jones and Wallace, 1992; Oldfield, 1998). It is only relatively recently that academic work has attempted to place children within the vast collage of citizenship discourse, succeeding as much in highlighting how popular conceptualizations of citizenship remain antipathetic to children's interests and needs. Dominant observations emerging from this literature reveal, for instance, that citizenship entails a distinct hierarchy of entitlement, affording rights to individuals in accordance with their earning capacity or economic value (Lister, 1997; Neale, 2004; Jones and Clutton in this volume). Children, who do not generally undertake paid employment, who do not pay taxes, and who rely on parents or the welfare state for their financial and social well-being, are inevitably placed at the bottom of this hierarchy. As a consequence, adults remain the primary filters of children's citizenship entitlement, reinforcing relationships of dependency, regardless of whether that dependency operates in the best interests of the child.

Similar observations can be applied to the construction of EU citizenship to the extent that the principal rights associated with that status – the free movement provisions – operate on a model of dependency and economic contribution.

EU Citizenship and Dependency

The articulation of EU citizenship as an expression of economic independence has been heavily criticised by feminist commentators (Pateman, 1992; Walby, 1997; Ackers, 1998). The argument essentially states that the rights and responsibilities associated with citizenship are enjoyed most fully by those who undertake formal, paid work and who pay taxes, thereby making a direct economic contribution to society. To the extent that men are more likely than women to be engaged in full-time paid employment, they are inevitably ascribed enhanced citizenship status. The concept is ill-equipped to acknowledge the contribution women make to society in the private domain, and indeed, the extent to which women assist men in fulfilling their economic activities in the public sphere by assuming domestic, particularly caring, responsibilities. Society's routine disregard for such activities reinforces women's economic dependence on their male counterparts, thereby perpetuating their legal and social subordination (see Alderson; Lister; in this volume).

Similar arguments have been applied to assessments of children's citizenship status: children, like women, are more likely to be excluded from the labour market, although in their case it is primarily as a result of legal and moral prescription rather than personal choice or responsibility. However, while the feminist campaign has made some progress towards promoting the contribution women make in the private sphere as a legitimate foundation for citizenship, such endeavours have been less effective in the context of children. This is mainly attributable to the fact that children tend to be the cared *for* rather than the carers *of* and, more often than not, are the very cause of women's withdrawal from the labour market. In short, children are inherently and necessarily dependent on adults and, in that sense, are regarded very much as passive *recipients of* as opposed to active *contributors towards* social and economic provision both in the public and private sphere. This, in turn, shapes political and legal regimes, and embeds cultural constructions of childhood, all of which emphasize protection over participation and acknowledge children's capacity to exercise agency only in the most negative of contexts (e.g. as subjects of the juvenile justice agenda).

A similar model of dependency is evident in the EU citizenship provisions. The right to move freely is now synonymous with the status of EU citizenship, particularly following its formal articulation in Article 18 of the EC Treaty. Free movement rights were available to EU nationals long before this constitutional development, however. Migrant workers' mobility rights were extended to workers' family members in the 1960s (by Articles 10–12 Regulation 1612/68) in acknowledgement of the importance of family relationships and responsibilities as a key factor influencing migration decisions. The assumption was that workers would be less inclined to move to other Member States to pursue economic activities if forced to leave their family behind. Interestingly, and consistent with nation-based constructions of citizenship and gendered notions of contribution, the European Community legislation delineating the entitlement of accompanying family members is based on a model of dependency: the worker can be accompanied to other Member States by his or her spouse or legally recognized registered partner; their descendants who are under the age of 21 years or are dependants; and dependent relatives in the ascending line of the worker and his or her partner (Directive 2004/38, Article 2(2)). Family members thereby gain access to a range of social rights, including employment, educational and welfare rights for as long as they remain (financially) dependent on the migrant worker (Directive 2004/38, Article 16). The practical implications of this legal formulation for children are, on the whole, quite positive in that they can receive education and any other child-related benefits on the same basis as nationals in the host state. The free movement legislation is limited in a number of respects, however.

First, tangible EU citizenship entitlement is only relevant to children who migrate between the EU Member States, leaving (the majority of) non-migrant children in the EU with little opportunity to actively practise or engage with their citizenship status. Second, the free movement provisions extend entitlement to the family as an indivisible entity and are thus based on the presumption that parental and children's rights are exercised concurrently. Until recently, the law did not clarify the legal status of accompanying family members should the family unit disperse following arrival in the host state (e.g. as a result of divorce, domestic violence or the departure of one or other parent to take up work elsewhere). This implied that the family members would only have a right to remain in the host state for as long as their relationships of 'dependency' on the migrant worker subsisted, however artificial that might have been (Case 267/83 *Aissatou Diatta v Land Berlin* [1985] ECR 574 C-267/83). The Court of Justice has thus played a key role in more recent years, in expanding the scope of EU citizenship to accommodate family members', including children's, interests in a range of different migration and relationship contexts.

Redefining Dependence: Developing a Model of Interdependence

While the discussion has already alluded to the limitations of a dependency-based model of EU citizenship in the sense that it undermines women and children's contribution in the public and private sphere, critiques of nation-based citizenship have sought to challenge instead the negative connotations commonly associated with dependency (Jordan, 2001; Moss and Petrie, 2002; Neale, 2004; Moosa-Mitha, 2005). These critiques have developed our appreciation of dependency as a necessary feature of human relationships and reconceptualized it in more positive terms as 'interdependence' to convey the mutual value and benefits of the adult–child dynamic, particularly within families.

Interestingly, a similar reconceptualization is apparent in the way in which the ECJ now delimits children's and their carers' rights under the free movement provisions. This point can perhaps best be developed by reference to the case of *Baumbast and R v Secretary of State for the Home Department* (Case C-413/99 [2002] ECR I-7091). This involved the claim of a third-country national woman and her children to remain in the UK following the departure of her migrant–worker husband to work in the Middle East. The ECJ upheld their right to remain on the basis that, as nationals of a Member State (the children were of German nationality), they qualified as EU citizens and, consequently, had an independent right to pursue their education in the host state. A strict interpretation of the free movement provisions would have divested the mother, a third-country national, of her right of residence since this subsisted only for as long as she remained dependent on her husband in the host state. The ECJ conceded, however, that the children's rights as EU citizens would be impracticable unless their mother was allowed to remain with them as their primary carer.

Similarly, the subsequent case of *Zhu & Chen v Secretary of State for the Home Department* (Case C-200/02 [2004] ECR I-9923) involved a Chinese woman who travelled to the UK (Cardiff) in May 2000 when she was pregnant with her second child. Two months later, she travelled to Belfast where she gave birth to a daughter in September 2000. Her reason for doing this was that, according to unique nationality laws in place at the time, any person born on the island of Ireland (including Northern Ireland) acquired Irish nationality. Baby Chen was issued with an Irish passport in September 2000 and her parents applied for a long-term residence permit arguing that the move between Cardiff and Northern Ireland triggered their EU family free movement rights. This was initially refused on the grounds that the baby, because of her tender age, had no independent right to move under the free movement rules, nor was she financially self-sufficient. The mother could not, therefore, derive any free movement rights on the basis of some artificial dependency on the child. The ECJ upheld the claimants' right to remain, however, concluding that, although the move between territories within the UK did not strictly trigger the operation of the free movement provisions (which demands a move between two distinct Member States), as a national of a Member State, and therefore *as a citizen of the Union*, baby Chen was entitled to enjoy long-term residence in the UK. In what has been referred to as a 'remarkably sensitive [affirmation of] the procedural and substantive rights of the child' (Forder, 2005: 98), the ECJ highlighted the injustice of withholding EU citizenship entitlement from children solely on the basis that they are not yet old enough to exercise those rights independently. Additionally, the ECJ upheld the mother's right to remain in the host state as the baby's primary carer, provided that the family demonstrated that they had sufficient financial resources so as not to impose any burden on the social welfare system of the host state.

These decisions add a new dimension to the model of dependency traditionally espoused by the free movement case law and legislation to reflect the different layers of interdependence between family members. Thus, the children in *Baumbast* and *Chen* derived their citizenship status from their migrant parents to enter the host state in the first instance and remain dependent on them for their day-to-day care and well-being; the very existence of that dependency later becomes the source of their non-qualifying parents' ongoing right of residence. In other words, the parents depended on their children's dependency as the basis of their own legal right to remain.

These cases also highlight the important distinction between child autonomy and self-sufficiency that pervades children's rights and citizenship literature (Neale, 2002 and 2004; Lister; Fortin; in this volume); the children had an autonomous right to remain in the UK founded on their status as EU citizens but were not expected to exercise that right without appropriate parental support (Sawyer, 2005). However, while the final decisions may represent a triumph for the children and families concerned, they do serve to reinforce the status of parents as the initial trigger/access point for their children's citizenship rights, and to high-light the vacuous nature of EU citizenship in relation to children in non-migrant families. Since children do not have a legal right to move to other Member States independently of their parents, the only means by which children in this context can actively exercise their EU citizenship rights is if their parents decide to move with them in the first instance and continue to support them in the host state.

Moreover, while the emphasis on an ongoing relationship of dependency following a move to another Member State, and specifically on the child's need to be cared for as the basis of the non-qualifying parents' right to remain, is perhaps an appropriate endorsement of the right to family life, it is potentially open to exploitation. Regarding the *Chen* case, for instance, there is something slightly unsettling about the rela-tionship of interdependence observed between mother and child: baby Chen was obviously dependent on her mother for her day-to-day care and emotional well-being; Mrs Chen, on the other hand, depended on her maternal relationship with the baby to establish a legal right to remain in the UK. The facts of Chen clearly indicate that the mother made a conscious decision to give birth to the baby in Northern Ireland to exploit the Irish nationality laws at the time, thereby enabling the baby to acquire EU citizenship. A regrettable consequence of this (although little is made of it by the ECJ) is that the child forfeited any right to acquire Chinese citizenship, thereby limiting any future visits to China to 30 days under a temporary visa. Perhaps a more far-reaching and poignant consequence than this is the limited opportunity baby Chen (and, indeed, her mother) will have to develop a relationship with the older son left behind in China. This raises some concerns as to whether EU citizenship, so readily endowed on children by the judicial authorities, is accompanied by an equal commitment to ensuring the concept operates to ensure that the child's (rather than the parents') best interests remain paramount.

EU Citizenship and Economic Contribution

Notwithstanding the limitations outlined above, one of the most important consequences of the *Baumbast* and *Chen* decisions is that they appear to represent a significant departure from the economic imperative underpinning free movement entitlement (which necessarily excluded children as economically inactive) towards a more inclusive equality-driven interpretation of EU citizenship. They constitute just two of a steady stream of cases to come before the Court of Justice in the past decade that have succeeded incrementally in extending the tangible benefits of EU citizenship to all categories of EU migrant. The ECJ, through this densely critiqued jurisprudence, has arrived at the conclusion that once an individual is legally installed in a Member State of the European Union, he or she enjoys equal access to any rights, including all social, tax- and welfare-related benefits that fall within the scope of the EC Treaty (Dougan and Spaventa, 2003; 2005). In the cases of *Grzelczyk* (Case C-184/99 [2001] ECR I-6193) and *Collins* (Case C-138/02, [2004] ECR I-2703), for instance, EU migrants were successful in their claim for a subsistence allowance and jobseekers allowance respectively on the basis of their EU citizenship status, despite the fact that neither had made any contribution to the host economy whatsoever. Yet despite the apparent success of EU citizenship in opening up free movement rights to previously marginalized groups, it is not unconditional: the ECJ, in all of the cases referred to here, has been careful to emphasize that rights of entry and residence are subject to a resources requirement; the individual and their family members must demonstrate that they have sufficient financial resources as well as comprehensive medical insurance to minimize the likelihood of them making any claim for social assistance from the host state. But the ECJ has also, to its credit, exercised considerable discretion in the application of these conditions where the principles of social solidarity and proportionality demand a more lenient approach to one-off 'worthy' causes such as *Grzelczyk* and *Collins* (Barnard, 2005; Dougan and Spaventa, 2005). Conversely, in *Baumbast*, it was clear that the main factor influencing the decision to allow the family to remain in the UK was that it would be disproportionately disruptive to the children's education and welfare in view of the fact that the family had never, nor would they ever be likely to claim any welfare benefits in the host state. Similarly, in *Chen*, the mother was granted leave to remain with the baby on the grounds that the family was entirely self-supporting and that it would be unreasonable to deport them to China particularly in view of the fact that the child had already lost her right to acquire Chinese citizenship.

These factors demonstrate, therefore, that beneath the Court's seemingly inclusive, equality-driven interpretation of EU citizenship, the deference to economic capacity that epitomizes traditional formulations of citizenship remains. That said, purely economic factors are not sufficient in themselves to justify blanket restrictions on the free movement of the economically fragile, and in such cases the Member State would have to advance fairly persuasive justifications to support a refusal to allow individuals access to their territory, or indeed, to support a decision to deport individuals (Dougan and Spaventa, 2005: 202). A reasonable justification would relate, for example, to the fact that unfettered access by migrant families to the benefits associated with free movement would place an undue burden on the welfare resources of the host state, particularly in view of the extensive provision generally available to those with children. Dougan and Spaventa make a similar point in the context of health care tourism in the European Union:

> Member States may legitimately take account of certain financial considerations when attempting to justify indirectly discriminatory barriers to free movement on broader public interest grounds. In particular . . . the possible risk of seriously undermining the financial balance of the social security system may well

constitute an overriding reason in the general interest capable of justifying a barrier to the exercise of fundamental Treaty freedoms; and . . . maintaining an adequate standard of welfare provision for the benefit of the entire population . . . is inextricably linked to the Member State's ability to exercise effective control over its levels of financial expenditure. This in turn implies that the competent public authorities must be in a position to curtail the range of individuals (and especially foreign migrants) capable of staking claims against its social solidarity system.

(2005: 202)

Similarly, children are an expensive venture as far as the welfare state is concerned, particularly in view of the abundant initiatives (in the UK at least) aimed at tackling child poverty, early years health and education, and child care strategies to facilitate women's reintegration into the labour market. Indeed, all of these social and welfare benefits are as much (if not more so) an expression of parents' citizenship status as they are of their children's citizenship status; the State is showing an increasing willingness to express its solidarity with individuals (in the form of enhanced tax relief and social assistance) precisely *because* they have dependent children. This is provided not only as an incentive for parents to remain in the labour market, enabling them to continue fulfilling their civic responsibilities as producers and tax payers, but also as an investment in the well-being of children as the labour force of the future.

Given the public cost of this undertaking it seems inevitable that host states will endeavour to curtail the number of (non-national) families with young children taking up residence in their territory, particularly where the contribution of the parents is outweighed by the child-related costs incurred by the State. As such, the *Baumbast/Chen* approach to children's citizenship is likely to operate narrowly to the exclusion of parents and children who do not have the financial means to guarantee economic self-sufficiency for the duration of their residence in another Member State. Certainly the ECJ's acknowledgment of the child's citizenship status in *Chen* was a novel way of rationalizing the residence rights of parents who were already making an important contribution to the EU economy through their (highly lucrative) business activities. It is unlikely that the ECJ would have been so sympathetic had the claim involved, say, an asylum-seeking mother who had given birth in Northern Ireland, a point recently illustrated by the English court of Appeal decision in *W (China) and X (China) v Secretary of State for the Home Department* (CA (Civ) [2006] 103 LG 45 (27)). Thus, notwithstanding the symbolic importance of the ECJ's explicit acknowledgement in these cases that children are EU citizens in their own right, their impact is likely to be quite limited, even amongst those exercising free movement.

Beyond Free Movement towards a Rights-based Model of EU Citizenship?

This chapter has highlighted the association between EU citizenship, free movement and non-discrimination. Yet free movement is only a practical reality for less than one per cent of the estimated 94 million children living in the European Union whose mobility choices are inevitably dictated by adult agendas (Ackers and Stalford, 2004: 97; Ruxton, 2006). This begs the question of whether EU citizenship is activated in any context other than that of migration in a way that might be of significance to children more generally or, indeed, whether citizenship is the most appropriate context in which to promote children's rights at EU level.

Article 17(2) of the EC Treaty, referred to above, suggests that citizenship denotes enjoyment not only of the free movement provisions, but of all the rights conferred in the Treaty. The lack of Treaty provision targeting children, however, significantly limits the scope of this provision. Moreover, aside from the modest provision addressing the health and welfare interests of children in the context of youth employment (Directive 94/33/EC), consumer protection (e.g. Directive 88/378/EEC), and cross-national divorce (Regulation 2201/2003) there is little EU legislation that constitutes a positive expression of children's autonomy.

Thankfully, there have been some recent constitutional developments to indicate that this may well change in the future. The Charter of Fundamental Rights of the European Union, referred to in the introduction of this chapter, contains a number of explicit references to children's rights and interests, including a dedicated children's rights provision to reflect the aspirations of UNCRC. This Charter – which continues to operate as a free standing statement of the EU's code of human rights – has already acted as an important source of inspiration for the EU institutions in their development of new Community initiatives. Additionally, the recently proposed 'reform Treaty' – which will substantially alter the constitutional framework of the European Union – explicitly recognises the rights contained in the Charter as having the same legal value as the Treaties. These developments represent a more positive endorsement of children's rights which could dramatically extend the ideological, and perhaps even the normative, foundation for future children's rights measures at EU level. Whether this will have any material impact upon the experiences of children remains to be seen, although recent case law and legislation suggest that the EU institutions are more readily alluding to the broader provisions contained in the Charter to ensure that children's rights are upheld and promoted at this level (Drywood, 2007).

Conclusion

The discussion in this chapter has aimed to consider the meaning and scope of EU citizenship and its relevance to children. While EU citizenship differs in many respects from nation-based citizenship (to the extent that it is a formal, legal construct, linked primarily to the exercise of cross-national, intra-EU migration), the two concepts share a number of features: notably, both denote a set of rights and responsibilities, collective membership, and a stake in the economic, political and social life of a community. Moreover, both concepts have been denigrated for favouring public, profit-maximizing activities and for reinforcing relationships of dependency to the detriment of women and children.

Progress has been made at both levels to develop a more positive, inclusive approach to citizenship with important consequences for law and policy affecting children. At EU level progress has been driven by judicial ingenuity. However, in spite of the Court's success in extricating (albeit to a limited degree) EU citizenship from traditional, adult-oriented notions of economic contribution and dependency, its association with free movement inevitably limits the status to EU nationals who are in a position to migrate between the Member States. Children's access to EU citizenship, therefore, is only triggered by their parents' decision to move, and will only be upheld for as long as their parents remain economically active or self-sufficient in the host state. As such, it is clear that achieving a more extensive and meaningful endorsement of children's rights at EU level demands a broader rights-based approach; one that takes us beyond the confines of EU citizenship, and looks instead to the possibilities presented by the Charter and other human rights instruments. This approach, coupled with the typically activist approach of the ECJ could make an important contribution to the children's rights campaign, challenging deeply embedded cultural attitudes towards children and childhood and substantiating children's citizenship status in a manner that extends far beyond nation-based and EU formulations of citizenship.

References

Ackers, L. (1998) *Shifting Spaces: Women, Citizenship and Migration within the European Union*. Bristol: Policy Press.

Ackers, L. and Stalford, H. (2004) *A Community for Children?: Children, Citizenship and Internal Migration in the European Union*. Aldershot: Ashgate.

Barnard, C. (2005) 'EU citizenship and the principle of solidarity', in E. Spaventa and M. Dougan (eds) *Social Welfare and EU Law*, Oxford: Hart, pp. 157–80.

Castro Oliveira, A. (2002) 'Workers and other persons: step-by-step from movement to citizenship – Case Law 1995–2001', *Common Market Law Review*, 39: 77–127.

Cullen, H. (2004) 'Children's rights', in S. Peers and A. Ward (eds) *The European Charter of Fundamental Rights*, Oxford: Hart.

Dougan, M. and Spaventa, E. (2003) 'Educating Rudy and the (non-)English patient: a double-bill on Residency Rights under Article 18 EC', *European Law Review*, 28(5): 699–712.

Dougan, M. and Spaventa, E. (2005) 'Wish you weren't here . . . new models of social solidarity in the European Union', in E. Spaventa and M. Dougan (eds) *Social Welfare and EU Law*, Oxford: Hart.

Drywood, E. (2007) 'Children's rights and the family reunification directive', *European Law Review*, 32(3): 396–407.

Forder, C. (2005) 'Family rights and immigration law: a European perspective', in H. Schneide (ed.) *Migration, Integration and Citizenship: A Challenge for Europe's Future*, Maastricht: Forum.

Fries, S. and Shaw, J. (1998) 'Citizenship of the Union: First Steps in the European Court of Justice', *European Public Law*, 4(4): 533–59.

Harris, N. (2000) 'The welfare state, social security and social citizenship rights', in Harris, N. (ed) *Social Security Law in Context*, Oxford: Oxford University Press.

Jones, G. and Wallace, C. (1992) *Youth, Family and Citizenship*. Buckingham: Open University Press.

Jordan, E. (2001) 'From interdependence, to dependence and independence: home and school learning for traveller children', *Childhood*, 8(1): 57–74.

Lansdown, G. (2002) *Challenging Discrimination against Children in the European Union*. Brussels: EURONET.

Lister, R. (1997) *Citizenship: Feminist Perspectives*. New York: Macmillan.

Marshall, T.H. (1950) *Citizenship and Social Class*. Cambridge: Cambridge University Press.

McGlynn, C. (2002) 'Rights for children?: the potential impact of the European Union Charter of Fundamental Rights', *European Public Law*, 8: 387–400.

Moosa-Mitha, M. (2005) 'A Difference-centred alternative to theorization of children's citizenship rights', *Citizenship Studies*, 9(4): 369–88.

Moss, P. and Petrie, P. (2002) *From Children's Services to Children's Spaces*. London: Routledge.

Neale, B. (2002) 'Dialogues with children: children, divorce and citizenship', *Childhood*, 9(4): 455–75.

Neale, B. (ed.) (2004) *Young Children's Citizenship: Ideas into Practice*. York: Joseph Rowntree Foundation.

Oldfield, M. (1998) 'Citizenship and community: civic republicanism and the modern world', in G. Shafir (ed.) *The Citizenship Debate*, Minneapolis, MN: University of Minnesota Press.

O'Leary, S. (1999) 'Putting flesh on the bones of European Union citizenship', *European Law Review*, 24: 68–79.

Pateman, C. (1992) 'Equality, difference, subordination: the politics of motherhood and women's citizenship,' in G. Bock and S. James (eds) *Beyond Equality and Difference: Citizenship, Feminist Politics and Female Subjectivity*, London: Routledge.

Ruxton, S. (2006) *What about Us? Children's Rights in the European Union: Next Steps*. Brussels: EURONET.

Sawyer, C. (2005) 'Citizenship is not enough: the rights of the children of foreign parents', *Family Law*, 35: 224.

Stalford, H. (2005) 'Constitutionalising equality in the European Union: a children's rights perspective', *International Journal of Discrimination and the Law*, 8: 53–73.

Van der Mei, A.P. (2003) *Free Movement of Persons within the European Community: Cross-Border Access to Public Benefits*. Oxford: Hart.

Walby, S. (1997) *Gender Transformations*. Routledge: London.

Weiler, J.H.H. (1998) 'Introduction: European citizenship – identity and differentity', in M. La Torre, *European Citizenship – An Institutional Challenge*, London: Kluwer Law International.

14

Devolution and the Language of Children's Rights in the UK

Samantha Clutton

Introduction

The UK devolution process has facilitated some notable areas of policy divergence between the nations in spite of the apparent limitations of relatively conservative constitutional change (Sullivan, 2002). One such area is that of policy responses towards children and young people, with the balance between rights and responsibilities tipped in different directions for children growing up in different nations within the UK. Before examining claims of divergence in more depth it is necessary to examine citizenship and the historic relationship between children, young people and citizenship.

Citizenship

Marshall's seminal formulation of citizenship (1950) provides a classic definition of a contested concept. Marshall's theory was rights-based and reflected the relationship between the State and the members of its community at a time of economic confidence and the birth of the post-war welfare state. Under different economic circumstances and through the ideological influence of the political New Right, the balance of citizenship in the UK was altered. Lister has claimed that the New Right 'turned commonly accepted notions of citizenship on their head and exchanged the language of entitlement for that of obligation and responsibility'(1990: 7).

Only two years into New Labour's first administration Dean (1999: 222) contended that 'in spite of New Labour's insistence that vulnerable people will always be protected, the overwhelming implication is that social rights can be conceded only if they are earned, or exceptionally deserved. There are no unconditional rights of citizenship.' New Labour's approach to citizenship is, however, essentially different to that of the New Right in one principal regard. New Labour has an understanding of social exclusion that acknowledges a structural as well as an individual basis of exclusion (Deacon, 2003). New Labour offers additional help in the form of new opportunities to individuals who have been structurally disadvantaged so that they may fulfil the obligations of citizenship.

The responsibility of the individual, is then, to take advantage of the new opportunities offered to them and sanctions are associated with non compliance so that those 'who play by the rules' do not 'see their opportunities blighted by those who don't' (Blair, 2004).

The modern social contract of citizenship has been interpreted in different ways over the period since the post-war settlement as a result of economic, social and political change. There has been a movement from the rights-based approach presented by Marshall to a form of conditional citizenship associated with a clear set of responsibilities. Throughout this period the relationship between citizenship and children and young people has been shaped by their inability to fulfil the changing obligations of citizenship in order to claim the status as of right.

Children, Young People and Citizenship

Following on from Lister (1990), Jones and Wallace (1992) have criticized the failure of Marshall's account to consider the dimensions of gender, ethnicity or age as a basis of differential access to the rights of citizenship. They argue that 'Full participation (rights and access to them) in society is, as Marshall (1950) indicated, dependent on personal resources and position in the social structure; and thus, following Lister (1990), also depends on the achievement of economic independence: this applies to young people of both sexes' (1992: 21). Instead, children and young people must claim 'citizenship by proxy', that is through their membership of a family unit.

Children and young people have been described by Marshall (1950) and others as 'citizens in making' (Lister, 2005). This relationship of deferred citizenship is illustrated well through the residualization of State support for those under 25 years of age (Stewart and Stewart, 1988; Coles, 1995; Finch, 1996). Social policy responses to rising youth unemployment in the 1980s served to foster the continued dependence of young people on their families and reduce reliance on the State. Eligibility to certain social security benefits was removed or restricted for those under 25 years of age, a presumption was made that those young people who were unable to support themselves could and should be supported by their families (Wallace, 1988). The presentation of children and young people as 'citizens in making' who must claim citizenship 'by proxy' through family membership until they can fulfil the obligations of citizenship and claim the status in full seems at face value to provide a neat solution. Children and young people belong to families who can fulfil these obligations in order that they and their children may enjoy the rights associated with that status. At the same time the State ensures that the basic rights of children within families are met through legislation that serves to protect the welfare of the child and provide for public intrusion into the private sphere of family where it is in 'the best interests of the child' (e.g. through the Children Act 1989).

The way in which protection and welfare have been provided to children and young people has historically seen them presented as 'objects of intervention rather than legal subjects' (Hill and Tisdall, 1999). The Children Act 1989 signified 'a shift away for the objectification of children in policy and the law' and set out parental responsibilities towards them as persons to whom duties were owed, rather than possessions over which power can be exercised (Such and Walker, 2005: 41). However, it remains true that children and young people have little influence over the choice of persons who determine the conditions under which they must live and grow (Flekkoy, 1995).

However, the presentation of children and young people as 'citizens in making' who must claim citizenship 'by proxy' is problematic. First, children and young people may be born into families who are unable to fulfil the obligations of citizenship on their behalf. Lister (1990) examined the ways in which the poor were excluded from full citizenship as the costs of participation increased whilst opportunities to meet these costs were restricted by structural factors. Latest figures suggest that New Labour's pledge to end child poverty by the year 2020 will not be met, although there has been a reduction in numbers with around one in four children and young people now living in poverty in the UK (a reduction from a figure of one in three) (End Child Poverty, 2006).

Children living in poor households are at increased risk of poor educational outcomes, increased risk of unemployment, poor heath and low income in adulthood (Adleman et al., 2003, Ridge, 2004; Welsh Assembly Government, 2004a; Bradshaw and Mayhew, 2005). Children and young people living in poor households are clearly disadvantaged in claiming citizenship 'by proxy' through family membership. New Labour's solution to the social exclusion of the poor is to offer new opportunities. However, if people 'do not take the opportunities that New Labour will create they will have excluded themselves and their children' (Deacon, 2003: 134). Children and young people fail by association where they are born to families who do not satisfy the demands of the modern social contract of citizenship. For these children and young people claims of citizenship 'by proxy' are meaningless.

Some children and young people grow up in families that cannot meet their needs or who fail to provide them with protection. In these cases the State intervenes and children and young people may be removed from their families and placed into public care. Looked after children are more likely to become young householders, to be homeless, to have poor educational outcomes, to have low levels of post-16 education, to be sexually exploited and to be unemployed than their peers (Stein, 2004). The Children (Leaving Care) Act 2000 put in place procedures to improve outcomes for looked after children but the impact of these procedures have yet to be fully realized. Children in public care cannot claim citizenship 'by proxy' through family membership and the evidence suggests that the State as corporate parent does not provide an alternative avenue to the rights of citizenship for those children in its care.

Presumptions about the operation of a form of citizenship 'by proxy' for young people up to the age of 25 years support a policy framework based on an assumption about the nature of families and the levels of support they can offer. Assumptions that particular types of responsibility are normal in families are essentially flawed (Finch, 1996) and the case for this argument is strongly made by Gill Jones elsewhere in this volume. Where policy responses are built on assumptions about family obligations, which cannot be enforced by private or public law the result is that: ' "Holes" occur where a void is left in provision of needed care, support or financial maintenance because State assistance is withheld on the assumption of family obligations which cannot be enforced' (Fox Harding, 1996: 223). One of the consequences of this barrier to citizenship 'by proxy' is persistently high levels of youth homelessness (Jones, 2002).

The evidence suggests that the presentation of children and young people as 'citizens in making' who must claim citizenship 'by proxy' serves to exclude those children and young people who grow up in marginalized families or who are removed or expelled from family units. Children and young people must be able to claim the status of citizenship in their own right in order to access the social rights that support positive childhoods and good outcomes. This is not to claim that children and young people are in a position to meet the full demands of the social contract of citizenship or to deny that they must also be the subjects of our protection. However, we need to recognize and acknowledge a broader set of criteria for satisfying the demands of citizenship.

There is a case then, for children and young people to be accepted as full members of our community or citizens so that they may access the rights that will support them in realizing their potential. The other half of the citizenship equation is of course responsibility and it can be argued that for example participation in education is a responsibility as well as a right. Extending and enforcing responsibility has been a driving force of policy emerging from Westminster under New Labour, an approach most recently served up in the 'Respect' agenda action plan (2006). Children and young people have been the focus of much of this agenda. Measures introduced under various pieces of criminal justice legislation have served 'to draw greater numbers of younger, less problematic, children and young people into the youth justice system, (and) to subject them to modes of correctional intervention which have not been shown to be particularly effective' (Pitts, 2000: 169). Those 'policies which ignore the social and economic realities in which children find themselves, while promoting greater equality and justice within formal systems of control, may not only ignore but compound the structural and material inequalities which have been historically associated with criminal behavior' (Asquith, 2002: 282). Those children and young people identified earlier as in situations which deny them citizenship 'by proxy' are the same children and young people who find themselves under the greatest scrutiny by these new systems of social control. In other words, those children and young people least able to access and exercise social rights are those most likely to be called to account as responsible members of society.

Strategic Frameworks for Children and Young People's Services

This decade has seen the emergence of strategic frameworks which set out the ways in which the needs of children and young people should be met and the avenues through which their potential can best be realized. In March 2000 the *Report of the Policy Action Team 12: Young People* was published by the UK Social Exclusion Unit. The report recognized young people as social actors negotiating multiple socio and economic factors in their 'career' to adulthood and in so doing set out the structural causes of social exclusion that needed to be addressed (Banks et al., 1992). The report acted as a policy driver for the development of strategic frameworks to promote positive outcomes for children and young people across the UK.

The devolution process has resulted in the development of four distinct approaches across the nations of the UK.

England

In 2001, a strategic document was published by the short lived Children and Young People's Unit in England which promised to provide young people with the opportunities to reach their full potential (CYPU, 2001). A Green Paper *Every Child Matters* was published in 2003 (DfES, 2003), this was followed by *Every Child Matters: Next Steps* in 2004 (DfES, 2004). Most recently *Every Child Matters: Change for Children* provides an English framework to 'build services around children and young people so that we maximize opportunities and minimize risk' (DfES, 2004: 2). The strategy sets out five outcomes for children and young people: being healthy; staying safe; enjoying and achieving; making a positive contribution; and achieving economic well-being (DfES, 2004: 4).

In defining what the five outcomes mean, the UK Government has identified for England 25 specific aims for children and young people and the support needed from parents, carers and families in order to achieve those aims. Over half of these aims are presented in terms of the responsibilities of the child, for example to 'engage in decision making and support the community and environment' or to 'develop enterprising behaviour'. At the same time the primary role and responsibilities of families towards their children are clearly stated. Any discussion of the rights of the child, of children's citizenship or reference to the United Nations Convention on the Rights of the Child (UNCRC) is conspicuous by its absence within *Every Child Matters*.

A Green Paper, *Youth Matters* was published for consultation in 2005 (DfES, 2005). The Green Paper set out a vision to help all teenagers achieve the five *Every Child Matters* outcomes and is examined in detail by Piper within this volume. The approach is based on six underpinning principles which are largely focused on service delivery and improved outcomes. However, one of the underpinning principles is 'balancing greater opportunities and support with promoting young people's responsibilities'

(DfES, 2005: 4). A reference to 'Young People as Citizens' is included but this is concerned with the ways in which young people can make a contribution as active citizens within their communities rather than with an understanding of young people as the bearers of rights. Following the consultation period *Youth Matter: Next Steps, Something to Do, Somewhere to Go, Someone to Talk to,* was published in 2006. This provides a 'vision to transform the lives of very young person through a radical reshaping of provision' (DfES, 2006: 2).

Every Child Matters (DfES, 2004), *Youth Matters* (DfES, 2005) *and Youth Matters: Next Steps* (DfES, 2006) are primarily documents about delivery and outcomes. They are also clear in stating the responsibilities of children, young people and their families in relation to the opportunities offered to them. It is clear that for Westminster the rights children enjoy reflect the duties they owe and the idea of children as citizens is given no credence.

Scotland

The Scottish Executive published *For Scotland's Children: Better Integrated Children's Services* (2001) which is guided by the principles of social justice and focuses on the reduction of inequalities and focuses on service delivery. The strategy states that the Executive is committed to 'A Scotland in which every child matters, where every child regardless of their family background, has the best possible start in life'. The 2001 strategy includes reference to UNCRC. There is a presumption that the UK ratification of the UNCRC is in itself an indication that 'a view of the child as a citizen with rights is being actively promoted and implemented by Government and by service providers across sectors' (Scottish Executive, 2001: 19). The strategy also identifies legislation and policy – in particular the Children (Scotland) Act 1995 – which are said to evidence that 'the importance of the welfare and rights of children and young people' are 'well reflected in the polices and structures which have emerged in recent years' (2001: 44). More recently Scottish Ministers have agreed a high-level vision for the children and young people of Scotland: 'in order to become confident individuals, effective contributors, successful learners and responsible citizens, *all* Scotland's children need to be: safe, nurtured, healthy, achieving, active, included, respected and responsible' (Scottish Executive, 2006). Rather than presenting a 'view of the child as a citizen with rights' (Scottish Executive, 2001) the latest vision statement appears to support a presentation of children as 'citizens in the making'.

Northern Ireland

The Children and Young People's Unit , Northern Ireland, published a *Consultation Draft Strategy for Children and Young People in Northern Ireland* in 2004 (CYPU, OFMDFMNI, 2004). The 2004 draft Strategy adopted a rights-based whole-child approach and was built directly on the articles of the UNCRC. It was not clear on how the articles of the UNCRC would be delivered in the Northern Irish context. More recently a strategy has been produced which draws form but is distinct from the consultation document. Published by the Office of the First Minister and Deputy First Minister, Northern Ireland *Our Children and Young People-Our Pledge* (OFMDFMNI, 2006) is a 10-year strategy which is outcomes-driven. Targets are set towards a set of outcomes which will mean that children in Northern Ireland are: healthy; enjoying, learning and achieving; living in safety and with stability; experiencing economic and environmental well-bring; contributing positively to community and society; and living in a society which respects their rights (OFMDFMNI, 2006: 7). The strategy presents respect of the rights of the child as a key outcome, so that child whose rights are respected 'should achieve in the other five outcomes' (OFMDFMNI, 2006: 9). Conversely there is a claim that delivery of the other five outcomes will evidence that the rights of the child have been respected. The strategy includes the 'pledge' that 'we are committed to respecting and progressing the rights of children and young people in Northern Ireland and will be guided and informed by the UNCRC' (OFMDFMNI, 2006: 23). The Northern Ireland approach recognizes children and young people as the bearers of rights and is guided by the UNCRC. A set of rights are not explicitly set out in relation to children and young people. The strategy is based on an outcomes model and the approach relies on the satisfaction of children's rights through the realization of identified outcomes.

Wales

The National Assembly for Wales turned its attention to youth policy early in the devolution process with the publication of *Extending Entitlement: Supporting Young People in Wales* a report by the Policy Unit. This document provided the basis of evidence to support the development of a strategy. In 2000, *Children and Young People a Framework for Partnership* was published by the Welsh Assembly Government (WAG, 2000). The Assembly Government stated that they had adopted the UNCRC as the basis of all their work with children and young people in Wales and that they had translated this commitment into seven core aims for all children and young people. This framework set out the ways in which local author-ities and their partners would be expected to deliver on the seven core aims. The strategy is heavily laden with the language of entitlement. Within guidance published to support the delivery of the strategy an 'Early Entitlement' is set out for all children aged 0–10 years. The guidance (WAG, 2002a: 3) states that every child in Wales has an entitlement to a set of seven entitlements including for example the right to '*Enjoy the best possible physical and mental, social and emotional health, including freedom from abuse, victimization and exploitation*'.

Guidance in relation to Section 123 of the Learning and Skills Act 2000 sets out '*Extending Entitlement*' for all young people in Wales aged 11–25 years. This provides guidance in relation to the delivery of the 'the universal entitlement', comprising 10 basic entitlements. These include for example the 'right to be consulted, to participate in decision-making and to be heard, on all matters which concern them or have an impact on their lives'. The guidance states that the universal entitlement is to be delivered in an environment where there is 'a positive focus on achievement overall and what young people have to contribute; a focus on building young people's capacity to become independent, make choices and participate in the democratic process; and celebration of young people's successes' (WAG, 2002b: 10).

A later publication, *Children and Young People: Rights to Action* (WAG, 2004b) sets out the ways in which the Assembly Government were delivering on their commitments to children and young people. The Children Act 2004 provides the statutory framework for the delivery of these strategies.

Through the language of entitlement children and young people have been presented as rights bearers in Wales. The UK's Second Report to the UN Committee on the Rights of the Child was considered in September 2002 and made three specific responses to Wales welcoming that the UNCRC has been used for the Strategy for Children and Young People developed by Welsh Assembly Government; the establishment of an independent Children's' Commissioner for Wales (the first in the UK); and the adoption of the Assembly of regulations prohibiting corporal punishment in all forms of day-care, including child minding.

The adoption of the UNCRC in Wales and the presentation of a strategy which is based on a set of identified entitlements for all children and young people in Wales sets this approach apart from those taken elsewhere in the UK.

Conclusion

Some advocates of devolution argued that the process would allow for Scotland and Wales to pursue a more progressive policy agenda based on a traditionally collectivist value position in relation to social problems (Adams and Robinson, 2002). Others have argued that since devolution policy developments in Wales reflect a specifically Welsh set of solutions which 'apply a set of values which have a traditional resonance in Wales', and values which 'link individual progress and life chances to collective effort and action' (Drakeford, 2001). There is evidence in other policy areas, most notably health, that although 'the Welsh settlement is constitutionally the weakest of the devolved administrations . . . policy differentiation from the English model is most obvious' (Sullivan, 2002). The Welsh Assembly Government's First Minister, Rhodri Morgan, has claimed that the Welsh approach is informed by a commitment to delivering 'a set of rights, which are, as far as possible: free at point of use; universal and unconditional' (Morgan, 2002: 3).

The devolution process has facilitated policy divergence between the nations of the UK. Policy in relation to children and young people provides a clear example of such divergence. The English strategy is, I would argue, strongly shaped by an understanding of children and young people as the subjects of protection who will be offered opportunities to fulfil their potential dependent on their ability to fulfil the responsibilities which are expected of them. Until they can reach economic independence children and young people in England are to claim 'citizenship by proxy' through their membership of a family unit. In Scotland, the importance of the welfare and rights of children and young people are acknowledged. However, the Scottish Executive's 'high level vision' for children and young people in Scotland appears to present an understanding of them as 'citizens in the making'. Within Northern Ireland, there is a commitment to respecting and progressing the rights of children and young people. However, the rights-based approach in Northern Irish strategy is based on an outcomes model, reliant upon the satisfaction of children's rights through the realization of identified outcomes. In other words children's rights are not presented in terms of the entitlements we associate with a citizenship model, but rather as the byproduct of good provision in the interests of the child's needs. The Welsh strategy provides children and young people with a set of entitlements and in so doing presents them as rights bearers. This is not shaped clearly in terms of children's citizenship. However, the language of universal entitlements for all children and young people in Wales provides an avenue to citizenship to Welsh children and young people in their own right.

The strategies examined here are still relatively recent in policy terms and it is the implementation rather than the rhetoric of the policies that ultimately impact on the lives of children and young people. A recent report published by Save the Children on behalf of the NGO UNCRC Monitoring Group in Wales comments on the reality of children's rights in Wales (Williams et al., 2006). The report acknowledges that the Welsh Assembly has made considerable progress on delivering the general measures of UNCRC implementation, but is also clear that much work still needs to be done in delivering the entitlements owed to children and young people in Wales. For now, the everyday lives of children and young people across the UK are still shaped by social inequalities and family background. However, the presentation of children and young people as rights bearers within the modern social contract of citizenship is an essential first step in the journey towards better childhoods and outcomes for all children and young people.

References

Adams, J. and Robinson, P. (2002) 'Divergence and the centre', in J. Adams and P. Robinson, *Devolution in Practice: Public Policy Differences within the UK*, London: IPPR, pp. 198–224.

Adelman, L., Middelton, S. and Ashworth, K. (2003) *Britain's Poorest Children: Severe and Persistent Poverty and Social Exclusion.* London: Save the Children.

Asquith, S. (2002) 'Justice, retribution and children', in J. Muncie, G. Hughes and E. McLaughlin (eds) *Youth Justice Criminal Readings*, London: Sage, pp. 275–83.

Banks, M., Bates, I., Breakwell, G., Bynner, J., Emler, N., Jamieson, L. and Roberts, K. (1992) *Careers and Identities.* Buckingham: Open University Press.

Blair, T. (2004) 'The Opportunity Society', Speech delivered at the Labour Party Conference, Brighton Centre, 28 September 2004.

Bradshaw, J. and Mayhew, E. (eds) (2005) *The Well-being of Children in the United Kingdom*. London: Save the Children.

Cabinet Office (2006) *Reaching Out: An Action Plan on Social Exclusion*. London: Cabinet Office.

Children and Young People's Unit (CYPU) (2001) *Tomorrow's Future: Building a Strategy for Children and Young People*. London: CYPU.

Children and Young People's Unit (CYPU, NI) (2004) *Making It R Wrld 2: Consultation on a Draft Strategy for Children and Young People in Northern Ireland*. Belfast: Office of the First Minister and Deputy First Minister.

Coles, B. (1995) *Youth and Social Policy: Youth Citizenship and Young Careers*. London: UCL Press.

Deacon, A. (2003) 'Leveling the playing field, activating players': New Labour and 'the cycle of disadvantage', *Policy & Politics*, 31(2): 123–37.

Dean, H. (1999) 'Citizenship', in M. Powell (ed.) *New Labour, New Welfare State?* London: Policy Press, pp. 213–33.

Department for Education and Skills (2003) *Every Child Matters*. London: DfES.

Department for Education and Skills (2004) *Every Child Matters: Change for Children*. London: DfES.

Department for Education and Skills (2004) *Every Child Matters: Next Steps*. London: DfES.

Department for Education and Skills (2005) *Youth Matters*. London: DfES.

Department for Education and Skills (2006) *Youth Matters: Next Steps, Something to Do, Somewhere to Go, Someone to Talk to*. London: DfES.

Drakeford, M. (2001) 'Co-ordinating polices and powers to reduce social exclusion: the Welsh approach to Credit Union development', *Wales Law Journal*, 1(3): 246–55.

End Child Poverty (2006) *Unequal Choices: Voices of Experience Exposing Challenges and Suggesting Solutions to Ending Child Poverty in the UK*. York: Joseph Rowntree Foundation.

Finch, J. (1996) 'Family responsibilities and rights', in M. Bulmer and A. Rees (eds) *Citizenship Today: The Contemporary Relevance of T.H. Marshall*, London: UCL Press, pp. 193–208.

Flekkoy, M. (1995) 'The Scandinavian experiences of children's rights', in B. Franklin (ed.) *The Handbook of Children's Rights: Comparative Policy and Practice*, London: Routledge, pp. 3–22.

Fox Harding, L. (1996) *Family, State and Social Policy*. Basingstoke: Macmillan.

Hill, M. and Tisdall, K. (1999) *Children and Society*. Harlow: Longman.

Jones, A. (2002) 'Homeless Children', in J. Bradshaw (ed.) *The Well-being of Children in the UK*, London: Save the Children, pp. 215–30.

Jones, G. and Wallace, C. (1992) *Youth, Family and Citizenship*. Buckingham: Open University Press.

Lister, R. (1990) *The Exclusive Society: Citizenship and the Poor*. London: Child Poverty Action Group.

Lister, R. (2005) 'Children and Citizenship', Paper presented at a Glasgow Centre for the Child and Society Seminar, 3 November 2005.

Marshall, T.H. (1950) *Citizenship and Social Class and Other Essays*. Cambridge: Cambridge University Press.

Morgan, R. (2002) Speech by the First Minister, National Assembly for Wales, Annual Lecture of the National Centre for Public Policy, University of Wales, Swansea.

Office of the First Minister and Deputy First Minister (OMFDFMNI) Northern Ireland (2006) *Our Children and Young People-Our Pledge*. Belfast: OFMDFMNI.

Pitts, J. (2000) 'The new youth justice and the politics of electoral anxiety', in B. Goldstone (ed.) *The New Youth Justice*, Lyme Regis: Russel House Publishing.

Ridge, T. (2004) *Child Poverty and Social Exclusion: From a Child's Perspective*. London: Policy Press.

Scottish Executive (2001) *For Scotland's Children: Better Integrated Children's Services*. Edinburgh: Scottish Executive.

Scottish Executive (2006) *Improving Outcomes for Children and Young People*, published on the web www.scotland.gov.uk/Publications/2006/02/03143159/0, last accessed 2 June 2007.

Social Exclusion Unit (2000) *Report of Policy Action Team 12: Young People*. London: SEU.

Stein, M. (2004) *What Works in Leaving Care?* Barkingside: Barnardo's.

Stewart, G. and Stewart, J. (1988) 'Targeting youth or how the state obstructs young peoples' independence', *Youth and Policy*, (25): 19–24.

Such, E. and Walker, R. (2005) 'Young citizens or policy objects? Children in the "rights and responsibilities" debate', *Journal of Social Policy*, 34(1): 39–57.

Sullivan, M. (2002) 'Health policy, differentiation and devolution', in J. Adams and P. Robinson (eds) *Devolution in Practice: Public Policy Differences within the UK*, London: IPP, pp. 60–6.

Wallace, C. (1988) 'Between the family and the state: young people in transition', *Youth and Policy*, (25): 25–36.

Welsh Assembly Government (2000) *Children and Young People a Framework for Partnership*. Cardiff: WAG.

Welsh Assembly Government (2002a) *Children and Young People a Framework for Partnership: Early Entitlement*. Cardiff: WAG.

Welsh Assembly Government (2002b) *Children and Young People a Framework for Partnership: Extending Entitlement, Section 123 of the Learning and Skills Act, 2000*. Cardiff: WAG.

Welsh Assembly Government (2004a) *Report of the Child Poverty Task Group*. Cardiff: WAG.

Welsh Assembly Government (2004b) *Children and Young People: Rights to Action*. Cardiff: WAG.

Williams, J., Crowley, R. and Croke, R. (2006) 'General measures of implementation', in R. Croke and A. Crowley (eds) *Righting the Wrongs: The Reality of Children's Rights in Wales*, Cardiff: Wales Programme of Save the Children.

15

Institutional Support for the UNCRC's 'Citizen Child'

Jane Williams and Rhian Croke

Introduction: Citizenship, Children's Citizenship and the Problem of Differential Capacity

Earlier chapters in this volume have illustrated both that the concept of citizenship is contextualized and contested and that any attempt to extend it to children introduces further layers of complexity. Lister, drawing on Marshall to identify the meaning of citizenship within the context of the UK, describes it in terms of membership of a community, with rights and duties attached, equality of status and participation. Stalford, examining the EU concept of citizenship, refers to a set of rights and responsibilities underpinned by an ethic of equality, participation and inclusion. Liebel and Lockyer demonstrate the implications of the underlying conceptual differences between civic republican and liberal accounts of citizenship and of whether (and how) it is constructed 'from above' or 'from below'. All recognize, however, that differences in the developmental capacity of children, whether actual or constructed, give rise to questions about the extension to them of certain aspects of citizenship, especially those characterized as 'participative'.

The United Nations Convention on the Rights of the Child (UNCRC) promotes the right of children to participate in decisions affecting them but at the same time circumscribes the extent to which this may be permitted in practice by reference to their evolving capacity (most obviously, Articles 12 and 5). Accordingly it is tempting to characterize the UNCRC as consistent with a version of children's citizenship as 'partial' or 'incremental'. At a conceptual level, this sits uncomfortably with the principles of equality and inclusion, implying a lesser status for the merely immanent citizen. The UNCRC makes a claim for children to possess and enjoy a range of rights *in their own right*, rather than simply as collateral beneficiaries of claims made by adults. Superficially, it therefore militates against children holding citizen rights only 'by proxy' (Jones; Clutton in this volume). On the other hand, with its acknowledgement of evolving capacity and the role of adult carers and kinship groups, it may be interpreted as reinforcing a view of the child as a rights holder who is at best 'lesser amongst equals'. The value of equality of status is thereby undermined by the problem of differential capacity. As Milne (this volume) demonstrates, the UNCRC was not designed as a charter for children's citizenship. Nonetheless it is seen by the UN Committee on the rights of the child (hereafter, 'the Committee') as providing 'confirmation of the equal status of children as subjects of rights' (UNCRC, 2003: para 66) and provides important if incomplete support for an emergent concept of 'Citizen Child' (Doek, Foreword to this volume).

In this chapter, we draw a rather loose analogy with the legal concept of trusteeship as a possible means of reconciling the issue of differential capacity and the principle of equality in the context of the UNCRC, and consider the role of processes associated with the UNCRC in enforcing the 'trust' we suggest is implied by it.

The 'Trust' Implicit in the UNCRC

In Anglo-Welsh law, a distinction is made between status and capacity. Many rights are conferred and obligations imposed on persons irrespective of their age, but a distinction is made, at the point of exercise of the right or obligation, between those possessing and those lacking capacity. Thus an infant who inherits property is the owner of that property but is prevented from dealing with it until reaching the legal age of majority. In this situation, law provides the device of a 'trust', whereby a person having legal capacity (the trustee) holds the property on behalf of the child (the beneficiary) and must manage it in a way which is consistent with the child's eventual entitlement. This device provides both a concept and a process (potential legal action) to prevent elision of the rights of the beneficiary and those of the trustee. Applying this by way of analogy to the UNCRC, parents, kinship groups and the State may be seen as the trustees of such rights as an individual child is unable, through lack of capacity, to exercise independently. At the same time these 'trustees' are required to support the development of the child's capacity. The separate rights of children must be properly represented in all matters affecting them, whether at collective or individual level, and evolving capacity determines only how, not whether, this occurs (Articles 3, 12). In this analysis, the mechanisms for representing the position of children are of critical importance.

Unlike infant beneficiaries of a real trust, the UNCRC's 'child citizens' have no recourse to individual legal enforcement of their entitlement. Instead, there is the monitoring and reporting process. States parties are obliged to submit detailed reports to the Committee within two years of ratification and thereafter every five years. The monitoring process keeps a check on the State as 'principal trustee', but the consequences of any breach of its obligations are limited to the inconvenience of public criticism in an international forum. The effectiveness of the process thus depends very much on how it can be internalized in domestic law and policy and used to effect change. The idea is that ongoing dialogue between State Party and the Committee, in which criticism is supported by constructive advice, will encourage governments to make efforts between reporting sessions better to implement the Convention.

The Committee requires that the State Party report gives concrete information about progress achieved, provides reliable data and statistics, disaggregated by age, gender, ethnic origin, and so forth, and is self-critical, identifying shortcomings and proposing measures to be taken to improve the implementation record. On receiving the State Party and alternative reports the Committee holds oral hearings. On the basis of all the evidence presented, the Committee then has an opportunity to interrogate the government on its progress on implementation. The Committee's subsequent Concluding Observations to the State Party indicate areas of concern, factors and difficulties impeding implementation of the UNCRC and recommendations for future action (UNCRC, 2005).

The Concluding Observations are the starting point for the next reporting phase. They can be used to set priorities and mobilize partners at national and local levels, to exert pressure on the government to act on the Committee's recommendations and to lobby for changes in legislation and practice (Theytaz-Bergman, 2005). In this process, national and sub-national non-governmental structures play a crucial role.

The Role of Non-Governmental Structures

Two such structures are considered here: Children's Commissioners and coalitions of non-governmental organizations (NGOs), drawing respectively on experience in the UK and Wales. Although not expressly mentioned in the text of the UNCRC, children's commissioners are seen by the Committee as institutions that can represent children individually and collectively, lobby for policy and legislative change, raise awareness of children's rights and generally promote implementation of the Convention (UNCRC, 2002: para 19; UNCRC, 2003: paras 9 and 65). The Committee's encouragement, bolstered by the endorsement of other international bodies, has influenced the rapid emergence of a number of such offices, including the UK's four Children's Commissioners (Williams, 2005). NGOs, on the other hand, have always had a recognized role in the Convention process: as noted by Milne (this volume), they played an important part in the negotiation of the text even before the Convention was adopted. Both NGOs and children's commissioners are 'competent bodies' for the purposes of Article 45 (a) of the UNCRC and this has acted as a catalyst for collaboration between them to prepare alternative reports to the Committee. As a result there has been a dramatic increase in the number of national coalitions for children's rights globally (NGO/CRC, 2004).

Children's Commissioners

Amongst the offices so far established around the world, there are many variations as to the precise remit of a Children's Commissioner.

The European Network of Ombudspersons for Children compiled the following list, noting that not all the offices have all the functions and that in particular there is considerable variation as to whether they deal with individual cases and complaints from children:

- promotion of full implementation of the UNCRC;
- promotion of a higher priority for children, in central, regional or local government and in civil society, and to improve public attitudes to children;
- influencing law, policy and practice, both by responding to governmental and other proposals and by actively proposing changes;
- promoting effective coordination of government for children at all levels;
- promoting effective use of resources for children;
- providing a channel for children's views, and encouraging government and the public to give proper respect to children's views;
- collecting and publishing data on the situation of children and/or encouraging government to collect and publish adequate data;
- promotion of awareness of the human rights of children among children and adults;
- conducting investigations and undertaking and encouraging research;
- reviewing children's access to, and the effectiveness of, all forms of advocacy including children's access to the courts;
- responding to individual complaints from children or those representing children, and where appropriate initiating or supporting legal action on behalf of children.

The UK has four Children's Commissioners – one each for Wales, Northern Ireland, Scotland and England, with the English Commissioner also having responsibility for 'non-devolved' matters affecting children throughout the UK. Each has a different statutory framework which reflects the policy priorities of the respective governments and their different approach to UNCRC implementation. Common to the Commissioners for Wales, Scotland and Northern Ireland is that their 'principal aim' includes safeguarding and promoting the rights of children and that they are required to have regard to the UNCRC in exercising their functions. This, we suggest, is sufficient to enable them to play a significant part in monitoring fulfilment of the 'trust' implicit in the UNCRC. They can act on behalf of children collectively and, to the extent permitted in the respective statutory schemes, on behalf of an individual child, in a way that supports the principle of equality of status, whilst acknowledging and compensating for differences in capacity.

An example can be seen in a legal case brought by the Northern Ireland Commissioner: *In the Matter of an Application for Judicial Review by the Northern Ireland Commissioner for Children and Young People of the Decisions Announced by the Minister of State for Criminal Justice, John Spellar* on 10 May 2004 [2004] NIQB 40. The object was the government's proposal to introduce anti-social behaviour legislation similar to that already in force in England and Wales. The Commissioner argued that insufficient time had been allowed for children and young people to be consulted effectively, and that the consultation paper failed to pay sufficient regard to their rights under the UNCRC. The Commissioner lost the case, on the ground that the court would not interfere with the legislature's constitutional sovereignty. However the significance for our purposes was that here the Commissioner acted on behalf of children and young people, challenging government in the courts – as citizens are entitled to do but as child citizens are unlikely to be able to do without structural support of this kind.

The effectiveness of a Children's Commissioner in this role depends critically on two factors: first, the Commissioner's functions must be clearly linked to implementation of the UNCRC as a whole (not merely coinciding with aspects of it) and second, they must be clearly independent of government. On paper, the Commissioners for the three devolved UK areas appear more effective in this sense than the English Commissioner.

Every Child Matters, the Green Paper which paved the way for the Children Act 2004 (which in turn established the English Commissioner), made no mention of the UNCRC or of children's rights. During the parliamentary passage of the Act, the Government rejected amendments which would have given the Convention prominence in the Commissioner's remit. Instead, this Commissioner's role is tied to the five 'aspects of well-being' identified in the Act:

a. physical and mental health and emotional well-being;
b. protection from harm and neglect;
c. education, training and recreation;
d. the contribution made by children to society;
e. social and economic well-being,

in respect of which section 2(1) of the Act provides that the Commissioner has 'the function of promoting awareness of the *views and interests* of children in England' (emphasis added). The sole reference to the Convention comes in section 2(11) which requires the Commissioner, when considering what the 'interests' of children might be, to have regard to the UNCRC. The provision is carefully constructed so that the UNCRC is a mere aid to interpretation, rather than an overarching set of principles.

The English Commissioner's role thus embraces facilitating the hearing of children's voices but is not directly connected to the UNCRC in the same way as that of the other three Commissioners. As Harry Hendrick has said, 'voices and rights are not necessarily co-existent since children's voices may be heard (and ignored) without any formal recognition of their rights in any respect' (2004: 247). Government Ministers' insistence that 'the views of children rather than the rights agenda should drive the commissioner's work' (Hansard, 30 March 2004) serves to illustrate the truth of this proposition, bearing in mind that the 'views of children' to which they referred were views gathered in response to a consultation paper, *Every Child Matters*, which did not mention the UNCRC or children's rights. Furthermore, the English Commissioner is not independent of government, being answerable to a government Minister rather than directly to the elected body as in the case of the other three.

This divergence within the UK may be associated with ideological differences between the devolved governments and the UK government about the relationship of the citizen – of any age – and government (Williams, 2007 and Clutton in this volume). The 2004 Act gives English children a forum in which their voices can be heard – one aspect of citizenship – but does little to further the realization of other 'citizen' rights supported by the UNCRC. The statutory stipulation that the devolved countries' Commissioners have regard to the UNCRC at least establishes a statutory basis for monitoring and promoting the UNCRC in full, consistent with the notion of the 'trust' implicit in the UNCRC. Accordingly they have a clearer legal basis than the English Commissioner on which to fulfil the function of ensuring that governments keep the promises made on ratification of the Convention. In Wales, there is evidence of the Commissioner's influence in policy areas such as child poverty, education and child protection (Rees, 2005; Williams, 2005).

NGO Coalitions

National coalitions are supported by the NGO Group for the UNCRC ('NGO Group'), a coalition of international NGOs originally formed in 1983 during the drafting of the Convention. There is a liaison unit based in Geneva which supports national coalitions participating in the reporting process and undertakes other activities geared to UNCRC implementation. The NGO Group acts as a focal point for the establishment and sustainability of national child rights coalitions across the world and works toward strengthening the link between national NGOs, international NGOs and relevant UN mechanisms.

Within the UK, there is the Children's Rights Alliance for England and the Scottish Alliance for Children's Rights, each of which is a registered charity promoting UNCRC implementation. In Northern Ireland, a coordinating role is carried out by the Children's Law Centre and Save the Children (UK) and in Wales there is the UNCRC Monitoring Group, a national alliance of agencies convened by Save the Children (UK).

Each coalition works to produce the NGO alternative report to the Committee, mobilizing other NGOs and civil society to become involved in the reporting process and seeking to influence national and local government to make legislative, policy and programmatic changes. They seek to develop ways to involve children and young people in the promotion, implementation and monitoring of the Convention. The UK coalitions meet biannually to share information and update each other regarding progress on UNCRC implementation.

The nature of the work carried out by such coalitions and its potential contribution as a mechanism for enforcing the 'trust' implicit in the UNCRC is illustrated below by reference to Wales. Experience elsewhere in the UK and across the globe may produce a more or a less positive picture. In Wales, the Welsh Assembly has made a clear political commitment to UNCRC implementation (NAW, 2001, 2004; WAG 2004 and see Clutton in this volume). This has contributed to the provision of material support for children's participation in the Welsh UNCRC process as well as to an attempt by the Welsh Assembly Government ('WAG'), working with the NGO coalition, the Children's Commissioner's office, local government and other organizations to establish ways of reflecting UNCRC requirements in standards and conditions for public service provision.

The Wales–NGO Coalition

The Wales UNCRC Monitoring Group ('the Group') was established in 2002. NGO submissions had been made to the Committee in the UK's initial and second reporting rounds, but the establishment of the Group reflected a determination to achieve more depth, breadth and impact in the third and subsequent rounds. The Group's membership at the time of writing comprises representatives from Aberystwyth University, Barnardo's Cymru, Cardiff University, Children in Wales, Funky Dragon, Nacro Cymru, NSPCC Cymru, Save the Children (Chair) and Swansea University, with officials from the WAG, the Welsh Local Government Association and the Children's Commissioner for Wales as observers. In 2004 a full-time post, funded by Save the Children UK, was secured to coordinate the Group's work.

A major focus for the Group is the preparation of the Wales NGO report to the Committee, due in 2007. The Group identified contributors from amongst its own members or their respective networks to prepare an interim report. The resultant document therefore represented collaboration by a range of agencies and disciplines. The report, *'Righting the wrongs: the reality of children's rights in Wales'* (Croke and Crowley, 2006) was launched at a public conference in January 2006.

The Conference was addressed by the Chair of the Committee, the WAG Minister for Children, the Children's Commissioner for Wales and two academics. Policymakers, practitioners and academics were invited to attend not only to hear the findings of the report and to learn more about the UNCRC and its application to Wales but also as experts who could contribute to discussion about implementation. It was intended in this way to strengthen the policy advocacy community for children's rights in Wales and to encourage more people to become involved in the monitoring and reporting process. The Conference was well covered in the media. In his concluding address, Peter Clarke, the Children's Commissioner for Wales, remarked:

> It really is one of the things that struck me immediately . . . just how many people have signed up to come here today to talk about children's rights . . . that wouldn't have happened 5 years ago, so there clearly is some sort of cultural shift happening and I just hope that it continues. But it's not just the numbers of people but it's also who you are and where you come from, it seems a lot more diverse agencies are represented here today than again would have been very

likely to have come forward in previous years on an agenda that is so clearly about the United Nations Convention on the Rights of the Child – so that's welcome too. The report itself I think is brilliant, it's one of the best reports I've seen for a long time.

(Save the Children, 2006: 24)

A significant achievement of the Conference was to secure from the WAG Minister for Children a public commitment that she would be personally responsible for Wales' submission to the State Party report. There was also an opportunity for a closed meeting between the Chair of the Committee, the Children's Commissioner for Wales, senior WAG officials and representatives of the Group to discuss the presentation of alternative reports and effective representation of the views of children in the process, bearing in mind the significant time constraints within which the Committee works.

'Righting the wrongs' and the Conference provided a snapshot of the state of children's rights in Wales, gained the attention of government and raised awareness of the UNCRC in Wales. The process of preparing the report and the Conference strengthened the Group and led to expansion in its membership. The Conference report (Save the Children, 2006), together with the *Righting the wrongs* report, informed the developing strategy of the Group.

Interwoven with the Group's work on preparation of the alternative report is the business of seeking to bring about change through discussions with governmental and non-governmental bodies, lobbying for new law and guidance and support for training and awareness-raising. Since devolution in 1999, there has been progress in the development of structures to support children's participation in Wales (Skeels, 2006; Thomas and Skeels, 2006), the establishment of the Children's Commissioner's Office and the development of the WAG's *Rights to Action* strategy with its seven core aims derived from the UNCRC. However, optimal use of the UNCRC to deliver children's citizenship requires further change and further structural support.

The Group has developed an approach to mainstreaming children's rights using the UNCRC general measures of implementation and is represented on the WAG's Children and Young People's reference group. The latter group is tasked with agreeing priority outcomes associated with the seven core aims in *Rights to Action*, together with a selection of indicators to measure achievement. It thus provides an example of the kind of detailed implementation work that Milne (in this volume) argues has been absent at national and sub-national level in the past. In Wales, the work of the reference group is undertaken in the context of implementation of the Children Act 2004, an England and Wales measure which enables greater central prescription for local planning and delivery of children's services. WAG guidance under the 2004 Act promised that the work of the reference group would continue 'in helping to develop shared outcome measures and advising on the need for changes to current indicators that will effectively support partnership working and a rights-based approach to monitoring outcomes' (WAG, 2006: para 7.4). A list of priority outcomes, based on the reference group's work, has since been published (WAG, 2007).

Consistent with the Committee's exhortation (UNCRC, 2003: para 67), the Group has lobbied for a comprehensive strategy to implement Article 42, which requires State Parties to make the UNCRC known by 'appropriate and active means' to adults and children alike. Here too, some progress has been made, building on the Assembly's *Extending Entitlement* direction to local authorities (WAG, 2005). The current focus of the Group's lobbying is on the allocation of sufficient resource for awareness-raising amongst children and young people and for the necessary training for personnel involved in public service delivery.

Other areas identified by the Group as requiring further action, and on which it is actively engaged in discussion with the WAG, are data collection on all areas covered by the UNCRC (there are striking gaps, such as a dearth of information on children's mental health), identification of the proportion of local and national budget expenditure on children, the use of children's rights impact assessments, further improvement in coordination of central and local government structures for planning and delivery of children's services and maximum use of the Assembly's (limited) legislative powers to incorporate UNCRC obligations in the legal frameworks for public service delivery, particularly through the mechanisms provided by the Children Act 2004.

The Wales Children and Young People's Report

The work of the Group described above does not include directly representing children's views either to the Committee or to government. Separate structures exist for this, based on WAG-sponsored young people's assembly for Wales, Funky Dragon.

Following an initial training session given by the Group's coordinator, a young people's steering group was elected from the Funky Dragon Grand Council. This steering group took responsibility for the design and delivery of a participatory research project, funded in part by WAG, in part by the European Social Fund and in small part by national lottery funds, to determine to what extent children and young people in Wales were able to access their rights.

The steering group examined the examples to date of direct input by children into the UNCRC process. The impact of these has been the subject of review elsewhere (Heesterman, 2005). They include Belgium's *'What do you think?'* project to Japan's five essays, Germany's 120,000 questionnaires and India's working children's report. The steering group took the view that none of these had involved young people as actors in the research process to the extent they sought. Rather, they wanted to adopt an approach similar to that which Clark (2004: 160) has described as 'a framework for discussion and interpretation led by children', acknowledging children as competent, active, meaning makers.

At the time of writing the project is ongoing. It involves awareness-raising coupled with participative research, designed and carried out by young people with support from adults in funded posts. In terms of the 'ladder of participation' (Hart, 1992), it appears on target to reach level eight: it is young-people initiated, there is shared decision-making with adults and it aims to empower young people while at the same time enabling them to access and learn from the life experience and expertise of adults.

Aided as described above by the provision of structural support, this project may well promote children's participation in Wales, beyond the UNCRC process itself, by equipping more young people with the rights literacy necessary to hold duty bearers to account and the knowledge to become more active participants in other formal processes. This project demonstrates how the 'UNCRC has given rise to new political possibilities, providing a resource whereby the necessary re-imagining of adult-child relations, which is at the heart of the citizenship debate can take place' (Roche, 2005: 55).

Conclusion

If sense is to be made of the UNCRC's claim for equal status for children as rights holders, mechanisms must be found which can address the problem of differential capacity, prevent elision of the rights of the child and those of relevant adults and support the extension in practice of rights to children who are excluded. Institutions such as Children's Commissioners and NGO coalitions, linked as illustrated here to the UNCRC, may make an important contribution in this regard, given the right conditions of material and political support. The Wales–NGO coalition has been presented here as an example of promising use of the UNCRC process in a context where for the time being those conditions exist. For the most part the developments described here – the increasingly focused NGO activity and the establishment of the four UK Children's Commissioners – have occurred in the current reporting period, and their impact will be tested when the alternative reports from the NGOs, Children's Commissioners and children are submitted. The onus will then pass to the Committee to respond in a way which best facilitates continued work at national and sub-national level. In this way we will see, over time, how effective the UNCRC process may be in bringing about enforcement of the 'trust' implied by the Convention.

References

Clark, A. (2004) 'The Mosaic approach and research with young children', in V. Lewis, M. Kellet, C. Robinson, S. Fraser, and S. Ding (eds) (2004) *The Reality of Research with Children and Young People*, Sage: London, pp. 157–61.

Croke, R. and Crowley, A. (eds) (2006) *Righting the Wrongs: The Reality of Children's Rights in Wales*. London: Save the Children.

Hansard, 30 March 2004 Baroness Ashton, Lords Debates on the Children Bill, Vol. 659, Col. 1302–1303.

Hart, R. (1992) *Children's Participation: From Tokenism to Citizenship*. London: UNICEF.

Heesterman, W. (2005) 'An assessment of the impact of youth submissions to the United Nations Committee on the Rights of the Child', *The International Journal of Children's Rights*, 13: 351–78.

Hendrick, H. (2004) *Child Welfare*. Bristol: Policy Press.

National Assembly for Wales (NAW) (2001) *Children and Young People: A Framework for Partnership*. NAW: Cardiff.

National Assembly for Wales (NAW) (2004) 'Plenary Resolution of the National Assembly for Wales', 14 January 2004.

NGO/CRC (2004) 'A Profile of National Children's Rights Coalitions', NGO Group for the Convention on the Rights of the Child/Child Rights Information Network, Joint Working Paper No. 1, London/Geneva, 2004.

Rees (2005) 'Making a crisis out of a drama? A commentary on the Clwych Examination', [2005] *Wales Journal of Law and Policy*, 4: 67–86.

Roche, J. (2005) 'Children, citizenship and human rights', in A. Invernizzi and B. Milne (eds) Children's Citizenship: An Emergent Discourse on the Rights of the Child? *Journal of Social Sciences*, 9: 43–55.

Save the Children (2006) 'Righting the Wrongs: The Reality of Children's Rights in Wales', Conference Report, London: Save the Children.

Skeels, A. (2006) 'Children as Active Participants in Welsh society', Submission to General Day of Discussion: the child's right to be heard, UN Committee on the Rights of the Child, 2006.

Theytatz-Bergman, L. (2005) 'UN Committee on the Rights of the Child and Its Interest for NGO Coalitions for Children's Rights – NGO Reporting Process', in Proceedings of the fourth regional meeting of NGO Coalitions for the Rights of the Child in Europe, Brussels: Belgian Children's Rights NGO Coalitions, pp. 38–40.

Thomas, E. and Skeels, A. (2006) 'Participation', in R. Croke and A. Crowley (eds) *Righting the Wrongs: The Reality of Children's Rights in Wales*, London: Save the Children.

UNCRC (2002) *General Comment on the Role of National Human Rights Institutions*. UN Committee on the Rights of the Child, CRC/GC/2002/2.

UNCRC (2003) *General Comment on General Measures of Implementation*. UN Committee on the Rights of the Child, CRC/GC/2003/5.

UNCRC (2005) *General Guidelines Regarding the Form and Content of Periodic Reports*. UN Committee on the Rights of the Child, CRC/C/58. Rev. 1.

WAG (2004) *Children and Young People: Rights to Action*, Welsh Assembly Government, Cardiff, January 2004.

WAG (2005) *Extending Entitlement: Working Together to Provide Young People's Entitlements*. Welsh Assembly Government, Cardiff, May 2005.

WAG (2006) *Children and Young People: Rights to Action, Stronger Partnerships for Better Outcomes. Guidance on Local Co-operation under the Children Act 2004*. Welsh Assembly Government, Cardiff, July 2006.

WAG (2007) *Rights to Action – Seven Core Aims Priority Outcomes*. Welsh Assembly Government, Cardiff, January 2007.

Williams, J. (2005) 'Effective government structures for children? The UK's four children's commissioners', *Child and Family Law Quarterly*, 17: 37–53.

Williams, J. (2007) 'Incorporating children's rights, the divergence in law and policy', *Legal Studies*, 27(2): 261–87.

Index